Praise for

A LEADER'S DESTINY

"A distinctive, thought-provoking view on leadership in the twenty-first century." —*Kirkus Reviews*

"Elias Aboujaoude's thoughtful and stimulating *A Leader's Destiny* is at once a great read and an incisive analysis of what we mean by 'leadership.' By unpacking the essential personality and psychological qualities needed for ascending to leadership positions and the individual and societal price that one—or all of us—may need to pay to get there, Aboujaoude uses his great experience in psychology and psychiatry for critical insight into how our own makeups generate behaviors with positive, and potentially negative, consequences."

> —Alan F. Schatzberg, MD, former president,
> American Psychiatric Association

"Stanford expert Aboujaoude is the perfect person to dissect how the leadership and life coaching industry has given us a new class of narcissistic leaders who model themselves on the master of impulse, Elon Musk. A potent antidote to the notion anyone can be taught to be a leader, *A Leader's Destiny* gives us pioneering insight into the personal, psychological, and situational factors that shape effective leaders."

> —Jonathan Taplin, director emeritus, Annenberg Innovation
> Lab, University of Southern California

"Engaging right from the beginning, *A Leader's Destiny* drew me in and made me read on and on. Everyone who aspires to a leadership role or, very importantly, who is responsible for choosing and developing leaders, must read this book. I wish I had read it while I was developing my leadership team."

> —John Featherstone, dean emeritus, School of Dentistry,
> University of California, San Francisco

"Aboujaoude's lively, accessible, and learned critique of the concept and practice of leadership raises interesting and provocative questions that resonate. Can leadership be taught? What is the role and virtue of executive coaching? How can the tools of the psychologist assist in improving current practice? What is the priority given to emotional intelligence in the training of potential leaders? Aboujaoude's case studies illuminate all these issues and many others beyond."

—Colin B. Bailey, director, the Morgan
Library & Museum, New York

A
LEADER'S
DESTINY

ALSO BY ELIAS ABOUJAOUDE

Virtually You: The Dangerous Powers of the E-Personality

Compulsive Acts: A Psychiatrist's Tales of Ritual and Obsession

Mental Health in the Digital Age: Grave Dangers, Great Promise
(edited with Vladan Starcevic)

Impulse Control Disorders (edited with Lorrin M. Koran)

A LEADER'S DESTINY

Why Psychology, Personality, and Character
Make All the Difference

Elias Aboujaoude

PUBLICAFFAIRS
New York

PublicAffairs
Hachette Book Group
1290 Avenue of the Americas, New York, NY 10104
www.publicaffairsbooks.com
@Public_Affairs

Printed in the United States of America

First Edition: May 2024

Published by PublicAffairs, an imprint of Hachette Book Group, Inc. The PublicAffairs name and logo is a registered trademark of the Hachette Book Group.

The Hachette Speakers Bureau provides a wide range of authors for speaking events. To find out more, go to hachettespeakersbureau.com or email HachetteSpeakers @hbgusa.com.

PublicAffairs books may be purchased in bulk for business, educational, or promotional use. For more information, please contact your local bookseller or the Hachette Book Group Special Markets Department at special.markets@hbgusa.com.

The publisher is not responsible for websites (or their content) that are not owned by the publisher.

Print book interior design by Marie Mundaca

Library of Congress Cataloging-in-Publication Data

Names: Aboujaoude, Elias, 1971– author.
Title: A leader's destiny : why psychology, personality, and character make all the difference / Elias Aboujaoude.
Description: First hardcover edition. | New York : PublicAffairs, [2024] | Includes bibliographical references and index. |
Identifiers: LCCN 2023038373 | ISBN 9781541703018 (hardcover) | ISBN 9781541703032 (ebook)
Subjects: LCSH: Leadership. | Leadership—Psychological aspects. | Personality. | Character.
Classification: LCC BF637.L4 .A136 2024 | DDC 158/.4—dc23/eng/20231030
LC record available at https://lccn.loc.gov/2023038373

ISBNs: 9781541703018 (hardcover), 9781541703032 (ebook)

LSC-C

Printing 1, 2024

To my father

CONTENTS

CONTENTS

PROLOGUE

A FEW YEARS ago, Tim,[*] an outstanding medical student I was supervising in my role as psychiatrist on the clinical wards, asked me for a letter of recommendation in support of his application to a competitive dermatology program, where he hoped to specialize in the treatment of skin cancer. I was happy to provide one and drafted what must have been the strongest letter I had ever written on behalf of a student. In it, I praised Tim's excellent bedside manner, the thoroughness of his medical notes, his reliability as a team member who went beyond the requirements of his role to help colleagues, his track record in research, his contagious passion for his field, and his overall functioning at a much higher level than would be expected at his stage of training. I shared the draft with him one busy Monday morning after rounds, fully expecting it to reduce the stress of the application process. As I watched him read it in my office, though, I was struck by a facial expression that seemed to go from overt excitement at the beginning of the letter to near despair at the end. Did I mistakenly show Tim the evaluation I had started writing for a classmate who was failing his rotation, I wondered, seriously breaching the latter's privacy and nearly giving the former a heart attack? "Is everything OK?" I asked, utterly confused by the unfolding scene and already beating myself up for a self-inflicted disaster that nobody needed on a busy Monday morning on the psych ward—or any morning on any ward. "Is everything OK?" I repeated, feeling anything but OK myself about my presumed mistake.

---

[*] The names of private individuals mentioned in this book have been changed and their identifying characteristics fictionalized to protect confidentiality.

Appearing more stressed than I had ever seen him, after a long pause, stutteringly, Tim asked if I could "add something, anything, about leadership qualities." These, apparently, were now weighed more highly than clinical abilities, research output, scholarly contributions, or collegiality. Tim was completely convinced that it would be impossible to get into a competitive program without a strong prediction by a supervisor of his brilliant future as a leader in his field. Dumbfounded but still very much wanting this deserving student to get into the program of his dreams and to become the great skin cancer specialist I knew he could become, I edited the letter, overdosing on leadership references by managing to squeeze the word in twice, even if the clinical wards where we crossed paths were not exactly the arena for leadership potential to blossom and be fully evaluated, and even if Tim had mostly expressed interest in being the best doctor he could be, not in "leading" in any traditional sense of the word. He got in.

In preparing to write a book on the psychology of leadership some years later, I thought I would check in with my star student and would-be leader. I was hardly surprised to hear that Tim had completed his training with flying colors, was practicing at a busy county hospital, and was conducting research with a biopharmaceutical company into a promising new melanoma drug. What was somewhat surprising, however, was that Tim had already turned down two leadership positions that had come his way: chief resident of his training program and medical director of his hospital's dermatology service. This news seemed like an opportune moment to bring up the story of the recommendation letter that nearly sent him to the emergency room and his request for "something, anything, about leadership qualities." Several years later, I figured we could both laugh about it. "So much for exercising those 'leadership qualities!'" I joked. "Oh, no, I'm not cut out to lead," was Tim's unexpected response, delivered with the self-awareness of someone whose psychotherapy journey has paid off. "It takes a certain kind of person," he added, "but this hasn't stopped everyone and their grandmother from wanting to be a leader!" "What about wanting to come across as a future leader in that letter?" I asked, confused by his evolution from being desperate to portray leadership potential to declining two opportunities with the equivalent of "Thanks but no thanks." "It's a game we are forced to play," Tim explained. "If it weren't for those edits," he continued, "I really don't think I would be here today. But I'm not cut out for it. I'm just not."

Tim operated under the "Know Thyself" principle. He knew he was not "cut out" for leadership because he was in touch with his own psychology, and he was aware that it took certain traits that he did not possess to be happy and successful leading. But Tim also operated under the "Know Thy Culture" principle and knew just as well that leading was what the culture valued more than anything and that if he were to send the message that he was not "leadership material," his application might be dismissed as he might, horror of horrors, be thought of as a follower. Most of us do not have that self or cultural knowledge and are too happy ignoring intrinsic personality traits and the unhealthy societal fixation on executive titles as we blindly eat up an industrial complex's worth of leadership workshops, bootcamps, minors, majors, coaches, and professors of leadership, in a self-defeating quest that ignores the basic psychological premise that not all have what it takes to lead—and its mathematical corollary that not all can become leaders and that the world also needs followers.

Indeed, something is culturally afoot that has made leadership both everywhere and scarce as a unicorn. I'm talking about the culture-wide obsession with leadership in all its dissectible components, teachable prerequisites, and perfectible tools. Its manifestations include a leadership industrial complex that has emerged to produce leaders. With a size estimated to be as high as $50 billion annually by the industry platform Chief Learning Officer, leadership training has been among the fastest-growing sectors within the $357 billion learning and development market, and one of the only ones to have experienced year-after-year growth in recent years, independent of economic trends and conditions.[1] We have bought into and put in place an entire system to "produce" leaders, but, for reasons that deserve urgent explanation, the system is broken, as evidenced by the scary dearth of leaders we can respect and be proud of.

Other manifestations of the leadership obsession include the ubiquitous executive coaches populating human resources (HR) departments and tasked with optimizing, branding, and reforming leaders; ever-more-creative, and empty, titles meant to meet the insatiable demand for leadership roles—what led a favorite San Francisco restaurant to appoint a "chief pastry officer," for example; and the growing number of daycare centers that feature "Little Leaders" in their names and that suggest that it is never too early to embark on leadership training. And yet, whichever direction you look, there is a leadership vacuum and failure after failure. Practically every news cycle has a fallen, failed, or criminal leader as a leading topic. The spotlight in recent months has belonged to Samuel Bankman-Fried, or SBF, who went from being the world's undisputed crypto leader and its first projected trillionaire to Fox Hill, a Bahamian prison so awful it has been nicknamed Fox Hell, having been charged with eight counts of conspiracy and fraud by the Department of Justice.[2] The more we embrace "leadership development," the more dispiriting examples like this seem to hit us in the face, like buckets of ice water hiding a wake-up call that is waiting to be deciphered. What is going on? As we have mythologized leadership, we have also bought into simple training recipes that supposedly crack its code and get us "there," regardless of baseline character and innate traits. Where we are arriving, instead, seems to be some version of Fox Hell.

True leadership has been disrupted out of existence, hollowed out of genuine meaning, and virtualized to where only the number of a leader's social media followers counts. The innumerable MBA programs, TED talks, motivational speakers, online workshops, and executive development bootcamps work together to send the message that leadership is something you can learn, and not the complex intersection of luck, circumstance, experience, and, above all, psychology. Yes, psychology. Before it was a big business, before it was a "science," leadership was about character and personality, yet you have to sift through leadership training curricula with a fine-tooth comb to find a meaningful analysis of the role of psychology; one that goes beyond paying lip service to the field to admitting that some people are simply not psychologically wired to become leaders and perhaps should be discouraged from it—and, very importantly, that this does not mean they are failures. We are not talking here about leaders who cultivate a "cult of personality," understood to mean unquestioning praise and flattery by blinded followers. We are, rather, talking about some traits that go with good leadership and some that can make a person unhappy or downright destructive if elevated to a leadership position. Unless we break away from the notion that these traits can be sufficiently massaged so that almost anyone can be content and successful leading, and the notion that leadership is something that can be learned by signing up for the right leadership program or signing on the right executive coach, we will not be able to rescue ourselves from the crisis of poor leadership plaguing our society, the pure narcissism it masks, and the far-reaching pathological consequences of worshiping title over substance. And we will continue to have to contend with leadership like the deans of New York University, who fired an eminent chemistry professor, despite his having written an influential textbook in his field that is in its fifth edition, after 82 of his 350 students signed a petition complaining that his organic chemistry class was too hard; or CEOs who negotiate raises even as their employees' financial lives become ever more precarious; or nonprofit hospitals that are outdoing for-profit ones at profiteering; or elected representatives who will not hesitate to shut down government to make a petty point or satisfy purely egotistical needs.[3]

My path to these questions, and, I hope, some answers, may have started when I noticed an uptick in email messages from various schools I have and have not been affiliated with, inviting me to avail myself of leadership training opportunities. I had no reason to suspect a reputation for haplessness as a leader—a clinical psychiatrist who's a researcher and writer such as I am is not a leader in the classic definition of the word, so they seemed irrelevant—and I wondered whether my publication record and academic position somehow tagged me as somebody who could benefit from what leadership courses had to offer. The heavy marketing was typically met with my delete button, until I started noticing something happening at the level of culture at large; something I couldn't easily delete.

An early red flag was an invitation I received a couple of years ago to speak at a fundraiser held by a business school for some of its high-net-worth alumni on the psychological impact of internet-related technologies, a topic I have long researched and wrote about in my book *Virtually You*. I seldom need convincing to give a lecture on a subject close to my heart, but perhaps to increase the odds that I would say yes, event organizers had described me as a "thought leader" in their invitation, a phrase that I had not yet come across. Instead of stroking my ego, however, the description left me a bit spooked. It smacked of mind control and, as a psychiatrist, reminded me of the psychotic symptoms of "thought insertion" and "thought broadcasting," whereby patients with schizophrenia believe thoughts are being placed in their heads by an outside force or communicated against their will to an external entity. Did "thought leader" somehow imply the ability to plant ideas in a passive person's mind or widely disseminate my views at such a deep cognitive level? Was I someone who had this power over his audience? I thought not.

Still, I was grateful for the invitation and immediately accepted. But what happened over the course of the conference convinced me that perhaps I needed to devote more thought to the current concept of leadership, in its various manifestations. For starters, it turned out that thought leadership was a crowded field: I met several other speakers referred to by the same moniker in their respective specialties, which ranged from technology to teaching to philanthropy. And every time an audience member wanted to interject a comment or ask a question, the school's chief development officer emceeing the event would go out of her way to introduce the audience member by a formal leadership title, however unusual. And so, besides the familiar chief executive officer, I became acquainted with a chief green officer, a chief engagement officer, a chief brand manager, and an executive vice president for operational excellence. One leader was even introduced as a "multi-hyphenate," to suggest he leads on several fronts and may have too many titles to list. And a couple of leaders' titles were preceded by "fierce," as in the "fierce chief financial officer of . . ."—as though fierceness had become a sought-after leadership quality and part and parcel of the title.

And in the cocktail party that followed, I had the pleasure of meeting a PR firm leader who jokingly referred to himself as a master of disaster—"I clean up executives' messes"—and an official "influencer," who served as a sort of ambassador of buzz to her social media followers, although on what topic or product was not immediately clear. These titles, seemingly dreamed up by a creative chief linguistic officer with too much free time on his hands, did not convey much beyond a need to feed a leadership-obsessed corporate culture. Amid this C-suite bumper crop of authorities, was anyone left to be led, I wondered?

The following morning, I received a grateful note from a senior administrator in the school. "The leadership wishes to thank you for your participation," it began. Although the email was a personal one and came from a specific individual whose signature it carried, he did not opt for the usual "I" or even the royal "we," twisting his language instead to refer to himself several times in the third person as "the leadership." Why the seeming insistence on an out-of-place word that didn't convey anything additional? Was he just inflating his own ego? Was he "hiding" behind a group of leaders so as not to assume a direct position on my semicontroversial talk, which blamed Silicon Valley for much of our social and political ills? Was he referring to an entire "class" of leaders, a politburo-like entity running the school, which would import into academia a language that might fit better in the propaganda of unhappy political systems known for their cult of leadership?

I was not the only one souring on a certain use of the word "leadership," it turned out. While researching, around the same time, an article on the booming coaching business, something seemingly banal landed in my inbox: a list of "the most overused words that you must retire STAT from your vocabulary." Distracted from my article, I scanned the list quickly, looking to see if I had used any of the offending words in my piece. I had had the good sense to avoid such apparently out of vogue terms as "rock star" (to refer to anyone other than an actual rock star), "landscape" (to refer to anything other than a Monet), "ecosystem" (to refer to anything other than marine health or global warming), and "space" (to refer to anything other than the space-time continuum). But I was chagrined that "leadership," which was ranked toward the top of the list of words that should be banned, had made it into my article. No longer an eternal concept immune to changing fashions, linguistic or otherwise, "leadership" was also apparently becoming cliché; a word that only amounted to white noise. Still, I left it in, having convinced myself that I was using it to criticize a certain approach to producing cliché leaders by cliché coaches, not to contribute to the further hollowing out of the word and the concept.

Other questions were bubbling up. In Silicon Valley where I practice psychiatry, what is this self-bestowing among twenty-somethings of titles like president, CEO, and CTO, when they operate in tiny startups with no employees to lead, an undefined business model, and a shoestring budget? What should I tell my patients who engage in cutthroat competition to get to the top, only to admit in my psychiatric practice that they were ill-suited for it and that it amounted to a race to the bottom? Why are HR departments in academia and the nonprofit sector, which like to see themselves as above corporate trends, becoming just as uncritically smitten by the leadership training bug and the executive coaching "solution" to so much of what goes wrong with leadership? What does it mean when we tell an undecided spouse or an amotivated child that we made "an executive decision" to perform activity X, and that they have no choice but to comply? Does the world really need a chief happiness officer (even if everyone agrees it could use more happiness)? Ditto for chief spiritual officer. And what exactly does a chief metaverse officer do?

These questions and observations, rather isolated on the surface, seemed to flow from the same cultural well. Connect the dots, and they tell the story of a leadership obsession turned serious business, and of followers being led seriously astray. Popping up at the same cultural moment, they have brought me to the realization that something is "up" that is making a twisted notion of leadership ubiquitous and real leadership AWOL—and that is worthy of deep analysis.

We worship the concept of leadership in a way we never have before—our definition of self-worth is now predicated on demonstrating strong "leadership qualities" in fields as varied as corporate life, teaching, doctoring, and even parenting. We are obsessed with executive roles and somehow ignore the logical fallacy that says everyone can be a leader. An entire industry has emerged to convince us that we, too, can be destined for leadership—and to help us conquer that destiny. Yet, paradoxically and tragically and despite noteworthy exceptions, too many examples of abdication of leadership continue to come out of boardrooms, government, NGOs, and academia. As I write these words at Stanford where I work and teach, campus is reeling from the sudden resignation of the university president amid accusations of flawed research. Perusing reactions to the *New York Times* article announcing his departure, I was struck by this reader comment: "Frankly, I find it refreshing that he is not resigning because of some sex scandal—although I didn't quite finish the article. Let me know how it ends."[4] Such are peoples' expectations of leaders today. Such is the bar by which they judge them. Such is their disillusionment.

Why the desperation to enter a leadership class we seem to have lost respect for? Do we genuinely think we can fix things, or are darker forces driving us? How can good leaders, and followers who believe in them, happen again? Having spent some time thinking and writing about leadership and having published scholarly research on coaching (including the "executive coaching" mediating some of the issues I highlight), I now see in my training and practice as a psychiatrist that the old word "leadership" has indeed taken on a new meaning—cornucopian and empty, attractive and repellent. We must pause and reflect on where we have pushed the boundaries of this notion, how we have stretched it beyond the limits of its elasticity until it snapped in our faces. And, from a psychiatrist's perspective, we must revisit the real psychological underpinnings of good leadership and return to those core values and standards. Overused and abused, the word "leadership" probably deserves to go. I personally won't be overdosing on it again in future letters I write for medical students, but I won't be dropping it quite so stat, either. Not before I attempt an investigation into the concept and what it says about today's leaders, followers, and overall culture. There is a syndrome to be diagnosed and treatments to be suggested. There are hot air balloons to be deflated and myths to be punctured. There is an urgency to resurrect personality, psychology, and character as must-have ingredients that money can't buy. To understand why leadership is on the rocks, we will have to put it on the couch.

PART I

THE LEADERSHIP PRODUCTION LINE

PART ONE REVIEWS how a veritable leadership industrial complex has arisen to meet our leadership needs and create new ones we didn't know we had. How much are you willing to pay for that leadership title? A Harvard leadership training program will set you back $52,000 for the "basic" model, plus an additional $27,000 for an accessory module that can grant you Harvard alumni status and a lifelong Harvard email address. Leadership is now as entrenched in the market bazaar as other commodities that the business schools peddling leadership degrees are also expert at. Crude oil, natural gas, corn, soybeans, leadership! It would be worth the price tag if one could point to a clear return on the investment within leadership culture overall. Instead, we have created an industry that is succeeding at whipping up frothy leadership demand while failing at its goal of producing reliably good leaders we can all be proud of. To the extent that leadership cannot be reduced to the laws of supply and demand and is, indeed, "priceless," this failure may be "built into" the leadership industry and should perhaps surprise no one. A less expected outcome, however, is the inferiority complex we are giving people who buy into the simplistic notion that leadership can be learned relatively easily, then crash at the altar of reality when they don't rise like they were all but promised would happen in leadership school. "What is wrong with me?" is their self-torturing question, when the "wrong" may be in how we have turned leadership into a multibillion-dollar business.

Part One also shows how, rather than a commodity, leadership is first and foremost a state of mind—basically, about psychology. Yet, in our current conception of leadership, one has to look really hard for real evidence of psychology's determinant role. Instead of psychologists advising on personality and character traits that may or may not be suitable in leaders, we have armies of "executive coaches" having to function as pseudotherapists of sorts for armies of executives, many of whom, research has shown, have worrisome levels of antisocial and narcissistic traits. The result, quite often, is a corporate menagerie of leaders who are faking having what it takes to lead, and coaches who are in over their heads doing what they can to try to help them. The rise of coaching as an integral component of the leadership industry, this part argues, is a dramatic symptom of how divorced leadership has become from personality, character, and psychology.

Having minimized the role of psychology and turned leadership into a business, we are also turning it into a science, which, of course, would make the business more credible and further justify the money being made developing, grooming, and hand-holding leaders. As Part One will explain, however, the "science" of leadership is no traditional science. It is also no "rocket science," rife as it is with easy leadership tools and handy mnemonics à la 5W+H, WIGO, FIAO, WOA, 3Rs, 4Cs, PACE, and even LEAD, all telegraphing the message that the science of leading is a user-friendly one—as easy as ABC! While scientific research into leadership has yielded some crucial findings, such as around the all-important role of emotional intelligence in leaders, these findings often drown in a sea of oversimplified, cookbook-y, and quite unscientific tips and recipes—such as about how to achieve a superior emotional quotient (EQ) if you were not naturally thus endowed.

EQ, charisma, and overall personality, Part One will show, are rather sticky and inelastic. Whether for a leadership position or any other desired outcome, they can be stretched and manipulated only up to a point, and the process for doing so is tectonically slow and requires patience and hard work. This is what personality research and experienced therapists working to effect deep change in people will tell you, and this is what a tour of some recent famous leaders' dispositions will illustrate. Don't expect a personality transplant from a weekend leadership workshop, or a standard-deviation-sized charisma gain from an online webinar on how to influence people. The leadership industry can mislead by suggesting that personality is so malleable that essentially all comers can be reasonable leadership raw material. But, when it comes to personality, the industry can mislead in another way, too: to the extent that it identifies a personality, it often seeks to stamp it out, making the bland, personality-less leader the prototype to aim for today and the "brand" that should somehow move and inspire us. The result of all this has been to diminish leaders and leadership culture, and to risk transforming the industry from a service that is there to fix a real and present crisis in leadership to one of its symptoms and possible root causes.

1

HOW AN INDUSTRIAL COMPLEX FUELS AN INFERIORITY COMPLEX

CLAUDIA WAS THE patient, but I heard just as much about Tessie, her nonidentical twin sister, over the course of her therapy with me. The two were raised in the same nurturing environment by their high-achieving parents. They took the same vacations, consumed the same food, and had the same friends. They attended the same preschool, middle school, high school, and college, and pursued the same business degree, which they completed with near identical, excellent GPA scores: 3.91 for Claudia versus 3.89 for Tessie.

In our work, which took place nearly fifteen years after the sisters graduated from college, Claudia would often return to her "higher" GPA score and this 0.02-point spread, only half-jokingly and as proof of noninferiority to her sister. The sisters' paths, you see, diverged significantly after college, bifurcating as a function of personalities that were quite distinct, despite so much else that was commonly held and seemingly indistinguishable. As Claudia told it, Tessie was the effusive one with the outward-facing disposition, who thrived on meeting people, reaching out, and initiating. Claudia, on the other hand, charged her emotional batteries by looking inward and enjoyed analyzing and trying to understand what made the world around her tick, without feeling a need to fully partake in all its workings. One seemed to grab life by the horns, the other allowed it to happen, which is not the same as saying that Claudia let life pass her by. She marveled at its mysteries and absorbed its lessons but did not feel tremendous agency in shaping it or harbor a burning desire to change the world. Passive in her approach? Perhaps. Depressed about it? Not at all.

Claudia took a job with a pharmaceutical company after college; Tessie, with a consulting firm. Tessie, the sister with the effusive personality, ease of socializing, and initiative taking, built crucial relationships with peers and superiors, and advanced rather quickly up company rungs. Claudia, whose glowing reviews consistently highlighted her meticulous work ethic, reliability, and thoroughness, stayed in more or less the same rank. For a long time, this did not seem to bother her. She was productive, enjoyed the familiarity of what she did, liked her colleagues, and felt respected and well compensated. This sense of professional peace, however, began to fray when Tessie was appointed to an executive position at her firm, prompting the twins' parents—themselves in senior positions at their respective companies—to insinuate questions along the lines of "What are you doing with *your* career?" At the same time, as part of "employee development," everyone in Claudia's company was being encouraged to pursue the leadership-training opportunities being offered by her employer's contracted "leadership academy." Meant to nurture employees' inner leader, these coaching sessions, training bootcamps, books, and podcasts seemed to send the message "You, too, can be an executive!"—a marketing approach that Claudia, because of her twin's path and because of the signaling from the larger culture, was becoming increasingly sensitized to.

With a little help, she thought, Claudia could "catch up" with her sister and with the world's notion of a worthwhile job. "They make it look easy," she said of the classes and events she started investing time and money in. "Nothing that someone with a 3.91 GPA can't figure out." Claudia would be in "good company" in that these interventions are being adopted across the board and up and down the leadership hierarchy from total leadership novices to tech executives with household names. There isn't anyone who seemingly cannot benefit.

A DISPROPORTIONATE NUMBER of these CEOs seem to be connected to San Francisco, the city I call home. They love the City by the Bay, and the city loves them back, proving its affection by cutting them slack and turning a blind eye to their urban transgressions, which it sees as transformative disruptions by brilliant innovators whose innovations the rest of us just don't yet "get." And so, on the transportation front alone, we have been treated to some of the earliest examples of Tesla drivers literally asleep at the wheel;[1] extraterrestrial-looking self-driving Google cars going in circles as they search for an outlet on dead-end streets;[2] Facebook employee shuttles blocking the public bus stops that other San Franciscans rely on;[3] and bright-green scooters from the bike-sharing startup Lime precariously abandoned on the hilly city's vertical sidewalks.[4] For Uber, however, an enough-is-enough moment of sorts was reached in 2017. It seemed that way to me, at least, when a friend and fellow San Francisco resident sent out a mass "#DeleteUber" email to everyone in our social circle. This came as a bit of a shock, given that she had sold her car soon after taking her first Uber, convinced she would be Ubering everywhere for the rest of her life. Barely six months later, she was campaigning against the company and inundating all of us on her phone's contact list with invites to join her newly downloaded Lyft app. What had happened?

It started when Keala Lusk, a former software engineer at Uber, went public regarding the toxic corporate culture of rampant backstabbing, discrimination, and harassment.[5] Shortly thereafter, Uber's senior vice president of engineering resigned for failing to report a sexual harassment allegation lodged against him during his time at Google.[6] A few days later, the *New York Times* broke a story about "Greyball," a software tool used by Uber to identify and evade authorities in cities where Uber was banned or restricted.[7] And, in the midst of all this—talk about a bumpy ride—Fawzi Kamel, an Uber driver, released a dashcam video of an argument with Travis Kalanick, Uber's founder and CEO, in which Kalanick berated Kamel for questioning his pricing policy.[8] "You know what, some people don't like to take responsibility for their own shit. They blame everything in their life on somebody else. Good luck!" Kalanick is heard saying. To which Kamel responds: "Good luck to you too, I know that you aren't going to go far."

The video, which quickly achieved viral status, led to a rare demonstration of contrition from the brash CEO, as well as a promise to fix his problem: "My job as your leader is to lead . . . and that starts with behaving in a way that makes us all proud," he told his employees in a post entitled "A Profound Apology."[9] "This is the first time I've been willing to admit that I need leadership help and I intend to get it."

Fortunately for Kalanick, leadership help was just around the corner. Over the past few years, an enormous and ever-expanding leadership industry has arisen that promises to bring leadership to the masses, turn almost anyone into leadership material, and rehabilitate even the most un-leader-like behavior. I doubt Kalanick was classmates with Claudia, but the idea is the same: give us your executive shortcomings and dreams, and we will deliver leadership. Instructor-led training workshops, one-on-one executive coaching, and individualized, bespoke programs from top business schools for up to $150,000 a pop are all available.[10] Indeed, some of the biggest names in the leadership industry—the leadership industry's leaders—are highly respected business schools that know a thing or two about maximizing profit. The fact that the business of leadership is partly run by some of our greatest business scholars has helped transform leadership training into the money-making juggernaut it has become. These minds have also helped lend credibility to the industry, encouraging a certain suspension of disbelief when it comes to some of its claims and a blind eye to the aggressive marketing sometimes used.

But can good leadership actually be taught, or is it a combination of hard work, luck, circumstance, and temperament? If we acknowledge that temperamental factors, such as whether someone is genuinely interested in lifting others, are crucial to leadership, then saying that these programs can be counted on to form good leaders amounts to saying that they can make somebody who's in it for greed and personal benefit be more caring and service-minded. Similarly, if we buy into the importance of charisma in inspiring people to work toward a common goal—another important leader attribute—then saying that these programs can be counted on to form good leaders amounts to saying that they can endow somebody who isn't naturally magnetic with that indescribable spell that successful leaders can cast on people. Can every weak leader be trained by a leadership program and every failing leader reformed by management rehab? Is leadership a fully learnable set of skills? Or should some people accept that they do not have what it takes and move on? A tour of a handful of leadership offerings and their improbable promises leaves one wondering.

Harvard may be the paragon of all that is exclusive and highly selective in education, but the leadership training courses it offers seem much more open and democratic than, say, its physics, comparative literature, or psychology majors, sending the message that it's perhaps easier to become a successful leader than a computer scientist, writer, or neuropsychologist. Openness and democracy may start with the "program advising team" staffing the 1-800 phone number the Harvard Business School Executive Education site invites you to call with questions "at any stage of the admissions process"—a level of access that Harvard's physics, comparative literature, and psychology applicants can probably only dream of. "Whatever your role or career stage, our comprehensive leadership programs will prepare you for the challenges ahead," the site reads.[11] "Whatever" is hardly exclusive and "challenges ahead" applies to literally everyone. What this does communicate is that leadership training is universally relevant, universally useful, and universally doable. There are no traditional prerequisites like grades, majors, prior courses, and so on, to worry about, either: "Most programs have no formal educational requirements"[12] and rely more on work history, letters of recommendation, and difficult-to-pin-down "leadership potential."[13] While this makes some sense—who said successful leaders should have a high school GPA of 4.18 out of 4, which is the reported GPA of Harvard's admitted freshmen class?[14]—it still rings strange coming from Harvard. It also begs the question of whether the acceptance rate into Harvard's leadership programs, described as "selective" by the site, may still differ by a significant margin from the extremely forbidding 4.59 percent acceptance rate faced by Harvard's undergraduate class of 2022.[15]

And if the simpler-than-one-might-expect process for signing up for Harvard leadership courses were not enticing enough, how about, as previously mentioned, being able to call yourself a Harvard alumnus? In what feels like an overt act of marketing, and for only an additional two-week module, the Program for Leadership Development will reward you with the ultimate status symbol—Harvard alumni status: "Each program journey offers a broad business management and leadership curriculum, personalized coaching, individual projects that address your business challenges—and the opportunity to earn Harvard Business School alumni status."[16] And what leader would not want *that* on their curriculum vitae (CV)?

What is unquestionably exclusive in Harvard's Program for Leadership Development is its price tag: $52,000 for the basic four modules of "blended" teaching, and an additional $27,000 for the optional alumni-making fifth module.[17]

Harvard is in good company. Wharton at the University of Pennsylvania was founded in 1881 as the first collegiate business school, and can claim an illustrious record of success that goes on to our day—its MBA program was ranked first in the 2023 *US News* list of best business schools.[18] With this pedigree, Wharton shouldn't need to come across as overpromising on outcomes to convince you to enroll in its Global C-Suite leadership program. Yet here is what someone interested in mastering leadership can expect in as little as nine months of largely self-paced learning that doesn't exceed five hours a week:[19]

- Consolidate your functional, business, and communication skills to lead from the C-suite
- Plan and execute global strategy from a range of lenses including leadership, organizational culture, business challenges, and talent management
- Understand how to manage complex, multi-partner alliances and nurture strategic business ecosystems
- Develop new approaches for global team building, strategy execution, and implementation
- Recognize the drivers of corporate value and their trade-offs: organic revenue growth, returns on capital, and long-term investing
- Identify the factors that help your organization gain and sustain competitive market advantage
- Focus on the demands of emerging markets and grasp new industry challenges

What reads like the fruit of an entire career of slowly accumulated knowledge and hands-on experience can be yours for much less time and effort. Like Harvard, Wharton sweetens the deal by offering completers a "pathway" to Wharton alumni status—and that coveted Wharton email address. Oh, and if I hurried and applied within nine days of checking the site and downloading the brochure, I could get $1,000 off the $20,000 tuition! What are the eligibility criteria highlighted for leaders to apply and potentially unlock all of this? Not as much as I expected: twelve years of work experience and fluency in written and spoken English.

If some of our greatest schools appear to be watering down leadership to a set of skills that seem rather easily learnable and downloadable, we may be able to excuse "lesser" sellers of the leadership product. Findcourses.com is a database that includes over 1,400 leadership courses.[20] A top 2022 course on the long list, 360 Leadership Communication Agility, was offered by Speak by Design University, which describes itself as an online executive communication training platform that "makes exceptional speakers and stand-out leaders by teaching you how to communicate powerfully" and how to "become a consistently compelling force."[21] The course made the following claim: "This program teaches you skills that give you immediate results: Vastly improve your ability to think on your feet; Communicate with confidence; and Develop communication agility to better manage up, down, and across. You will practice skills and techniques in real-life scenarios that prepare you for any high-stake interaction or negotiation."[22] *Up. Down. Across. Vastly.* And *Immediate.* Not to mention that many of the popular leadership offerings on Findcourses are self-paced or virtual, only a few hours long, and relatively inexpensive if you consider the advertised returns. So much for the old advice to underpromise and overdeliver! The claims are almost miraculous. There is, to be sure and as we will see, a big place for small miracles and the quasi-religious in how leaders happen and succeed, but Speak by Design University ain't where they take place.

Are such products really all there is to becoming a great leader? Or is there a spoiling role for personality, charisma, situational factors, and sheer luck? As I hope to show, any and all of these factors can play a determining role in who gets to lead and who manages to succeed once in a leadership position. And should some people be *dis*couraged from leading, precisely because their particular combination of personal disposition and situational context is not an auspicious one for leadership? Nobody seems discouraged when it comes to the three-day Strategy of Leadership course offered by Northwestern University (Kellogg) and open to "anyone who wants to affect [*sic*] change without authority."[23] Everyone seems welcome to the leadership party, where, like mythical Lake Wobegon, "all the children are above average," and where, in the end, everybody gets to be a leader.[24] If one had to pick a meme for the leadership industry, it might be "YOU get a car! YOU get a car! Everybody gets a car!," the iconic words shouted by Oprah at the end of an episode of her talk show in which every audience member in the studio unexpectedly won a car. Except that leadership is not something you can be gifted or buy, and this is not a show.

THERE ARE THREE main reactions to courses, certificates, and degrees that make leadership seem accessible and relatively easy. The first, a rather naïve one, is to celebrate how egalitarian leadership has become and how built-in obstacles seem to have softened to the point where, if you absorb a set of absorbable tools, leadership is yours for the taking. The second is to conclude that leadership has become a commodity whose marketplace plays by the rules and ethics of other marketplaces, not traditional educational institutions. The third is to be astonished by the narcissism being conveyed. To communicate that you have mastered the secret sauce for successful leadership and can reliably share the recipe over a few modules to almost all comers speaks of remarkable grandiosity. Have we really figured out what makes successful leaders, much less proven that we can reliably produce them?

A more democratic leadership landscape, where everyone has a reasonable shot at becoming a leader, would, of course, be a wonderful thing, but no such transformation in the leadership landscape has accompanied the rise of the leadership industrial complex. Despite endless offerings meant to improve our leaders, there has been no uptick in leadership successes we can point to; no increase in the number of inspiring leaders; no augmentation in transcendental acts by transcendental figures; no true broadening of the profile of who gets to become a leader; and no heightened confidence in those shepherding us through political, economic, climatic, and public health turmoil. None of this is true, and, in fact, the opposite might be true.

There is an inconvenient paradox at the heart of the leadership industry: while it pretends to bring people endless opportunities to become leaders or to help them up their leadership game, good leaders have become more and more difficult to find. Wherever we look, from the boardrooms that triggered the Great Recession, justified unequal pay for equal work, and covered up harassment, to a political class that can't seem to compromise even when faced with an unprecedented health crisis, to world authorities that idly watch, Nero-style, as the planet literally burns, leaders have been leading us into the wall. Consider recent nightmare CEO tales, like Martin Shkreli, the "pharma bro" infamous for hiking the price of a lifesaving drug more than 5,000 percent, then allegedly using a contraband cellphone to continue running his pharmaceuticals firm from jail after being convicted for defrauding investors and manipulating shares.[25] Or Adam Neumann, the cofounder of WeWork who resigned in 2019 after stories came out describing a shocking managerial style and Marie Antoinette–like antics, including reportedly banning meat from WeWork offices while continuing to consume it at the company himself, hiding a large stash of marijuana in a cereal box on a flight, making tequila the centerpiece of WeWork culture, and interviewing prospective employees while riding around in his superluxury car then telling them to hop into a separate "chase car" in his convoy when done.[26] Or Elizabeth Holmes, the former Silicon Valley darling whose blood-testing company rested on scientific deceptions for which she was found guilty, and, seemingly, personal deceptions, like imitating Steve Jobs's wardrobe, faking her voice, and practicing not blinking to "hypnotize" investors, journalists, and employees with unbroken eye contact.[27] The new crop of failed CEOs seems to have learned nothing about leadership from the class of 2008 that brought us the Great Recession, and whose cautionary vignettes are covered by executive coaches and in MBA workshops.

Or consider Washington, DC, where Congress can't seem to pass any meaningful legislation, including on a supposedly bipartisan priority like the COVID-19 pandemic, even when the US accounted for 25 percent of worldwide deaths despite only having 4 percent of the world's population; and where we have been on a desperate quest for a leadership style that might work in our chief executive, swinging from George W. Bush's knee-jerk decisiveness and folksiness, to Barack Obama's deliberative ivory tower style, to Donald Trump's post-leadership world where leaders do not even have to pretend to act leaderly.[28]

How can such a pronounced absence of ethics, spine, or intellect at the very top coexist with innumerable courses taught by the best professors of leadership at the best universities, armies of coaches waiting to mold the perfect leader, and endless TED talks claiming to distill the essence of leadership to anyone who will sign up for the podcast? Is the leadership industrial complex the necessary corrective to our culture of failed leaders—give us more, please!—or is it contributing to our leadership crisis by encouraging the wrong values or helping people who have no business being leaders in the first place visualize a way to the top? A business school's senior vice dean, an executive coach, or a professor of leadership might argue that more leadership training is the answer; that we do not teach enough "proven" leadership skills to enough leaders or would-be leaders, that, in essence, the leadership industry is not big enough. I would argue that the industry is part of the problem insofar as it has helped reduce leadership to a commodity when there is much more to leadership than what money can buy or professors can teach.

But the industry is not the whole story. If it represents the supply side in the law of supply and demand, we represent the demand, and, as such, we deserve some of the blame. We are part of a culture-wide obsession with leadership, and the leadership industrial complex, in a sense, is there to meet the voracious demand. We are the ones signing up for leadership development bootcamps at work, minoring in Leadership Studies in college, sending our children to daycare centers named Lil' Leaders, and taking for granted titles like chief pastry officer.[29] If we weren't in a hurry to become leaders and master leadership ourselves, it would be hard to imagine a program calling itself "Leadership Express Series" marketing itself to us.[30]

Meet our voracious demand and then some: by making leadership look unrealistically easy, the leadership industry can contribute to an inferiority complex that develops in those who succumb to feelings of guilt and worthlessness—when reality intrudes and they fail to become leaders, perhaps because mathematics dictates that the world also needs followers and not all can be leaders. While there is nothing wrong with the leadership industry stoking ambition by making leadership appear more accessible, this should not happen at the expense of giving people an inferiority complex, which can happen when those who internalize the message that essentially everyone can be a leader start faulting themselves when they don't make it. As a psychiatrist, I have seen more than my share of smart, talented, and passionate individuals succumb to dangerous self-blame when they can't land a leadership title or their "leadership development" fails to elevate them. Their self-worth had become attached to that, and how could it have not when the message permeating so much of culture is that leading is what matters—and that almost anyone can lead with the right prep course? The sum of these ingredients is often clinical depression.

PERSONALITY, CHARISMA, LUCK, and many other mercurial variables that cannot be taught by an executive coach or captured at a training bootcamp have a way of asserting themselves in the lives of people like my patient Claudia to correct the logic-defying industry message that everyone is, essentially, leadership material.

"Logic-defying" but also psychologically harmful, for the corollary to the message that everyone can be a leader is this one: "There is no self-worth in being a follower." For Claudia, leadership would continue to elude her, not for any shortage of IQ points or because she did not apply herself enough or diligently do her homework in the executive workshops she signed up for, but because leadership is much more complex than a matter of input and output ("Invest in this leadership track or minor, and you're all but guaranteed a C-suite spot"). For her, the result was an inferiority complex she developed for being excellent at something other than leading and for failing at the supposedly accessible task of becoming an executive. Claudia's "Why not me?" competitiveness with her sister had, until then, been foreign to their relationship. Normally self-confident, Claudia started wondering whether she was truly in command of her job qualifications and really possessed the competencies for it, even when year after year of very good reviews told a different story. The newfound self-doubt about what she brought to the table was accompanied by nascent guilt for having "wasted" precious years and fallen irreparably behind. Further, the leadership courses she took to try to make up for lost time were doubly unhelpful: First, they glorified leadership even more, which was probably the worst message one could send her. Second, the supposed hacks she picked up that were meant to jump-start her executive path were not working in terms of timely promotions, compounding her sense of failure. Finally, seeking out emotional support from her usual support system—first and foremost her natural-born-leader sister—had now become a complicated ask, making her feel isolated. All this added up to something that looked like depression in somebody who had never really been depressed before; who never wanted to be a leader and was suddenly pursuing leadership only because everybody seemed to be doing it; and who, given her more reserved personality, would probably not enjoy it even if she were to make it to the top.

Treating Claudia would involve more than pointing out how personality can make or break one's leadership chances and how there are many paths to happiness, success, and self-respect that do not go through the C-suite. Her treatment could not have been effective without an attempt at pointing out the larger forces contributing to her problem—without an attempt at "treating" the culture. My goals in working with her were similar to the message I hope this book communicates: Don't tie your self-worth to promotions—it's OK to be a leader, but there's nothing inherently wrong with being a follower. Appreciate the fact that forces beyond you may complicate, or turbocharge, your leadership path. Don't compromise principles to rise at all costs. And don't partake in the self-sabotaging cultural obsession with leading.

Our leadership obsession is obvious when one starts looking. PubMed is a free search engine popular with researchers in the biomedical and life sciences that allows access to over 34 million scientific articles. A PubMed search for "leadership" today retrieves over 80,000 entries, compared with about 60,000 for the same search in 2019—a very healthy increase in interest in the topic. An Amazon search for "leadership book" is similarly bountiful, with over 60,000 entries retrieved. That some have become international sensations speaks to the universality of this obsession. (And top international business schools have proselytized leadership training just as much as their US counter-parts.)

The interest in leading also covers the entire age spectrum. Look up "leadership books for teens" on Amazon, for example, and you will find over 10,000 entries, including *41 Leadership Tips for Teenagers*, written by an actual teen![31] In reading these books, teenagers can be said to follow the stated missions of their high schools, many of which now wear their leadership focus on their sleeves, with other historical roles of education, like forming responsible citizens, taking a backseat. They also better read these books if they want to get into a good college and not leave the "Leadership Experience" section of their college application blank. If they haven't held a position on the student council and are "just" a shy violinist, they may need to lower their standards. Unless, that is, they exaggerate or totally make up some leadership experience. For in the congested race to claim leadership experience and become leaders, many feel they have no choice but to resort to pretense and faking. The astounding story of George Santos, the expelled New York Congress member who lied about, well, *everything* on his way to the top and who is facing twenty-three felony counts, including for soliciting donations for a fake political fund then using it to buy designer clothes and pay off debt, is a case in point.[32] His CV, stuffed with a college he didn't attend, a GPA he didn't obtain, high-profile positions he didn't hold, and Holocaust connections he didn't have, had a certain style of leadership written all over it, insofar as being a leader in 2024 often comes with a dose of desperation and wholesale lying. Who *is* George Santos? The only accurate answer we might be able to come up with is "A Leader of His Times."

The culture-wide leadership fixation also manifests itself in title inflation and proliferation. Some new titles may reflect a positive evolution in society's values (e.g., the explosion in titles related to diversity, equity, and inclusion). Others are a way to project commitment to an issue of particular relevance to the company or institution (e.g., naming a chief ethics officer following a scandal). Other titles yet are a cheap way to avoid giving a raise (titles are free!) and can help with retention. But there are also titles that seem to serve no purpose other than to feed an obsession with leadership and its titular accoutrements. In a podcast on title inflation with senior Wharton faculty and administrators, business professor Betsey Stevenson recalled how in the firm where she worked before going into academia "they changed a lot of people's titles from 'senior analyst' to 'vice president.' 'Senior analyst' actually means something, but in the investment banking world, it is a pretty low rung. So people got new titles even though nobody's job changed."[33]

Wharton management professor Ben Campbell warns about the effects of the title inflation problem on the "currency" of titles in the same language that a central banker would use to warn about how letting the money printing presses run on overdrive would lead to a runaway increase in the cost of living. "Firms should be deliberate about how they give these title awards out to employees," he said in the Wharton podcast, "because each additional person who gets a C-level title dilutes the currency."[34] Four "vice president for . . . " titles make the title less "exclusive" and valuable than having just one "vice president," not unlike a hundred dollar bill that, under inflationary pressure, stops going as far. But a more relevant parallel than currency inflation might be grade inflation.

George Mason University professor Sita Slavov wrote in 2013, "Under regular [currency] inflation, prices can rise without limit. However, because grades are capped at A or A+, grade inflation results in a greater concentration of students at the top of the distribution."[35] This is not so different from the crowding of company C-suites by ever-more creatively titled executives. Grade inflation appears rampant: According to a 2012 study of over 200 colleges, grades that were As represented 43 percent of all grades, an increase of 28 percentage points since 1960 and 12 percentage points since 1988.[36] Another study, published in 2021 by researchers at Brigham Young University, Purdue, Stanford, and the United States Military Academy at West Point, argues that grade inflation is actually "warping" college graduation rates.[37] Graduation rates, which had declined from the 1970s to the 1990s, started rising again. What should have been a milestone to celebrate, however, turned out to be an artifact of grade inflation: "A significant number of college graduates would not have earned degrees if grading had stayed flat to the 1970s and 80s standards."[38]

Top schools have not been spared the grade inflation epidemic. Harvard itself was quite impacted, a 2017 article in the student daily warned, revealing that the most awarded grade at Harvard was now a straight A.[39] Many factors help explain this phenomenon. There is the genuine desire to give students an advantage in a difficult job or graduate school market. But there is also the concern by professors that bad grades will negatively impact student evaluations of them, thereby compromising their chance at tenure or advancement. Assessment tools of the 360-degree feedback type, where input is elicited from several stakeholders such as colleagues, supervisors, students, and parents, are increasingly used on educators. While such "multirater" feedback is considered less biased, one sure way to "bias" downward a student's evaluation of an educator would seem to be for the educator to fail the student. Another reason for grade inflation is that a class that is reputed to be an "easy A" attracts more students, which can translate into more funds and clout for the department and more income for the teacher. Professors also hate having to argue with students over grades. Regardless of the exact cause, the effect is to dilute the university transcript and its grade "currency." Another effect is to disadvantage students who come from schools that don't engage in grade inflation and to demotivate them when it comes to the need to work hard.

Angered by the situation but probably feeling like the inflationary pressures are too strong to resist, Harvard government

professor Harvey C. Mansfield, a passionate critic of grade inflation, devised a creative workaround that involves giving students
two grades: one that the student truly deserves and that only the
student sees; and an inflated one that shows up on the transcript
for employers and graduate schools to see.[40] Mansfield's dilemma
points to an academic system where the unofficial version of things
is accurate, and the official one fake.

There is a direct path that leads from grade inflation to title
inflation. In a world desperate for an A+ or a chief you-name-it
officer title, it's hard to resist the pull, to not be duplicitous like everyone else, to stand by your ethics. The line from an undeserved
straight A to an undeserved promotion to "chief" is straighter than
one might think, and the shortcuts, moral compromises, and cultural currents at play are quite similar. Neither is a sign of a healthy
society.

The leadership industrial complex with its ready supply of
leader-making opportunities can be seen as the free market's
response to heated demand. Leadership development programs,
books, how-to manuals, executive coaches, professors of leadership, and so on—are all the natural answers to frothy demand
for leadership from all levels of culture and society. But there
is a self-reinforcing viciousness to this cycle: by making leadership seem like a commodity, by suggesting that you have
cracked its code and are willing to sell it to the masses for the
right price, by literally putting leadership on the market, the
"suppliers" in this equation are further stimulating the already
exuberant demand. The result is a snowballing of the industry
that totally misses the real point, which is that, as we will see,
many of the essential ingredients of what makes leaders happen
and succeed are beyond the control of the leadership industry
and its ability to provide them, putting leadership out of the
reach of most of us. And this is perhaps why, despite all the
professed understanding of leadership—its tools, characteristics, methodologies, and goals—there are pervasive leadership
failures everywhere we look and as far as the eye can see, and
individuals who seem to lack every leadership quality not only

still manage to make it to the very top but are running many of our lives.

Sam Bankman-Fried, as noted earlier, the thirty-year-old CEO and cofounder of the cryptocurrency exchange FTX, presided over a total cryptocurrency implosion, having reportedly tapped into customer accounts to fund Bahamian real estate shopping sprees and high-risk investments via a sister company, Alameda Research, in what prosecutors have called "one of the biggest financial frauds in American history."[41] The run on bitcoins and liquidity crisis that resulted has forced his $32 billion empire into bankruptcy and caused untold collateral damage among those who believed his promise of opening up crypto to the masses. That, as the alleged behavior was unfolding, SBF was becoming the poster boy for Effective Altruism, a movement that wants to use reason, evidence, and the scientific method to direct its philanthropy, represents the cherry on top.[42]

Not to mention becoming the poster boy for congressional and regulatory inaction. As the *Washington Post* described it, "While Washington dithered, [SBF] appeared to place risky bets that incinerated his fortune, jeopardized billions of dollars in Silicon Valley capital and upended an entire ecosystem of cryptocurrency start-ups."[43] Washington leaders didn't quite know what to do with SBF, a wunderkind of a precocious leader who figured out how to sell bitcoins to the masses, probably for two reasons. The first borders on the forgivable—they simply do not "get" crypto, where bitcoins and digital tokens take the place of dollars, and where fortunes can be made and lost without a trader, banker, or government official in sight. The second, unforgivable, is that Democratic and Republican leaders may have been all too happy cashing real money from the leaders of a virtual money movement to effectively regulate this financial Wild West. During the 2022 midterms, FTX executives were estimated to have donated nearly $72 million to Democrats and Republicans, with SBF alone reportedly doling out $36 million.[44] And, during the 2020 presidential campaign, SBF was the second-largest individual donor to the Joe Biden campaign—to the tune of $5.2 million.[45] In *Politico*'s words, SBF was becoming "an increasingly familiar face on

Capitol Hill" and an "aspiring Washington kingmaker." The bigger scandal may have been that speculative money with no intrinsic value and hawked by propaganda was being embraced by the leadership of leading financial entities, and government regulators did little, if anything, to control it.

In the wake of the collapse of FTX, and to avoid another Lehman Brothers–type moment, the Treasury Department was described as busily placing calls to other crypto exchanges to assess the risk of wider contagion from FTX.[46] Fortunately, SBF was not declared "too big to fail," but this eerie flashback to the Great Recession also represented a bitter reminder of the utter failure of a previous leadership class—the class of 2008—and how it wiped out $8 trillion in stock market value, made Americans $9.8 trillion poorer as home values plummeted and retirement accounts vaporized, and pushed unemployment to 10 percent.[47] Crypto may be impossible for some to "get," but the FTX bankruptcy story is an all-too-easy-to-follow morality tale that encapsulates yesterday's and today's bankruptcy of corporate and political leadership.

FTX is headquartered in the Bahamas, and Alameda Research in Hong Kong, but put either entity in Google Maps, and you will be led to a nondescript domestic address: 5327 Jacuzzi St., #1C, Richmond, CA. Now look up "leadership training" within a narrow radius from that locale, and the map will light up with entries that are too numerous to list. Do the same with the DC Capitol as your locus, and you will be truly overwhelmed. It's not a shortage of help that made SBF and others possible, but it might be that we have become too confident that the leadership industry fully "gets" leadership and that with this sophisticated understanding and with all the leadership training opportunities now in place, altruistic people will be elevated and characterologically compromised ones will be stopped in their leadership tracks. The sad truth is that we have no good reason to trust that any of it is doing anything to prevent an anointed DC "kingmaker" and unquestionable cryptocurrency leader from going from hero to zero and for his bitcoin to ultimately be designated a . . . "shitcoin"![48]

2

BRING ME YOUR TOXIC LEADERS AND FAST-TRACKERS

Therapists, Coaches, and Impostors

PSYCHOLOGY IS THE determinant force in how leaders lead, and a leadership industry that gives it its due is one that can illuminate our understanding of leadership, help the right leaders rise, and deflect those who come with warning signs all over them. Some psychological traits are highly desirable in leaders and should be selected for, while others should make us hereby tender our resignations. A couldn't-be-more-central attribute when it comes to leaders, it is what differentiates a Churchill from a psychopath.

Given the centrality of psychology—and the tightly linked concepts of personality and character—it would seem like a big "missed opportunity" for the leadership industry not to have made psychology its absolute foundation, the source from which all its how-to books, development workshops, training webinars, and leadership degrees flow. Instead, we seem to have kept psychology at arm's length, paying it lip service while ignoring some of its basic tenets, and replacing it with a new helping profession that is well-meaning but, given what leaders' psychology can involve, maybe in a bit over its head. Enter the "executive coach," a professional who can be seen as channeling psychological principles to offer a user-friendly, therapy-like experience to leaders. This experience may lack the stigma that many leaders still associate with actual therapy, but can fall short of what is needed—and way short if the leader in question happens to channel psychopathic energy.

A new and increasingly ubiquitous presence in corporate and occupational settings, the executive coach offers career advice, serves as soundboard, and helps navigate the vicissitudes of the workplace and its web of vertical, horizontal, and "dotted line" relationships. While any attention to these issues in our increasingly complex professional lives and reporting structures would be hugely welcome, pushing coaches into this role has been unfair to them. Coaches, who typically have no formal training in psychology or mental health and no licensing or supervision requirements, are often not equipped to help leaders better understand themselves and others. To use the not-so-uncommon corporate example of inconsistent standards in judging one's reports, one might want to understand what it is about employee X that makes it so the person "can do no wrong" in the eyes of the boss, whereas identical behavior emanating from employee Y will make him snap. Could employee X remind the boss of a first love whose memory remains rosy all these years later, and might employee Y bring up unconscious associations with an abusive parent or a toxic colleague from a previous life? A working knowledge of psychological "transference" would come in handy in addressing this basic workplace inequity. Defined as the process by which we project feelings about one person onto someone else, transference is not something most executive coaches would have had exposure to, much less had the chance to practice identifying or learning to ask sensitive questions about.

The chief people officers—their title is an increasingly popular alternative to chief human resources officers—running many HR departments have found a godsend in the executive coach. As they do their work of developing highly promising employees, supporting the organization's leaders, rehabilitating fallen managers, serving as "policy police" around compliance issues, and generally keeping the company out of trouble and out of court, the executive coach has become a trusted and handy ally, a sort of cure-all pain relief for the company's equivalent of migraine, sinus, tension, cluster, thunderclap, and you-name-it headaches. The sports metaphor at the origin of coaching has been a powerful mantra for the leadership industry, which seems to have taken to heart the view of the ultimate football coach and NFL executive Vince Lombardi: "Leaders aren't born. They are made. And they are made just like anything else, through hard work."[1] Football players' physical attributes and innate talents, as reflected, say, in first downs, net yards per attempt, and rushing yards statistics, become a bit secondary if your favorite team is in the hands of a Lombardiesque coach. Find one, and it, too, has a reasonable chance of winning three straight and five total NFL championships in seven years, in addition to two Super Bowl titles, as did the Green Bay Packers under Lombardi.[2] But in taking the coaching metaphor from the Super Bowl to the C-suite and applying it to leadership training, the effect has been to minimize the role of psychology in leaders' success and failure, all the while turning executive coaches into proxy therapists who work around the edges of personality and mental health. It seems like character deficits that might cause an executive to self-sabotage, make for toxic relationships with subordinates, or result in unhealthy office competition are now, naturally and by default, the realm of the executive coach.

You have a "style" that is leading to rapid employee turnover or high burnout rates in your reports? We have a coach for that! You have a boss who is temperamentally unsuited for leadership because his impulsive decision-making precludes patient strategizing and long-term planning? We can, "just like anything else, through hard work," Lombardi-style, make him into a leader who works through the processes, mechanisms, and steps to see a long-haul undertaking through and deliver results!

The company coach has been a good mediator between HR and company employees, including leaders, many of whom prefer to avoid HR if they have the choice. I love my HR point person and fully appreciate the foundational role HR plays in the success of an institution or company, but, seriously, poor HR! It has become synonymous with so much work unpleasantness that it is almost unlovable.

Let us count the ways in which HR can be hard to love:

- HR runs background checks that, depending on the job, might dive deeper than you would like into your work history, education, credit score, driving record, criminal record, medical history, mental health history, and TikTok account.
- Puts you through drug screening.
- Makes you complete sometimes brain-numbing trainings to stay in sync with ever-changing regulations, then makes you repeat them annually, or, if you're lucky, every two years.
- Makes you document in uncomfortable detail bad behavior by colleagues, supervisors, or supervisees.
- Calls you to the office when you are the object of complaints.
- And, if you have ever been laid off or terminated, chances are, at that most stressful moment, you spent more time talking to somebody you didn't know from HR than saying goodbye to colleagues and friends.

For many people, these negative associations overshadow the many positive things brought to us courtesy of HR, including development opportunities and protection from discrimination and from inadvertently breaking the law, not to mention conveying the happy news of a job offer in the first place! For many, it would still be asking too much to conceive of HR as something other than a department to avoid if at all possible.

Hence, one convenience of having an executive coach around. Often external contractors working with HR on an independent basis, executive coaches are usually not direct employees of the organization. As such, they can be seen as unbiased and having the client's, not company's, interest at heart. This helps inspire trust between coach and coachee and defuses some of the awkwardness and discomfort that too-close-a-relationship with HR might bring.

Embraced by HR but somewhat removed from it, executive coaches have become the more accessible employee ally. If instructor-led development programs like the ones described in the previous chapter are the main pillar of the leadership industry, executive coaching is its second leg and is offered by more than 70 percent of organizations, according to a 2021 survey by the Chief Learning Officer website, with another 22 percent expressing a desire to offer it if they could find the budget for it.[3] And the influence of the coach is rapidly expanding up, down, and across the org chart. No longer reserved for executives, "high performers," or "high potentials," coaching has been democratized to the point where the notion that it can help individuals at all levels of an organization is firmly taking hold.[4] Like highly democratic leadership programs that are open to "leaders at all levels," it would seem like there isn't anyone who couldn't potentially benefit from coaching.[5] *But what is it and what is the problem?*

The International Coaching Federation, the leading global organization for coaches, defines coaching as "partnering with clients in a thought-provoking and creative process that inspires them to maximize their personal and professional potential. The process of coaching often unlocks previously untapped sources of imagination, productivity, and leadership."[6] It is, first of all, more than a little noteworthy that the International Coaching Federation puts "leadership" in its very definition of "coaching" (we're not even talking "executive coaching"), suggesting an organic link between the growth of coaching, the growth of the leadership industry, and the growth of cultural fixation with leadership and how to achieve it. It is also noteworthy that coaching sounds a whole lot like another profession you might be familiar with. If "personal and professional" growth via a trusting relationship with a neutral person who helps you "untap" inner resources conjures up a therapist or reminds you of a therapy experience you might have had, that's because it should.

So what, if anything, distinguishes a coach from a therapist, and what potential harm might result to leaders and followers alike, and to our very idea of leadership, from the confusion between where coaching ends and therapy begins? And how much can we trust this increasingly popular intervention when it comes to building up emerging leaders, rehabilitating fallen ones, and improving leadership culture and leadership understanding overall?

The blurry boundaries between what coaches do in corporate settings and what we as mental health professionals do in our clinics was made clear to me by Sam, a Silicon Valley medical device company executive who requested an appointment after coming across a research article I had published on coaching.[7] After graduating from a top engineering school, Sam initially joined his company as a contractor before quickly switching to full-time employee status in order to obtain health benefits for himself, his wife, and his son. Once employed, Sam quickly climbed the leadership ladder through four successive promotions in as many years. Before he knew it, he had a few dozen direct reports, even more employees that he oversaw indirectly via "dotted line" relationships, and a pipeline of products at various degrees of development that he managed. His salary more than quadrupled, and his incentive stock options grew impressively.

Much of Sam's rise was the direct fruit of his smarts, many sleepless nights in the office, and superior people skills. As reflected in consistently glowing reviews, he was both very good and very liked. But he was also very lucid about two fateful junctures for which he could not take credit and that directly played into his ascent: his first supervisor, who recruited Sam and deeply believed in him, decided not to return to work after going on maternity leave, giving Sam an early shot at a coveted supervisory position barely a few months into his company tenure. Another juncture occurred because one device he was overseeing targeted a rare cardiac condition that the child of a big Silicon Valley investor happened to have died of, prompting the businessman to make a substantial investment in the company in quiet honor of his child, which only further raised Sam's profile and triggered a fourth promotion.

A "high performer" and a "high potential" if ever there was one, Sam caught the eye of his company's HR team as someone who would benefit from coaching. Sam wasn't in trouble or exhibiting obvious burnout—common targets for coaching interventions for leaders. He was, however, silently struggling with a mild case of impostor syndrome, given the chance events that contributed to his quick rise. He could have also used some guidance in dealing with the CEO's insecurity, which made Sam feel like he was walking on eggshells whenever around him, especially during big company events like board meetings. On the more personal front, Sam was concerned about his teenage son's impulsivity—reckless driving and too much alcohol and drug experimentation—and in some disagreement with his wife about how to handle it. He was also wondering whether his son's problems might be somehow linked to Sam spending too much time at work and not being available to "model" responsible behavior at home. Sam processed all this internally, though, at no point complaining, "breaking down," or allowing it to impact his work productivity or how he was being perceived.

The coaching, then, wasn't meant to rescue Sam or target an obvious or voiced symptom. Rather, as he put it, "it was the thing to do" at his company for a high-placed employee with his responsibilities. Or perhaps it was meant to prevent a bad outcome: "Maybe they were afraid I might sexually harass someone." Regardless, with a mix of indirect pressure to do what everybody else seemed to be doing and some intrigue, he took time off his schedule to embark on weekly coaching with an executive coach.

Part of the "democratization" of employee coaching has been to not just broaden the scope of its recipients from leaders and top executives to lower-placed employees, but also to broaden its mandate. Coaching is no longer about fixing a problem. There is preventive coaching, meant to foresee and avoid problems before they occur; retention coaching, to make employees stick around; transition coaching, to help us settle into new roles, and so on. All this corporate coaching mirrors the rise, within culture at large, of the "life coach," a professional who, as the label suggests, can help with all aspects of existence, and who, as we will see, is giving those trained as professional therapists an existential crisis.

There is seemingly nothing within or outside the office that coaching cannot help with, appears to be the message, so why not offer it to leaders and would-be leaders even in the absence of clear target problems as a way to fortify and support them? Why not diminish the chances of a Sam messing up by intervening early? Preventive medicine is better than curative medicine, we are taught in medical school; it stops sickness before it starts. Why wouldn't the same principle apply in coaching? In the words of Sarah Morgan, the chief excellence officer of a leadership consulting company and the author of the popular *The Buzz on HR* blog, "Coaching is better than correction. Providing positive feedback and sincere suggestions for improvement early and often yields more success, better outcomes, and stronger relationships than any corrective action or progressive discipline ever will."[8] So, for Sam, a reasonable argument could have been made to coach early and coach aggressively—as warranty against something derailing a career's meteoric rise.

Another reason for intervening early and aggressively in Sam's case would be to keep him from being poached by another company. In a region that counts several top medical device companies—Abbott, Medtronic, Variant, Intuitive Surgical, to name a few—it's the rule rather than the exception that an "executive recruiter" representing a competitor will discreetly cold-call or reach out on LinkedIn to put out feelers, test the waters, and see what it might take for talent to jump ship. As Fortune 500 workplace consultant Alexandra Levit writes in an article on retention coaching, "Top Yahoo! employees want to go to Microsoft, top Microsoft employees want to go to Google, and so on."[9] Indeed, it is not unusual in my Silicon Valley practice for a patient to be working at, say, Facebook when a medication is started, Apple by the time it shows peak benefit, a new startup when the decision to stop it is made a year after responding, and at Instagram which, like Facebook, is part of Meta, when a relapse occurs a couple of years down the road. Golden handcuffs and unvested equity notwithstanding, it's a highly mobile and rather incestuous environment out here in the Valley; one that may recall the risqué late nineteenth-century play *La Ronde* by German playwright Arthur Schnitzler about a 360-degree pursuit of love that unfolds in ten scenes until the "round" is closed.[10]

First published in Vienna around 1900, *La Ronde*'s plot begins with Léocadie, a prostitute, who is negotiating an encounter with Franz, a soldier; he, in turn, has what we might today call a "hookup" at a dance hall with Marie, a chambermaid; she, in turn, has a tryst on a new job assignment with her employers' son, Alfred; he, in turn, has an ongoing affair with Emma Breitkopf, a society matron; she, in turn, engages in "pillow talk" about Alfred with her husband, Charles Breitkopf; he, in turn, has dinner in a restaurant's private room with Anna, a working class woman; she, in turn, has a hotel encounter described by Charles as their fantasy meeting, but instead of Charles, she has it with Robert Kuhlenkampf, a poet; he, in turn, connects backstage at a play with Charlotte, an actress; she, in turn, is paid a visit in her boudoir by a count who saw her perform; he, in turn, falls into the arms of a certain Léocadie while on a drinking spree, completing the circle.

Silicon Valley circa 2024, it cannot be overemphasized, is nowhere as interesting as Vienna circa 1900. And Vienna then, it should be recalled, is where Freud, the father of psychoanalysis, was formulating his psychoanalytic theories, studying personality structure, defining the id, the ego, and the superego, and exploring the unconscious, all inspired by similar boudoir shenanigans and the dogged pursuit of love and the pleasure principle by his analysands. My patient Sam, alas, did not have the advantage of working with Freud or a trained psychotherapist at his job, although the executive coach assigned to him seemed to channel one. As Sam would recount it, his work with his coach evolved in ways both predictable and not so predictable. As might be expected, his coach explained how leading involves switching from managing things to managing people, and from achieving through doing something yourself to inspiring others to achieve for you or with you. Much was covered about the importance of communication, clarifying expectations, maintaining boundaries, giving and eliciting feedback, and the all-important need to nurture and improve emotional intelligence. Sam's progress in coaching would be tracked via a series of "metrics" that measure coaching's impact on his performance, engagement, well-being, and job satisfaction, including the ubiquitous 360-degree feedback assessment, which incorporates input from his direct reports, his summer intern, his peers, and the executives above him.

But alongside the expected, something rather unusual was playing out that the already emotionally intelligent engineer picked up on. As the weeks went on, Sam's coaching started triggering déjà vu flashbacks to the psychotherapy he had undergone several years earlier while in college and struggling to recover from the painful breakup of his first long-term relationship. Only now Sam wasn't seeing an actual psychotherapist. As the sessions unfolded, he found himself discussing:

- The root cause of his insomnia (was it anxiety about an upcoming board presentation or a symptom of generalized anxiety disorder?).
- His conflict-resolution skills (in the context of feuding subordinates but also over parenting disagreements with his wife).
- How his personality meshed with that of others (his insecure boss but also his impulsive son).
- The importance of modeling behavior (to his team but also at home).
- And how not to feel like a fraud (whether he deserved his four promotions but also, given how little time he was giving his family, his wife's affections).

While in psychotherapy a couple of decades earlier, Sam would describe openly and quite willingly relationship dynamics with his mother and within his family of origin to explore how they might inform the struggles with his girlfriend. Those comparisons grew naturally and organically, and Sam never questioned the value of discussing them or the "authority" of the therapist stirring them up and helping him connect the dots. But it felt different now. Personal life would come up with his executive coach, as it always does, but never quite as freely and unselfconsciously and never without some doubt as to whether he should be baring his soul like that.

And the executive coach would not shut it down, probably because it would be insensitive to cut off a client who seemed in need of airing out serious concerns, but also because it would be difficult and artificial to erect impermeable boundaries between work and personal life—"Yes, we can talk about the quarterly earnings report on your mind, but we must pretend your son, who's the real source of stress in your life, doesn't exist!" In many ways, it *made sense* to bring up wife, son, and impostor syndrome along with boss, subordinates, and work deliverables—those personal issues weighed on him at work, just as an anticipated board meeting would occasionally enter his bedroom and keep him up at night. Life bleeds into work, and vice versa, in a strong bidirectional emotional current familiar to most employees, therapists, and coaches. But it didn't feel quite right to bring up home stuff with *this* professional, as well-intended and eager to help as she was. How *truly* independent from HR, which hired her, is she, he started asking himself. And is she sworn to secrecy the way a real therapist would be, or might sensitive content shared during his session inadvertently make it into her work with other company executives she was also coaching? No, it didn't make sense to ask her how to handle a fragile-egoed boss that Sam had independently "diagnosed" with borderline personality disorder, or inquire whether his son's impulsivity was the result of incipient bipolar disorder or teenage "acting out."

The executive coach was not, after all, a therapist, but, as he saw it, it was impossible for her to do her job without coming across as one. In a moment of truth, and since much was at stake personally and professionally for him, Sam asked his coach what psychological training, if any, she had received, since she seemed to issue interpretations and recommendations historically associated with Freud. Although her answer listed impressive-sounding (but optional-for-coaches) credentials—a PCC for Professional Certified Coach in the bag and aspirations for an MCC for Master Certified Coach—she could not list any psychotherapy license or formal training in mental health.[11] To his company's dismay, Sam decided to "terminate" with her—to borrow a term from professional psychotherapy—and to start seeing us. He did not, however, feel comfortable informing HR about his decision to transfer his "care" to us, fearing that he might be labeled a "mental case." As he experienced it, it was totally normalized within his company culture to indirectly explore psychological territory with a coach, but God forbid he should be thought of as somebody who might need an actual shrink.

Sam knew intuitively that discussing how personal life interacted with professional life with an executive coach who had no psychological training was not the best use of his time and could be potentially dangerous. While it's true that an executive coach is often much better versed than the typical therapist in corporate politics, retention packages, and boardroom intrigues, the fact is people are not that good at compartmentalizing their personal and professional lives, and focusing on one to the exclusion of the other can be too myopic to produce lasting benefit and risks missing the forest for the trees. Psychology shapes the workplace, and the workplace, in turn, impacts psychology. Therefore, a better choice for improving well-being, broadly defined, than a coach with no background in psychology is almost always a professional counselor with specific training in personality structure, drives, and motivations. One who has a better understanding of how DNA interacts with the environment to produce distress at home or at work; who can help you understand what "makes people tick" personally and professionally; and who can diagnose and address frank mental illness when it exists. Not to mention the ability to identify relationship styles that can be just as prevalent—and problematic—in the office as at home:

- Active-passive, where one is caretaker and one is helpless;
- Bully-victim, where you have an abuser and you have a target;
- Parallel, where rather than a shared path, two individuals are on separate tracks, and never the twain shall meet;
- And codependent, where one person needs the other, and the other needs to be needed.[12]

That executive coaches, with no required degree or formal training in these concepts, have become such an intrinsic part of forming and reforming leaders is a sign of how divorced the notion of leadership has become from psychology. It communicates that psychology is secondary or optional and not the dominant force it is in making and unmaking leaders.

To have made of coaching as opposed to psychological exploration a cornerstone for the leadership industry may also suggest that everyone is emotionally healthy to the point of not needing to investigate the psychological root causes of any work problems. It also assumes that clients are equally malleable and receptive when it comes to implementing a coach's advice, when decades of therapy research and experience teach us about the outsize, self-sabotaging role of "resistance to change"—and what to do about it. Assuming that leadership salvation will come through executive coaches who know org charts but who are not necessarily trained to know psychology and personality would seem like the wrong prescription for our leadership culture failures. As for maximally untapping human "resources," it can't be done without a finely tuned psychology that unleashes inner potential.

Even as they hew ever so close to therapy territory, coaches never claim that what they do is therapy or that leaders or people in general should eschew therapy in favor of coaching. But this expressed desire to coexist with therapists within a landscape where each profession plays in its well-defined lane is happening as the coaching field increasingly embraces the all-encompassing moniker of "life coach," with its implication that coaching helps with nothing short of life itself. This doesn't leave much for therapists to do, no "niche" for them to occupy. In addition to professional functioning, life coaching would naturally include overall wellness, relationship dynamics, grief, loss, adjustment, transitions, and specific psychopathologies like anxiety and ADHD. Indeed, quick Google searches will easily identify endless lists of local coaches advertising their help with these diagnoses and many more. Yet this same spectrum of workplace and personal issues is the raison d'être for therapy, what it was invented for. An ungenerous explanation for this contradiction—coaches saying they do not do therapy while taking on therapy's problems—is that coaches want to avoid the legal exposure of calling therapy by its name so use "coaching" as a convenient workaround.

The coaches I've interacted with, however, are genuinely motivated to help and honestly believe that there are clear boundaries and distinctions between coaching and therapy.[13] Coaching, they argue, is for psychologically healthy individuals who do not suffer from mental health problems. Coaching is more collaborative than the hierarchical, top-down therapy approach. Coaching has a clear beginning, middle, and end and doesn't meander open-endedly. Coaching is future focused and has no room for historical explorations of the tell-me-about-your-childhood variety. Coaching is informal, not ruled by rigid protocols around the time, location, and the conduct of the session. Finally, coaching is stigma-free.

Yet these distinctions really aren't, and it would be difficult for a coach working with a leader today to come across as anything other than a therapist doing therapy by another name. At least since "person-centered" therapy emerged some eighty years ago, the evolution of therapy has been to move away from the all-knowing, God-like figure of the therapist and toward a more collaborative partnership where therapist and client are on an equal footing.[14] The currently dominant school of cognitive-behavioral therapy (CBT) has further rebalanced the relationship to where therapist and client are equal players who partner together to decide therapy's goals and course, aiming to complete it in a finite period (fifteen to twenty sessions) within which there is little space for rehashing the past or retelling the history—only for practical, sensible, and actionable advice.[15] There is no patience for therapists with God complexes in the CBT philosophy, insofar as CBT has made the therapist "optional" through manuals that allow clients to confront their symptoms on their own via self-paced modules that essentially bypass providers. Newer programs take this notion even further by utilizing AI chatbots trained in CBT to deliver therapy for depression and anxiety through machine learning platforms with no therapist in sight.[16] Therefore, the distinction that coaching is collaborative, while therapy is dominated by the all-powerful therapist doesn't stand.

The same can be said about the supposed distinction between coaching and therapy based on how "formal" each is. Already well underway, the rise of remote therapy during the pandemic may have dealt the final blow to the idea of a regimented encounter between client and therapist occurring in a softly lit office painted in peaceful pastels. While I was supervising a trainee via Zoom early into the pandemic, there were three of us in the virtual office one Monday morning: a patient with panic disorder, the psychiatry trainee who had earned his MD degree but was now training to become a psychiatrist, and me, the supervising psychiatrist. I was disturbed at the beginning of the 60-minute consultation by our patient having logged in from bed while eating a breakfast of cereal and milk off a tray on her lap. An untouched glass of orange juice stood precariously on the tray. Uncomfortable proceeding given the lack of any "decorum," I started formulating in my mind how I would ask her to pause eating until we were done. Before I could say anything, though, something possessed my trainee to adjust his camera ever so slightly, revealing a glimpse of the ultimate business-on-top-party-on-the-bottom attire: Below his crisp dress shirt and tie, he wore what looked like a pair of gym shorts. Therapy over cheerios by a psychiatrist in shorts remains, thankfully, inappropriately casual, even by Zoom standards and even with all sorts of pandemic-justified rule relaxations and dispensations. But remote therapy offerings are just the latest and perhaps most extreme step in a long-unfolding process of casualization and flexibilization of what used to feel like a temple visit on a high holiday. All this complicates the notion that "etiquette" or "protocol" are reliable differentiators between the user-friendly and "accessible" approach of coaching and the stuffy, overwrought, and much more formal approach of therapy.

As to the distinction that coaching is for clients with no psychiatric illness whereas therapy is for individuals with mental health issues, it carries a dangerous assumption: that coaches can recognize mental illness when they see it, a faulty and risky differentiator, and leads to a disturbing conclusion—that coaches may be "treating" people who should be receiving mental health care instead. To that end, studies that show that 25 to 50 percent of recipients of coaching meet criteria for significant mental health issues should make us wonder about unwell leaders and other coaching recipients going undiagnosed and untreated by the coaches coaching them.[17] Well beyond the world of HR, executive coaching, and leadership development, it should make us wonder about the well-being of the many patients we are increasingly seeing, who, once we recommend therapy for their obsessive-compulsive disorder (OCD), panic disorder, or depression, answer: "Oh, but I'm already seeing a coach!"

THERE ARE OFFICE affairs more ominous yet than an unwitting boss punishing an employee who happens to trigger reminders of a better-forgotten antagonist from the past. The boss could actually be malignant. The lack of deep psychological knowledge at the heart of much of the industry also helps explain how rather scary personality traits in leaders can go undetected or be detected too late—after the CEO has been convicted, the Ponzi pyramid has collapsed, and many employees have lost their jobs. I am talking about leaders and would-be leaders with psychopathic tendencies. Many of their traits are exactly what the company is looking for in a leader: charm, polish, self-confidence, cool decisiveness, and a penchant for the fast track. Unfortunately for us, the Machiavellian, remorseless, parasitic, and morally compromised underside can go undiagnosed.[18]

Although the existence of this "underside" doesn't seem to be in doubt, its exact prevalence remains a subject of debate. Overall, preliminary research suggests that psychopathic traits are over-represented among leaders compared with the general population. Jack McCullough, founder and president of the CFO Leadership Council and author of *The Psychopathic CEO: An Executive Survival Guide*, summarizes it as such in a 2019 *Forbes* article: "Roughly 4% to as high as 12% of CEOs exhibit psychopathic traits . . . , many times more than the 1% rate found in the general population and more in line with the 15% rate found in prisons."[19] However, a large meta-analysis of ninety-two data sets published the same year in the *Journal of Applied Psychology* determined that having psychopathic tendencies was meaningfully, but not very dramatically, associated with leader emergence.[20] Still, given the number of follower lives that leaders control and the power that they wield, it doesn't take too many bad apples to bring down the whole economy or poison an entire leadership culture.

Regardless of the exact incidence, the rise in popular culture of the "corporate psychopath" as someone people love to hate speaks to real fear among followers of a boss character that they seem all too familiar with. Google's Ngram Viewer, which tracks the frequency of keywords in printed sources, dates the corporate psychopath's cultural emergence to the early 1980s.[21] Since then, provocative headlines ("7 Ways to Deal with a Psycho Boss"), catchy book titles (*Snakes in Suits*), and over-the-top media portrayals (the movies *9 to 5* and *Wall Street*, and the TV series *The Office* and *The Simpsons*) have fed the notion that most of us work for a Miranda Priestly–like figure from *The Devil Wears Prada*—a hypercritical boss who pits subordinates against each other, encourages office backstabbing, and goes through employees like she goes through clothes. Much more relevant for the "cult" of the corporate psychopath, however, is that it is an unwanted gift that keeps on giving. Hardly a news cycle goes by without a report on some, well, psychopathic move by a real, not fictional, psychopathic leader. We are not imagining the problem, and Meryl Streep is not to blame!

Case in point: when you ask them, followers are often unsparing in their assessments of their leaders, again suggesting a problem of rather considerable magnitude. The Edelman Trust Barometer is an annual report card of sorts on "trust issues" between citizens and business, government, media, and NGOs. Its 2023 update sampled more than 32,000 respondents from twenty-eight countries and showed that CEOs were among the least trusted institutional leaders at 48 percent, just above government leaders at 41 percent.[22] This lends credence to the old adage: "Employees don't quit jobs, they quit bosses." Indeed, a 2017 meta-analysis by Alex Rubenstein of the College of Business at the University of Central Florida and colleagues summarized data from 316 studies that explored why employees voluntarily quit.[23] The results showed that the quality of the leadership was a significantly bigger driver of employee turnover than pay, job description, an employee's age, or the number of children an employee has. Commenting on the findings, investment strategist and CFA Institute trustee Joachim Klement said, "They say that people with a mortgage and kids in school don't change jobs, but if the leadership is bad enough, they will. And no money in the world will be enough to keep them."[24] Accordingly, his message to those contemplating investing in a company is: "Ask company management to disclose their voluntary turnover rate. This is in my experience the single best predictor of company morale and future profitability." The moral of this body of evidence may be that when employees talk about a "toxic workplace," chances are they are talking about a toxic leader.

A leadership industry that is truly attuned to psychology would invest considerably more energy and resources trying to understand, research, and teach about leaders' complex psychology, like how a compromised core can come wrapped in superficial charm. Instead, seeing how little attention this seems to get, makes it look as though we have deluded ourselves into thinking that there's no character flaw, no toxic dose, that training and a good executive coach can't fix.

To be sure, identifying and fixing psychopathic tendencies is an uphill climb for mental health professionals as well, as suggested by Hervey M. Cleckley, an American psychiatrist and pioneer psychopathy researcher and the author of *The Mask of Sanity*, a book on psychopathic personality first published in 1941. Through illuminating vignettes of "the psychopath as gentleman," "the psychopath as man of the world," "the psychopath as scientist," "the psychopath as physician," and "the psychopath as businessman," and through profiles in psychopathy involving "Max," "Roberta," "Arnold," "Tom," "George," "Pierre," "Frank," "Anna," "Jack," "Chester," "Walter," "Joe," "Milt," "Gregory," and "Stanley," Cleckley arrives at conclusions that have stood the test of time, the most chilling of which may be: "More often than not, the typical psychopath will seem particularly agreeable and make a distinctly positive impression when he is first encountered. Alert and friendly in his attitude, he is easy to talk with and seems to have a good many genuine interests. There is nothing at all odd . . . about him, and in every respect he tends to embody the concept of a well-adjusted, happy person. . . . He looks like the real thing."[25]

Fast forward to the fifth edition, with nearly half a century of clinical experience under his belt, and Cleckley, by then the world's foremost expert on psychopaths, is full of modesty about what he can and cannot do with them. He describes himself as "still in the unspectacular and perforce modest position of one who can offer neither a cure nor a well-established explanation" for the problem. And, addressing a doctor who had referred him a client for treatment, he writes: "I think it very likely that he will continue to behave as he has behaved in the past, and I do not know of any psychiatric treatment that is likely to influence this behavior appreciably or to help him make a better adjustment. . . . I appreciate so very much your letting me see him and am sorry I cannot be more hopeful about his prognosis."[26]

The best that the ultimate authority on psychopathy could do, he seemed to tell us, is identify the problem, raise awareness, and support victims. He made no claims to being able to reform these individuals. There is a lesson in humility for the leadership industry, the coaching profession, and, indeed, the therapy profession in this. For the rest of us, the lesson might be to recognize that a serially untrustworthy, abusive, or manipulative boss might not be easily reformable even in the hands of the best experts, so protect yourself, know your rights, find support, and vote with your feet to get the hell out when you can. Don't hope against hope for a magical transformation, and don't trust that the industry will be able to save you.

How can executive coaches who never had to study the *Diagnostic and Statistical Manual of Mental Disorders* (DSM)—the "bible" of psychiatric diagnoses—illuminate us on antisocial personality disorder, a condition closely linked to psychopathy? Will they recognize the "pervasive pattern of disregard for and violation of the rights of others" and the "deceitfulness," "conning," "repeated lying," and "lack of remorse" that go along with it when they see them?[27] How can they, if they have not had to consult the International Classification of Diseases (ICD), identify C-suite "dissociality," a related, troubling personality feature defined as "disregard for the rights and feelings of others, encompassing both self-centeredness and lack of empathy"?[28] Will they be able to flag budding psychopaths who appear "agreeable . . . well adjusted, happy" when they come knocking on their HR doors, and will they divert them as far away as possible from the leadership trajectory, thus sparing us the prospect of a psychopathic boss? It is doubtful. If well-meaning, but insufficiently trained, executive coaches are the leadership industry's best defenses against an over-representation of psychopaths masquerading as charmers in the leadership class, we may be in trouble.

THE DISTINCTION THAT coaching is for healthy individuals and therapy is for those with mental illness does not make sense, then, because coaches, by and large, are not trained to recognize mental illness, including psychopathic tendencies. And, as we have seen, distinctions based on informality, lack of hierarchy, future orientation, and duration are similarly unsatisfactory. One distinction, however, does make sense: coaching lacks the stigma still attached to therapy. In my clinical experience, most people who opt for coaching over therapy do it to avoid the label of being a patient in need of a mental health provider. This is particularly true among men, where resistance to therapy or any kind of mental health help has been well-documented and attributed to masculine norms that discourage help-seeking and encourage the repression of feelings.[29] Rather than being forced to admit weakness or emote, they are more likely to respond to a grin-and-bear-it, stoic message.[30] This helps explain the popularity among many of them of a certain nonfiction genre represented by titles such as *Stoicism: How to Stop Fearing and Start Living, The Stoic CEO, How to Think Like a Roman Emperor,* and *The Stoic Challenge: A Philosopher's Guide to Becoming Tougher.* Given that leadership ranks remain overwhelmingly male, men's general resistance to therapy and psychological exploration is a very relevant detail. Coaching, a normalized and familiar concept with positive associations for many guys due to its sports roots, becomes a much more palatable, stigma-free option. And just like that, the coach becomes a medium channeling both Sigmund Freud and Vince Lombardi! But is stigma a good reason to divert clients who might benefit from a psychological assessment or treatment to those without the proper training? Or are we perpetuating stigma by going that route?

And male leaders aren't the only ones with difficulty discussing and navigating feelings and emotions. Many companies and HR departments are similarly challenged—possibly because they are still mostly run by male leaders—and show a general unease when dealing with all things mental health. They are often uncomfortable talking to employees about it, for fear it might worsen their "fragile" state, come across as insensitive, or breech privacy. They also do not like that there are no "objective" blood tests or brain scans that would allow us to verify problems. They worry that mental health diagnoses can be easily faked for leave-taking or other inappropriate ends. They fret about lawsuits.

This reality is also reflected in how employer-provided mental health benefits are often offered to employees as a "carve-out" that is removed from the main health insurance policy, sometimes with strict caps on the number of visits or total care cost, or not offered at all. The discomfort on the part of leaders, companies, and HR in dealing with mental health head-on may have found in coaches a tempting subterfuge—a convenient way to "address" mental health, without calling it that. Or offering a therapy-lite of sorts, without calling it that, either. This, in turn, has given more impetus and bigger roles to coaches and helped propel coaching into the industry it has become.

If coaching and therapy target similar issues and use similar strategies, there is another real distinction between them besides stigma, one big enough you can drive an industrial complex through it. Therapists must be licensed and meet clearly defined educational and training milestones and undergo extensive supervision before they can practice. And, once they start practicing, they do so under close oversight and with strict requirements for certification maintenance and malpractice insurance. Coaching, on the other hand, comes with no legally mandated educational, training, or supervision requirements, and occurs in a regulatory vacuum that is largely outside scrutiny. Despite coaching organizations calling for it, licensing and specific training are essentially optional. While many coaches have pursued impressive studies and careers, they are coaches largely because they say they are.

One can understand why therapists who worked long and hard for their credentials might develop therapy-worthy fears of professional replacement. Do not expect them to seek help from coaches, though, as they worry about going the way of cab drivers in a manner that recalls gig economy takeovers of an established profession by a newcomer who offers a similar service but is allowed to operate under easier rules. Only, when it comes to the uberization of therapy, the "passengers" to worry about might be vulnerable patients or, indeed, leaders whom we want to be in tip-top psychological form.

Still, the solution is not to eliminate coaching, including in corporate life, or give coaches impostor syndrome for passing as therapists. A new helping profession is a welcome development and speaks to a certain progressive acknowledgment that we need help and are ready to ask for it. And God knows there is more need for help than resources available. Instead, it should be about having an honest conversation about what coaching can and cannot do and what protections and transparency we owe clients who do not necessarily understand the limits of coaching or are pursuing it for the wrong reasons. To the extent possible, corporate coaching should stick to modalities that are easier to differentiate from therapy. There is skills coaching to perfect sales skills, for example. Or performance coaching to help managers meet targets following a performance review. Or developmental coaching to help with professional competencies. All this development can, of course, take place while acknowledging that the personal will invariably intertwine itself with the professional and that it doesn't diminish the coach in any way to seek consultation from, or refer to, an actual therapist when that happens.

His name may have since been eclipsed by a namesake Bollywood star, but, in the 1990s and 2000s, Ram Charan was a star coach to a who's who list of star leaders. Described in a 2007 *Fortune* profile by journalist David Whitford as "a corporate sage, with unparalleled access to boardrooms across the globe and intimate, enduring relationships with an array of powerful CEOs," he has been lavished with praise by many of them. Jack Welch, formerly of GE, talked of his "rare ability to distill meaningful from meaningless and transfer it to others in a quiet, effective way without destroying confidences." According to Dick Harrington, formerly of Thomson Corp., "He probably knows more about corporate America than anybody." Verizon's Ivan Seidenberg saw him as a "secret weapon," and former Citicorp CEO John Reed as his "conscience": "Just when you sort of think you have everything done and you're feeling pretty good about yourself, he calls you up and says, 'Hey, Reed, did you do this and that and the other?'"[31]

Charan was born in a small city in India and grew up with sixteen members of his family and his uncle's family on the second floor of a two-story house. A precocious kid, he enrolled in college to study engineering at age fifteen, then left for a work exchange program in Australia, with his grandmother pawning her jewelry so they could afford the plane ticket. He would continue on to Harvard business school and tenure at Boston University.

But academia was not his calling; consulting was. During business school, while working for a gas company in Honolulu over the summer, he discovered a looming problem with the company's ability to make its dividend payments. Six weeks later, Charan had figured it out: "The pressures in the pipes between 10 P.M. and 4 A.M. are too high," he told his boss. "You take them down, and your gas leakage will go down, and you will make the dividend." Problem solved. "That's where this whole consulting thing really began," he reflected back. As Whitford saw it, what made Charan valuable as a consultant was his ability to give specific advice and solve real problems. "His method is no method," he writes. "He is wary of abstraction and belongs to no school of management theory." In fact, of "theory," Charan told him: "Converting highfalutin ideas to the specifics of the company and the leader—that's the trick." "Then you bring it to common sense, and common sense is very uncommon." In the words of Whitford, "That means no ready-made solutions. Instead, Charan brings observation, curiosity, and care."[32]

To save coaching from itself, to be a true value added to leadership culture, and to protect vulnerable individuals who are confusing seeing a coach with seeing a therapist, coaching would benefit from going back to atheoretical, practical, business-related advice, leaving—to the extent possible—the rest of "life" alone. Meanwhile, some form of regulation around who can practice what would seem like an inevitable necessity to ensure basic training, quality control, and client protection. HR, normally a huge stickler for all manner of regulatory and compliance matters, has been strangely silent on this one. And, when it comes to leadership coaching specifically, we must be wary of an unholy alliance of incentives that has turned executive coaching into a massive indus-try by subordinating psychology—probably the most critical de-terminant of leadership success—and offshoring it to professionals who are often not equipped to deal with it. As executive coaching continues its inexorable expansion—a recent article on the future of coaching predicts the imminent arrival of the genetic diversity coach, the chief purpose coach, the distraction prevention coach, and the employee enablement coach—we should object to a system that is producing a class of leaders who are coached to death but just as lost in their understanding of who they are.[33] Sorry, chief people officers, but if one had to file under a particular relationship category HR's embrace of coaching and the leadership industry, codependent might fit best.

3

NATURE OR NURTURE

The ABCs of Leadership, Deconstructed

THE GREAT ASSUMPTION undergirding the leadership industry is that leaders can be made; that it's more an issue of nurture than nature; and that the industry is at the ready to serve as the nurturer if we let it. To prove its point, the industry often invokes science and scientific studies. A close look at some of the research, however, points to a certain oversimplification of its conclusions and what it actually demonstrates. Another interpretation of some of the same data turns out to be the following: great leaders are not made. They are mostly born or happen—no midwife necessary.

The only thing better and more lucrative than turning leadership into a business is to turn it into a science. But it is not just any science. Don't expect a discipline like statistics—so difficult that generations of students have referred to it as "sadistics." We're not talking organic chemistry, either—so conceptually challenging that it is often used as a weed-out course to eliminate students who might not make it through medical school. The "science" of leadership is no rocket science. It is on a totally different scale of approachability, comes with a plethora of handy tools that make it easy to digest, and lends itself well to trainings, modules, and offerings like the one called "Leadership Express Series."[1] Students will not feel like masochists signing up, and you would have to try quite hard to be weeded out. Now, take this user-friendly science, market it like there is no tomorrow, and watch the leadership business explode into a full-blown leadership industrial complex. Repeated buzzwords, intense advertising, and the rehashing of big claims have also served to hide the fact that all this science of leadership has yet to produce a leadership class that is more humane, inspiring, or competent, and that this may be an instance of the "scientific method" failing us.

"IN THE BEGINNING was the Word, and the Word was with God, and the Word was God" goes the famous opening line of St. John's Gospel. Words matter, in other words. And, in the biblical context, repeated words become God's way of bolding and italicizing the font. Appearing 365 times in the Bible, "Fear not" (or variations on not fearing) ends up sticking, encouraging readers to become believers and to find succor in the comfort of the ritualistically echoed word.[2]

God spoke through repetition, it would seem, something that has not gone unnoticed by today's marketing gods who, in developing our fearless leaders, are applying techniques from the Book of Psalms playbook. A casual overview of leadership industry advertising reveals a striking recurrence of certain buzzwords. The industry will make you a "transformative," "compelling," and "cross-functional" "catalyst," "visionary," and "change driver." It will teach you how to "innovate," "influence," "empower," and "unleash," and how to do so across many "verticals" and "tipping points." It will hold your hand as you "up-level" and "upskill" and go "global." You will come out the other end with a "personal brand." You will almost certainly "disrupt." You might even achieve "virality." Together, these buzzwords add up to a certain idea of what leadership today is supposed to be about and the kind of magic that leadership nurturing is capable of. By virtue of hearing the same marketing message over and over again, we suspend disbelief and stop questioning the difficulty involved in actually teaching someone who didn't start out that way how to become a "transformative" force or an "innovative unleasher." It becomes a scientific truth, and we become believers. While repetition is key to any successful marketing campaign, it serves in this particular one to convince us that (a) here are the building blocks of leaders and (b) here is how you can acquire them regardless of your natural dispositions.

And no one should underestimate the relentlessness of the marketing and the diversity of the platforms that it gets rolled out on. While doing research for this book, I became tagged as a potentially serious leadership customer. What ensued was a barrage of ads targeting my search engine and all accounts. A stubborn Google ad kept wanting me to click on "Berkeley CEO Program—Learn from Industry Disruptors." Once I did, I landed on "Emerge as a transformational leader"—a good example in maximizing buzzword-to-total-word-count ratio. Amazon insisted on selling me the latest edition of a popular "How-to" leadership book, and offers kept popping up from other sites for discounted old copies. Not that I could go on my social media account to take a break from the leadership topic. Leadership followed me there, too, flooding me with ads that seemed to come in unstoppable volleys. In one rather representative sequence unfolding over only a few minutes, I could count five ads interrupting the friend updates I was trying to catch up on: Northwestern Kellogg ("Show up, stand out, break through in every room"); Wharton ("Learn to effectively lead global teams"); *Forbes* ("Innovat(e) for greater solutions"); and InterviewKickstart ("Bag tech leadership roles at FAANG" [for Facebook, Apple, Amazon, Netflix, and Google]). An ad for Air Canada that would slip in by mistake to invite me to take off to Toronto, or a rather premature one for AARP, became welcome breaks that made me want to learn more. Given that the cost-per-click for Instagram ads can be $3, the industry may have spent $15 on me in one very short sitting, a not-so-good investment if you consider what they are getting in return![3]

If you have struggled to remember someone's name at a party, you know that repetition is key to information recall. The same applies to marketing, where the frequency of the messaging helps ensure that people remember your brand. Repetition has been called the "first principle of all learning," so crucial it is to how ideas fuse into our awareness and information acquisition occurs.[4] A tool to help along the way is the old mnemonic. A pronounce-able phrase or word where each letter represents an item that must be remembered, often in the order given by the phrase, mnemonics make medical school possible. From memorizing the symptoms of a particular disease, to the functions of various nerves, to the must-follow steps in clinical emergencies, you can always count on a mnemonic to help you help your patients or pass an exam. With time, the more colorful ones have proven to have more stay-ing power. They will never come in handy in my psychiatric prac-tice, but I will always remember the impossible sequence of small bones that make up the wrist. "Some Lovers Try Positions That They Can't Handle" can still make me rattle off "Scaphoid, Lu-nate, Triquetrum, Pisiform, Trapezium, Trapezoid, Capitate, and Hamate."

And so it is with much of modern leadership preparation, where mnemonics become a symbol of the "Let's give you a crash course in leadership" approach. Leadership courses abound with memorable acronyms meant to help managers and executives re-tain information they are told is crucial to good leadership. Run-ning a meeting? Remember your OARRs.[5] By defining at the outset your desired Outcome, the Agenda you will follow to ac-complish it, the various attendee Roles (timekeeper, facilitator, recorder, participants), and the meeting's Rules (everyone con-tributes, no one dominates, no cellphones, no side conversations, etc.), you are almost guaranteed a successful event. Larry Dressler, a "convener of high stakes negotiations and an advisor to leaders" recommends you take eight minutes at the beginning of the meet-ing to define your OARRs, "Time well invested if you count the minutes wasted by people straying off topic, engaging in noncon-structive behavior (e.g., repeating what has already been said), and disagreeing about process."[6] In a LinkedIn post, he praises the following sign he saw in a client's conference room: "No Objectives? No Agenda? No Ground Rules? NO MEETING!" It seemed to suggest an organization that takes its OARRs seriously.

As you go about leading, you will also use your 5W+H, WIGO, FIAO, and WOA techniques and be guided by your Fundamental 4, 3Rs, 4Cs, and PACE principles to unleash your DKDK zone. Allow me to translate. Leaders shouldn't be shy to ask questions, and by remembering their 5W+H formula, they will successfully investigate people and situations by asking "What," "Where," "Why," "When," "Who," and "How." What is the problem? Where did it occur? Why did it happen? When will it be solved? Who will fix it? And How? Rajiv Talreja, author of a leadership book with the no-nonsense title *Lead or Bleed*, swears by it. It's a "brilliant framework," he writes, and the "master key to analyze or create any marketing strategy under the sun since times immemorial."[7] It is necessary for a company's "clearly articulate purpose" and the growth that can flow from that. A bloody strong endorsement from the man described in *Entrepreneur* magazine as "India's leading business coach."[8]

As championed by CORO Northern California, a leadership training organization whose mission is to "cultivate emergent leaders at all stages of their lives and careers," WIGO, for "What Is Going On?," invites leaders to pause and assess each leadership decision from the perspective of those who may not be in the room.[9] FIAO, on the other hand, is CORO's reference to Facts, Inferences, Assumptions, and Opinions, and is meant to remind leaders to be fact driven and evidence based. "It is critical for leaders at every level to ask, 'How much F[act] is in our FIAO?'"[10]

And deciphering fact from fiction can only be helped if you master MIT's 4Cs, for the four essential competencies of sensemaking, inventing, visioning, and relating;[11] the Center for Creative Leadership's "Fundamental 4" of self-awareness, communication, learning agility, and influence;[12] and Harvard's PACE, for the Pick, Appraise, Collect, and Elicit model for increasing professional influence and impact.[13]

What of the WOA? The "Wedge of Awareness" is a management tool based on the humble doorstop. With its thin end facilitating access, a wedge serves to hold something open—and can be seen as a metaphor for the pushback felt when a disruptive leader questions a world running on autopilot. The more a leader attempts to challenge business-as-usual and open the door to new ideas, the more resistance can be expected. Leaders, if nothing else, are agents of change, and by squeezing a WOA into an automatic process, by "counting to ten," saying "Hold on," "Wait a minute," and "Let me think about this" before taking the well-trodden path, and by doggedly pushing against friction and impedance, leaders can blow the door open to new possibilities and new ideas, transforming the world in the process. Whoa!

The prize for applying these handy tools is to access the Oz-like land of the DKDK. This refers to what you "Don't Know you Don't Know" (and is not to be confused with "Don't Know Don't Care," Urban Dictionary's definition of DKDK).[14] Common sense tells us to work with what we know we know and to study and strive to learn what we know we don't know. However, what we "Don't Know we Don't Know," or the DKDK, lies beyond our consciousness and our present viewpoint, and as such is inaccessible and cannot be exploited or put to use. Because we are unaware of its existence, we don't seek it out. Yet it represents potentially limitless untapped knowledge, resources, and power.

And then there are the 3Rs. While there seems to be broad consensus about the acronym itself, there is significant disagreement about what it stands for. Depending on what executive coach, leadership training program, or professor of leadership you consult, you will get a different definition:

> Reflections, Resiliency, and Relationships;
> Relationships, Rules, and Respect;
> Respect, Recognize, and Reward;
> Rewards, Returns, and Requirements;
> and Recreate, Refocus, and Reclaim.[15]

If leadership training were a truly evidence-based science, most coaches, professors of leadership, and leadership training programs would swear by the same 3Rs (or other letter combination), since high-quality research would have reproducibly proven them to be the most relevant, revealing, and reliable. Instead, in an example that suggests a not-so-scientific approach to the "science" of leadership, we have a situation where we seem to like the handiness or sound of a particular acronym, so we start there, then "back up into" words that can be reduced to it. This does not inspire faith in leadership training and some of its foundational concepts and tools and does not suggest a scientific field that is based on a bedrock of substantive knowledge. Rather, it communicates a certain lack of intellectual rigor and possible "quality control" issues when it comes to the marketing of some tools as rather proven, settled, and factual.

The same problem can be seen with the scientific backing of other popular tools. Google Scholar—not to be confused with the basic Google search engine—is considered the largest academic database and includes nearly 400 million records covering all scholarly disciplines.[16] If a particular question has been researched, tested, and reported on in a scientific, peer-reviewed manner, chances are the studies will show up in that most comprehensive of scholarly search engines. As such, I thought I would see what scientific data might exist on the usefulness of OARRs in running meetings. My Google Scholar search for OARRs yielded a healthy 277 results, a finding that, frankly, surprised me as it suggested that OARRs had been indeed subjected to meaningful scientific scrutiny. A closer look, however, quickly revealed that, except for one, these search results referred to another use of the OARRs acronym—Ohio Automated Rx Reporting System. Rx stands for prescription, and the acronym, it turned out, had been co-opted by the medical field and used as a tool for tracking the distribution of controlled drugs to patients. Unlike leadership training, however, medicine had put OARRS through rigorous testing, scientifically researching the benefits derived from it in situations as varied as the opioid crisis, the spread of "pill mills," fentanyl overdoses, racial disparities in opiate prescribing, and pain control after both dental procedures and corneal transplants. The science of leadership that is repeatedly advertised, with its fool-proof-sounding acronyms and accessible tools, isn't really one—at least not yet and at least not by the criteria and standards of other sciences. The "scientific method" that has guided scientific inquiry since the seventeenth century consists of observation, hypothesis generation, hypothesis testing, and iteration. Much of what fills up the online leadership programs resulting in certificates in leadership, however, does not pass that test.

But the mother of all leadership mnemonics, IMHO (internet slang for "In My Humble Opinion"), is this "meta" one from the Stanford Graduate School of Business: LEAD.[17] It stands for Learn, Engage, Accelerate, and Disrupt, and represents their formula for "transforming business leaders into change makers." Like any good mnemonic, it is short, memorable, and evocative. It is also beautifully reflexive, as though leadership were standing in front of a mirror, pondering its own essence. (Fortunately for us, BLEED has not yet been acronymized.)

RELATIVELY EASY FORMULAS might make some sense if we were talking about managing a meeting or running an operation, but a crucial component of leadership training is to teach how it differs from management. George Bradt, senior *Forbes* contributor and founder and chairman of the executive onboarding group Prime-Genesis, whose clients include American Express, Bausch + Lomb, Cornell University, and Dropbox, had this to say about the distinction: "Leaders influence. Managers direct. While it may not be that black and white, leaders generally do focus on what matters and why, as managers focus on how. . . . Leaders have a bias to influencing by inspiring and enabling through advice and counsel and co-creation, while managers have a bias to command and control, organizing, coordinating and telling."[18]

Managing, then, is about delivering. It's about the nuts and bolts and seamless, timely execution. Leadership, on the other hand, is about inspiring others and what President George H. W. Bush famously called "the vision thing" before the 1988 presidential election, when he was urged to reflect on his plans for his prospective presidency.[19] Not to offend anyone in management, but one might imagine a mnemonic coming in handy for a manager keen on dotting the i's and crossing the t's, and who wants to make sure all the steps of a complicated process are systematically covered. But can inspiration and vision really be reduced to a formula or something that sounds like a nursery rhyme? By trying to distill the essence of leadership into memorable nuggets that can then be quickly taught in leadership courses, we are, to some degree, confusing it with management, when a tenet of leadership studies is to teach us how different the two are. If vision possessed an easy mnemonic, George H. W. Bush, who admitted to struggling with articulating his, might not have been a one-term president.

The problem with this approach is that it sends the deceptive message that leading is easily learned, as easy as ABC—literally. Learn the formulas and you're essentially good to go. This minimizes context, sacrifices nuance, and brings about leadership failure, according to a report put out by the global consulting firm McKinsey & Company titled "Why Leadership Development Fails."[20] Talking about the bullet-point approach to leadership training and the oversimplified competencies covered in many of these programs, the authors write: "Each is usually summarized in a seemingly easy-to-remember way (such as the three Rs) and each on its own terms makes sense. In practice, however, what managers and employees often see is an 'alphabet soup' of recommendations." The leadership coach Kristi Hedges, author of *The Power of Presence* agrees, quoting this report in her *Forbes* article on the importance of company context to the leadership training being delivered: "Leadership programs must integrate with the larger scope of the organization. Bringing in someone to deliver the standard pump-up-the-troops program may be briefly engaging, but not produce any behavior change."[21] She titled her article "If You Think Leadership Development Is a Waste of Time You May Be Right."

Unfortunately for leadership training programs and for us as a society that has bought into leadership training hook, line, and sinker, the ABCs of leadership do not add up to a good leader. An approach where complex environments, unique situations, and disparate personalities are distilled into one-size-fits-all, guaranteed-to-work phrases speaks to a certain concept of leading that turns it into a recipe and a certain view of leadership training that turns it into a cookbook. By way of contrast, if we know anything from the science of medicine, it is that patients suffer when algorithms replace individualized care. As Miriam Solomon, professor of philosophy at Temple University and the author of *Making Medical Knowledge*, writes, "It is not a compliment to say that a physician is practicing 'cookbook medicine.' Rather, it suggests that the physician is applying 'one size fits all,' unreflective, and impersonal clinical methods, and that the patient may suffer as a result of the lack of nuanced, reflective, and humanistic care."[22] Contrast that with the growing emphasis on "personalized care" in the medical field, where each patient is seen as a unique individual unlike any other; one who should not be subjected to the reductive, homogenizing effects of a sweeping algorithm. Personalized medicine aims to incorporate a patient's unique genetic fingerprint, environmental factors, and lifestyle conditions to arrive at the most accurate diagnosis possible and predict which treatments will work best for that one patient. It's the medical care everyone deserves. As Solomon writes, personalized care is "care that is tailored to the particulars of the case as well as care that acknowledges the personhood of the patient." More recently, this focus on the "particulars of the case" has been termed "precision medicine," meaning medicine that combines broad findings from empirical research with the precise circumstances of the specific case.

Recipes in medicine spell inferior medicine, and doctors and patients are encouraged to avoid them in favor of something more personalized. What might be more surprising is that cookbook

authors themselves, those whom we might expect to be the fierc-
est defenders of the recipe, are also washing their hands of recipes!
Daniel Patterson, the Michelin-starred restaurateur, food writer,
and James Beard award recipient, had this to say: "The recipes that
we do follow have become automated in their simplicity, largely
a way to get as quickly and mindlessly as possible from one place
to another. . . . Cookbooks should teach us how to cook, not just
follow instructions. By paying attention, a cook should be able
to internalize the process, rendering the written recipes obsolete.
. . . Good cooks rely on recipes—to a point."[23] A chef concerned
about the consistency of his restaurant's dishes, and a cookbook
author concerned about selling books, who nonetheless wants to
render recipes obsolete? It sure sounds like it. His kitchen equivalent of the precision medicine practitioner is a cook who has been
emancipated from the confines of the recipe and is able to make
the best out of the unique ingredients in his crisper drawer and the
unique context that the meal is taking place in.

Or consider Sam Sifton, the founding editor of the popular
New York Times Cooking website, whose job is to solicit, perfect,
and publish recipes, and whose site counts over 20,000 of them, all
presented in blow-by-blow detail. For the debut cookbook of his
site, however, the ultimate recipe curator chose the title *No-Recipe
Recipes.* "You don't need recipes. Really, you don't," the back cover
implores. Instead, Sifton invites his reader to "join me in cooking
this new, improvisational way, without recipes."[24] It's a freestyle,
more soulful approach to cooking that apparently can still result in
a dinner of fried egg quesadillas, roasted shrimp tacos, and chicken
with caramelized onions and croutons. I'll believe it when I taste
it, but if medicine and even the cookbook industry are lightening
up on recipes, is it unreasonable to expect the leadership industry
to do the same?

The ABCs of leadership can be reductive and can lack strong
scientific backing, but what of other cornerstones of what we
think of as leadership science? Take the concept of emotional intelligence, which has emerged as a crucial attribute of the successful leader and has spawned endless leadership webinars, coaching

sessions, and TED talks, and guided many a leadership training curriculum. Most of us would include empathy, self-knowledge, and social awareness—components of emotional intelligence—in our "wish list" for our leaders, and most of us would not doubt their importance in a leader's success. In a widely cited 2004 article on the topic in *Harvard Business Review*, Daniel Goleman makes the following observation: "Every businessperson knows a story about a highly intelligent, highly skilled executive who was promoted into a leadership position only to fail at the job. And they also know a story about someone with solid—but not extraordinary—intellectual abilities and technical skills who was promoted into a similar position and then soared."[25] Indeed. A leader that "looks good on paper" is far from a shoo-in for success, and, conversely, the annals of outstanding leadership are full of individuals who succeeded spectacularly but who got the job only because the one that the search committee *really* wanted said no.

A colleague who is a prominent surgeon must have gone through the world's longest interview process for a position leading a surgery department in a medical school in the South. Although he was ready to sign after the first time he and his wife were flown out to meet other leaders and explore the school and local real estate, they kept flying him back for more "in-depth" interviews with more stakeholders. Something was not fully "clicking," as the search committee seemed impressed enough to keep him in the running but not to extend an actual offer. Nearly two years, three visits, and thirty interviews later, my colleague was ready to pull the Band-Aid on what he saw as his dragged out, one-sided, and unrequited interest. Right before he officially withdrew his candidacy, though, a formal offer finally arrived and, in a matter of weeks, he was running his new department.

Once in his position, my colleague would gain some discreet insights from a search committee member who shared that the committee's favored candidate was actually another surgeon to whom they extended multiple offers. All the while, my colleague was essentially kept in the wings as a rather distant second and a "Plan B." The preferred candidate, however, had no serious intention of relocating to the state and was himself stringing the search committee along as he used their offers to negotiate a retention and promotion package with his employer. However, although he seemed to have successfully leveraged the situation for advancement into a senior leadership role, there was no obvious evidence of spectacular achievement in his new role.

Meanwhile, within two years of taking over his new position, my colleague had pulled off dramatic improvements in his department on several key metrics: patient satisfaction, surgical waitlist, physician burnout, research endowment, and national ranking. "Plan B" worked out swimmingly for the school, and the search committee was patting its back for recruiting a turnaround magician!

What helps account for these surprising outcomes, it has been argued, are "soft" traits that cannot be captured on a CV, IQ test, or even a series of interviews, namely emotional intelligence or components thereof. Few would argue against the value of emotional intelligence in leadership or against the idea that smarts and drive alone do not a great leader make. However, the idea that, as Daniel Goleman and Richard E. Boyatzis suggest in a subsequent *Harvard Business Review* article, leaders succeed by learning to activate an existing "system of brain interconnectedness" that triggers "mirror neurons" in followers, thereby prompting them to follow their lead, is somewhat optimistic.[26] There is no doubting the centrality of emotional intelligence, but it is a little bit of a leap to suggest that we have figured out how to tap into the 86 billion neurons that make up the human brain to successfully develop and deploy it.[27]

First discovered in monkeys in 1992 by an Italian research team, "mirror neurons" refer to brain cells—or neurons—that would fire when the monkey took an action (like holding a banana) or witnessed the same action being performed (like seeing a man hold a banana).[28] Since then, evidence has pointed to mirror neurons in humans as well. As Goleman and Boyatzis see it, great leaders powerfully leverage mirror neurons on their way to success. "Mirror neurons have particular importance in organizations,"

they write, "because leaders' emotions and actions prompt followers to mirror those feelings and deeds." They analyze a video of
former Southwest Airlines CEO Herb Kelleher strolling down the
airline's hub in Dallas, Texas. "We could practically see him activate the mirror neurons . . . and other social circuitry in each
person he encountered," they say. "He offered beaming smiles,
shook hands with customers as he told them how much he appreciated their business, hugged employees as he thanked them for
their good work. And he got back exactly what he gave."[29] Sounds
good, although: (a) I doubt Mr. Kelleher started out a stiff, socially
awkward shrinking violet and was bestowed with superior people
skills and a high-wattage smile by a leadership boot camp; and (b)
is any other reaction, besides smiling back radiantly at your boss,
imaginable if you want to keep your job, get your bonus, or perhaps even get promoted to a leadership position yourself?

Things, alas, are a bit more complicated than the neuronal
synchronized swimming between leader and followers exempli-
fied by this story, and we have no reliable way to activate mirror
neurons to bring about unison of emotion or purpose between
leaders and followers. Whatever Kelleher caused in his employees'
neurons, it was part and parcel of his unique and nonreproducible
nature.

Herb Kelleher cofounded and ran Southwest, described during
his tenure as the biggest success story in the history of commercial aviation, having figured out the golden formula for extreme
efficiency, low-cost pricing, innovative logistics solutions, and superior customer experience.[30] His secret may well have been his
affability—he could "carry an interesting conversation with anyone, anywhere about anything," according to a *Forbes* obituary—
and that he consistently elevated employees while consistently
bringing himself down from the founder-and-CEO pedestal.[31]
"Kelleher always chose to have an office without windows," the
article goes. "He believed that it eliminated the jockeying for
choice offices that goes on in organizations. Consistent with his
egalitarian spirit, it sent a message that the team is more important than the individual. So, who gets the room with the best view

at Southwest's general office? Everyone, because it's the cafeteria which overlooks runway 13R at Love Field," the airport in Dallas, where Southwest is headquartered.

Another reason his employees loved him is that he communicated directly and seemed to genuinely care. He went, or flew, the extra mile for his employees. "If you lose a relative, you hear from us," he told an interviewer. "If you're out sick with a serious illness, you hear from us. . . . If you have a baby, you hear from us. What we're trying to say to our people is that we value you as a total person, not just between eight and five." As recounted by a Southwest pilot, Kelleher once heard that an employee's son had died in a car crash. The employee was in Baltimore, and his family was in Dallas. Kelleher had a plane rerouted to land in Baltimore, pick up the employee, and reunite him with his family. It's stories like that and love like that that will make employees smile back, and from the heart, not the CEO mastery of how to turn on your team's mirror neurons. When leaders from other companies would visit Southwest's headquarters to learn about his methods, Kelleher was happy to reveal his non-rocket-science secret. "They were interested in how we hired, trained, that sort of thing," he explained. "Then we'd say, 'Treat your people well and they'll treat you well,' and then they'd go home disappointed. It was too simple." Even Southwest's New York Stock Exchange ticker, LUV, can be seen as a manifestation of that culture and philosophy.[32]

What made the package even more irresistible is that it was wrapped in humor, idiosyncrasy, and a unique personality. Shortly after Southwest rolled out its "Just Plane Smart" campaign, a tiny aircraft sales company, Stevens Aviation, which, unbeknownst to Kelleher, had been using "Plane Smart" as its motto, threatened to sue.[33] The legal dispute, however, would be resolved over an arm wrestling match between the two CEOs dubbed "Malice in Dallas." And so, on March 20, 1992, 4,500 spectators (mostly company employees) packed into a decaying former wrestling arena to watch Kelleher make his grand entrance to the theme song from *Rocky*. Although Kelleher lost the match, he still got what he wanted: in exchange for a $5,000 donation to charity and giving up the legal claim to the slogan, Southwest could still use "Just Plane Smart."

It was a slogan, and a company, that resembled—mirrored?—the man. There was nothing that felt packaged or practiced or coached about them or him. It doesn't take a neuroscientist to understand why passengers responded—and why employees smiled back. It was his nature and unique personality, not a mirror neuron–activating technique that he picked up, practiced, and perfected—or that is teachable. Indeed, there is no surefire tool for a dedicated leader to make restive followers more committed to the company or for focused followers to make a distracted leader mimic their concentration. Much of the mirroring we do is unconscious and unintentional and happens outside our control and with people we are close with—good friends who use the same words or adopt the same gestures or dress code; spouses who finish each other's sentences; toddlers who act as mirrors (or sponges) and reproduce what they see their parents and older siblings do. If reliably effective mirroring tools existed, autism spectrum disorder and social anxiety disorder, which are both characterized by social challenges, would have seen their treatment substantially improve.

Patients with autism spectrum disorder, in particular, often show deficits in imitating the actions of others, grasping social cues, or repeating simple motor actions. They may not engage in reciprocal social exchanges, like smiling in response to a smile, scowling in response to a scowl, or responding to a wave or handshake. For that reason, it has been hypothesized by some researchers, including Justin Williams, Senior Clinical Lecturer in Child Psychiatry at the University of Aberdeen, that mirror neurons—the neuronal correlate of imitation—may be dysfunctional in autism, leading to difficulty matching the actions of others and interrupting this potential "bridge" between minds.[34] Yet social skills training, including the use of "mirroring" to help improve social reciprocity in autism, has unfortunately not yielded dramatic cures. Most leaders, of course, would not be dealing with the added burden of autism or social phobia in learning to leverage mirror neurons. Still, what toddlers can do unconsciously and re-flexively is difficult for adults to master and apply consciously and intentionally. Mirror neurons are not switches we can willingly turn on and off. That something that cannot reliably achieve re-sults in one-on-one therapy between an autistic child and an expert therapist can succeed at the level of a complex organization com-posed of strangers—with no unifying bond other than a profes-sional affiliation with the same company—seems overly confident. Is a leader's social intelligence a mighty asset? Absolutely. Does it reside in the brain where everything else, from IQ to happiness to sadness to anger to love to mirror neurons, resides? Unques-tionably. Is it an established neuronal science, with a relationship to mirroring that is similar to the relationship that neurological conditions like Parkinson's disease or multiple sclerosis have with the medications that have been proven to work for them? Not really.

Now, if one were to ask whether there was a science "to" lead-ership, meaning some skills and qualities that are statistically more likely to be present in leaders, the answer would be yes, and some of the main findings from that science are neatly summarized in a *Harvard Business Review* article titled "What Science Tells Us About Leadership Potential," by Tomas Chamorro-Premuzic, a professor at University College London and Columbia University. Regard-ing who gets to become a leader, studies show that people who are "more adjusted, sociable, ambitious, and curious" are much more likely to emerge. In fact, 53 percent of the variability in leadership emergence can be explained by these personality factors. Although a high IQ certainly helps, it increases the likelihood of an individ-ual emerging as leader by less than 5 percent.[35]

Regarding how successful a leader is after emerging, science tells us that these same traits are important, but evidence also sug-gests that leaders with high levels of integrity who are more emo-tionally intelligent—and therefore can stay calm under pressure and possess better people skills—do better. Narcissistic leaders, on the other hand, "are more prone to behaving in unethical ways, which is likely to harm their teams."[36]

On the topic of leadership style, studies show that "thick-skinned" leaders are more likely to be entrepreneurial and focused on growth and innovation, whereas curious, sociable, and sensitive ones are likely to be more charismatic, although charisma "often reflects dark side traits, such as narcissism and psychopathy."[37] More—much more—on charisma and what it can hide later.

On the all-important topic of nature versus nurture—the perennial question "Are leaders born or made?"—studies have estimated leadership to be up to 60 percent heritable, largely because the traits that shape it, including personality and intelligence, are themselves heritable. Indeed, "most of the commonly used indicators to gauge leadership potential—educational achievement, emotional intelligence, ambition, and IQ—can be predicted from a very early age," Chamorro-Premuzic writes, which is why "it would be naïve to treat them as more malleable." In fact, without advocating it, Chamorro-Premuzic wonders whether "perhaps in the future, leadership potential will be assessed at a very early age by inspecting people's saliva." He is right to wonder; such a test no longer seems inconceivable as human genome research continues to unravel the biological underpinnings of personality traits, including those implicated in leadership.[38]

The fact that, if it existed, a saliva test administered to an eight-year-old could predict with reasonable accuracy the child's future chances of emerging and succeeding as a leader, would seem to cast serious doubt on the leadership industry (and, with it, on so many schools now promising success in professional, academic, and community leadership, regardless of how their students would perform on this putative saliva test). If the personality traits, emotional intelligence, and IQ cutoffs that have been linked to leadership are set to a significant degree at a very early stage of life and are not terribly "malleable," what is the source of all the optimism and self-confidence with which leadership is marketed, sold, and taught? To the extent that leadership has been scientifically studied, the conclusions, too often, do not seem to support leadership as a reliably teachable discipline. In fact, a different conclusion, one with a slogan along the lines of "Leadership, You Either Have

It or You Don't," might seem more consistent with the body of evidence.

Scientific data, then, would seem to support a "genetic theory" of leadership, by which leadership traits are, to a significant degree, born, not made, and a matter of one's DNA, although, like any gene, they can still be acted upon and modulated by the environment. More recent scientific data points to what might be called an "infectious theory" of leadership, at least among wolves. Wolf pack order and group dynamics among wolves have long fascinated leadership scholars for what they might reveal about leader-follower interactions in their human cousins.[39] Wolves live in packs. The "alpha leaders," one male and one female, lead the pack during a hunt and often eat first when a kill is made. They are also typically the only ones that breed. As they assume the guiding role, alphas let other wolves perform duties that align with their abilities. The physically strongest—that's not necessarily the leader of the pack—assume key hunter roles. Others assume the role of caregiver for the weak or sick. The elderly have a place in the pack, too, and seem to be the object of respect from pack members. As observed in the wild, with leaders who know what they are doing, responsibility becomes shared in a way that makes for a better, more collaborative, and more secure pack.

The parasite *Toxoplasma gondii* is known to infect mammals, and some early studies had suggested that it can make affected rodents less afraid and increase their exploratory behavior. Connor Meyer and Kira Cassidy, wildlife ecologists at the University of Montana in Missoula, and their colleagues set out to explore how infection with this parasite might alter wolf behavior. Their groundbreaking study looked at 256 blood samples from 229 wolves that had been closely monitored throughout their lives, including for social status within their packs.[40] Their results showed that wolves infected with the parasite were 46 times more likely than uninfected ones to become pack leaders. Had the infection somehow translated into new traits that were conducive to leadership in wolf culture? We have no idea, but the possibility is more than intriguing. "We got that result and we just open-mouth stared at each other," Meyer told the journal *Nature* about his findings. "This is way bigger than we thought it would be."[41]

We also have no idea what these results mean for human leaders—humans also playing host to this parasite—and no one should wish for toxoplasmosis in hopes of gaining a leadership edge. The point is to highlight once again that while leadership has been scientifically studied and fascinating data has at times emerged, we do not always know what it means and cannot use it to legitimately claim that we can produce reliably good leaders or promise those graduating with leadership certificates that leadership success awaits around the corner.

Leadership training overflows with references to science that are of varying degrees of defensibility. The Kellogg School of Management introduces its "Navigating Workplace Conflict" program by stating "There is a science to transforming conflict into collaboration."[42] Similarly, its description of "High-Performance Negotiation Skills" starts with "There is a science to negotiation."[43] And I would agree, although this would not be so different than saying there is a science to good relationships or a science to getting rich or a science to positive parenting. Saying there is a science "to" leadership would not be wrong and is different than saying leadership "is" a science. The former implies a dimension that is measurable and can be captured in studies, but still allows for magic, uncertainty, and other unknowable dimensions. The latter implies a field of incontrovertible certainties that accumulated from hypothesis-driven, carefully designed, properly controlled experiments, and much about how leadership skills are being marketed makes them appear like a full-on science—one that can be learned, applied, and reproduced the way you might learn civil engineering and then reliably build safe building after safe building. Such is the message communicated by many leadership books that make sure to incorporate a reference to "science" in their titles. By the sound of these titles, the acronym STEM, commonly used on campuses to refer to Science, Technology, Engineering, and Mathematics majors, might as well now also include Leadership Studies.

Having turned leadership into a business, we are turning it into a science, which, of course, would further justify its "businessification," since it gives the illusion of selling a product or skill that is similar to a STEM degree—worth your investment and with a rather guaranteed return on that investment. When you turn leadership into a science, you no longer have to worry about the vagaries and uncertainties built into getting a leadership position. When you turn it into a science, you no longer have to defend against the oft-repeated (and terribly unfair) criticisms leveled at humanities-type and liberal-arts-type disciplines—that they are subjective, that they do not teach you hard skills, that they do not increase your employability and marketability, that they do not prepare you for the real world, that they are not worth the tuition, and so on. These criticisms stop applying, and leadership studies suddenly moves to a different league altogether from quintessential liberal arts and humanities disciplines with which they may have more in common, like sociology, anthropology, and cultural studies. Yet these same liberal arts, with their emphasis on critical thinking, asking difficult questions, finding creative solutions to complex problems, and never losing sight of the "human" at the center of the "humanities," may be precisely what today's leaders are lacking. In that sense, an art history course might serve them better than a TED talk titled "Everyday Leadership."[44]

The overly simplistic acronyms and formulaic, not entirely scientific content that make up a significant proportion of leadership development suggest a no-sweat process and a soft-sloped learning curve that is simply not credible. I bring them up not to poke fun at them—I admit to taking a fondness to the Wedge of Awareness tool, in particular, and have incorporated it into my practice—but to highlight the lack of rigorous evidence behind some core concepts and tools. Some fundamentals espoused by the leadership industrial complex have very little research backing; aside from a relatively limited number of mostly short-term outcome studies that track implementation of learned techniques by leadership training graduates, I've seen little evidence that these programs work when it comes to their ultimate test—transforming someone who is not naturally inclined to lead and was not the beneficiary of good luck and propitious circumstances into a big success story. Similarly, there is little evidence that the advent of this industry and its explosive growth have correlated with a measurable improvement in the effectiveness, integrity, and humanity of our leaders, or in how we feel about them. Not to be flippant or dismissive, but the science of leadership makes me appreciate more the science of medicine. God knows that medicine has gotten the science wrong at many turns and acted without scientific backing many times—think of the changing dogma on hormone replacement therapy, prostate cancer tests, mammogram frequency, when to expose infants to peanut products, or even the importance of breakfast and how much water and coffee to drink over the course of the day. In my field of psychiatry, a "softer" medical science almost by definition, the examples would take up an entire chapter. But the combination of a cultural obsession with leadership, its commodification by business schools that know a thing or two about how to turn something into a money-making machine, and its premature marketing as a science seems rather unique—and uniquely risky. Generations of medical students have relied on the 3Ws to remind them of the symptoms of a serious neurological condition called normal pressure hydrocephalus: Wet, for urinary incontinence; Wobbly, for gait imbalance; and Wacky, for memory problems. It is ancient and somewhat insensitive, but I'll still take it over a leadership course's 5Ws.

4

INTROVERT OR SOCIAL ANIMAL

Knowing Who You Are

THE BUSINESS OF leadership, with its executive coaches, approachable tools, and lofty promises, runs roughshod over a fundamental psychological tenet, namely that personality is rather sticky and stubborn. It will not easily yield to attempts to turn it into something it is not, and, if it does, expect it to want to snap back into the form it naturally occupies. When it comes to leadership, the industry has found two convenient, but rather contradictory, ways to get around this fact. The first is to suggest, against what much of the research in mental health has shown us, that training can teach you the necessary personality traits relatively easily. The second is to suggest that the list of legitimate leadership styles is so long you are bound to find one that suits you—no change required. The science of leadership is in some conflict with the science of personality, an issue that leadership culture, miscast leaders, and stuck followers pay dearly for.

Someone who is considered to have a "personable" personality has a good chance of being considered charismatic, an attribute that has been linked to personality traits and that can be a huge asset for leaders. Like personality, it is difficult to meaningfully reinvent. It has been said that pornography is easy to spot but difficult to define, notably by Supreme Court Justice Potter Stewart's well-known line: "I know it when I see it."[1] So it is with charisma, where all the roads to a definition seem to lead to the otherworldly, the transcendental, and the mystical. Building on its Greek roots, which imply a freely given favor, Christian theology adopts the concept as charism, an extraordinary gift bestowed by the Holy Spirit.[2] Max Weber, the early twentieth-century German sociologist who first brought charisma into modern consciousness and connected it to leadership, described it as "a certain quality of an individual personality by virtue of which he is set apart from ordinary men and treated as endowed with supernatural, superhuman, or at least specifically exceptional powers or qualities. These as such are not accessible to the ordinary person, but are regarded as of divine origin or as exemplary, and on the basis of them the individual concerned is treated as a leader."[3] Linda Woodhead, head of the Department of Theology and Religious Studies at King's College London, describes charisma in theological and religious terms. "You can't learn it," she told the BBC program *In Our Time*. "You can't set about to being charismatic. Yes of course you can stage it to some extent, . . . but it always seems to have this irreducibly from-outside quality. . . . Charismatic . . . people often talk about that. They don't know what comes over them, they feel possessed. . . . There's something, a spirit from outside, an inspiration that comes from outside. In that sense, . . . charisma is inherently religious. . . . It does depend on thinking there is something that's bigger than you that you are somehow channeling. It's not just you."[4]

This irresistible *je ne sais quoi*, this magnetism, also crucial to the success of many artists, has been referred to simply as "It" by Joseph Roach, an arts historian and Yale professor, in a book by the same title that references the "It factor."[5] In his book, Roach partly describes charisma as the ability to convey two opposite qualities simultaneously, like strength and vulnerability, or grandeur and humility. Among contemporary US political figures, even to many of his detractors, Barack Obama oozed "It." Conversely, even to many of her admirers, Hillary Clinton was "It"-challenged. On the list of cringeworthy moments from US presidential debates in recent memory, a top spot may have been secured by this one from 2008. The debate pitted the two candidates for the Democratic nomination and put the question of a leader's charisma squarely on the debate table in the form of a direct question about "likeability":

MODERATOR: What can you say to the voters of
New Hampshire on this stage tonight who see
your resume and like it but are hesitating on the
likability issue, where they seem to like Barack
Obama more?
HILLARY CLINTON: Well, that hurts my feelings.
MODERATOR: I'm sorry, senator, I'm sorry.
CLINTON: But I'll try to go on. He's very likable. I
agree with that. I don't think I'm that bad.
OBAMA: You're likable enough, Hillary.[6]

Maybe the question should have never been asked, but Obama's backhanded compliment came across as narcissistic, insensitive, and anything but charismatic. It cost him that primary and illustrates how, even for the most naturally charismatic of leaders, charisma has to constantly be earned. It's "God"-given, undefinable, difficult to fake—and potentially fleeting.

Much more ominously, charisma can hide a chilling underside. A leader who many may find charismatic but also happens to be a psychopath represents a combination that is the absolute scariest one to contemplate. Writing for BBC magazine, World War II historian and British Book Award winner Laurence Rees finds this combination in Adolf Hitler himself, complete with a terrifying religious dimension. "Hitler was the archetypal 'charismatic leader,'" Rees says. "He was not a 'normal' politician—someone who promises policies like lower taxes and better health care—but a quasi-religious leader who offered almost spiritual goals of redemption and salvation. . . . More than anything, it was the fact that Hitler found that he could make a connection with his audience that was the basis of all his future success." Quoting a certain

Emil Klein, a man who heard Hitler speak in the 1920s, he writes, "The man gave off such a charisma that people believed whatever he said." Not that Hitler went out of his way to hide the fact that he was full of hatred and prejudice. It is just that, in the eyes of his blinded followers, what they saw as seductive charisma outweighed other considerations, contributing to his improbable rise in a country that was considered the best educated and most cultivated in Europe at the dawn of World War II.[7]

Charisma, then, is all around much too slippery to fully capture and can even turn tragic in the wrong hands. This has not stopped leadership experts and MBA programs from trying to teach and impart it. Executive coach John Mattone, whose blog has been ranked the "World's #1 executive coaching and business coaching blog" by the content reader Feedspot from 2017 through 2021, explains how the word comes from the Latinization of the Greek *Kharisma*, or "divine gift," and says it can be taught.[8] Similarly, an online leadership training course from the prestigious international business school HEC Paris translates it as "gift of grace," and also says it can be taught.[9] If you really believe its etymology as "divine gift" or "gift of grace," continuing to say you can effectively teach charisma essentially amounts to playing God, but that irony seems lost on charisma instructors.

A lecture titled "Learn to Be Charismatic" offered by the University of Michigan as part of its Inspiring and Motivating Individuals Coursera online course rests in part on a highly cited 2011 study that recruited middle managers and trained them in "charismatic leadership tactics," showing them videos where those were illustrated by charismatic protagonists and offering them a coaching session where their leadership profile was discussed.[10] Three months later, the middle managers were assessed by their colleagues as being better leaders than the controls. However, the study's tiny size—thirty-four participants—precludes sweeping conclusions, a fact that its authors acknowledge. The real "proof" would be if the 210,191 individuals who, according to the site, have enrolled in the course, became more charismatic upon completing it. To my knowledge, no rigorous, long-term, large-scale study comparing "before and after" charisma scores of participants has been published, but it would probably be safe to assume that, had most of them indeed become significantly more charismatic as a result of the training, there would have been an obvious culture-wide upgrade in leaders' personability. I for one have missed it.

If Coursera doesn't succeed at fully figuring out charisma, it would be in good company. Even Max Weber, the man who first brought it to the world's attention, seems to have failed at cracking its "It" factor. According to a *New Yorker* article by Corey Robin, professor of political science at Brooklyn College, politics was his "secret love," and he tried his hand at it over and over again during the three decades of his scholarly career, including to "give advice, stand for office, form a party, negotiate a treaty, and write a constitution."[11] But Weber never fully succeeded, gained a substantial following, or realized his political ambitions. Maybe he wasn't likeable enough.

Like charisma, we would do well not to project overconfidence in being able to radically transform personality. Mental health professionals are not above acronyms, and OCEAN is one that helps us remember the all-important "Big 5" personality traits of Openness, Conscientiousness, Extraversion, Agreeableness, and Neuroticism.[12] We all fall somewhere on the spectrum with respect to each of these traits, and the unique combination of how much of each we possess is a personality fingerprint of sorts. People high on the openness trait are more adventurous and have a broad range of interests, while those high on conscientiousness are more organized and detail oriented and better able to control impulses and urges. As for extraversion, it refers to being outgoing, emotionally expressive, and social. Regarding agreeableness, more of it means being more trusting, altruistic, and generous. Finally, those who rank high on neuroticism tend to be more anxious and to have more mood swings and irritability. Where do you fall on this personality grid?

It might not matter if leadership is your goal, according to current leadership conceptualizations, where everyone is essentially considered reasonable raw material for leading and everyone is invited to apply. The leadership industry is not very particular in whom it markets to or recruits. All personality styles are potentially workable, and you will not be turned away for being too "big picture" or too detail oriented, too "knee-jerk" or too deliberative. Everyone is more or less welcome in the new world of leadership development, and everyone can be a leader in the making. This is suggested by the existence of several acceptable, but seemingly contradictory, leadership styles.

The earliest formal research into leadership styles was conducted by psychologist Kurt Lewin and colleagues in the late 1930s and described three distinct types of leadership: autocratic leadership; democratic leadership; and laissez-faire (or "zero") leadership.[13] Autocratic leaders hold all the decision power and lead dictatorially, discouraging input from others. Democratic leaders encourage the free exchange of ideas within their team, with the team making decisions together as the leader plays a facilitator-type role. And laissez-faire leaders are "hands off" and delegate decisions to the team, whom they trust to make decisions without the direct involvement of the leader.

Lewin's experiments involved practicing the three types of leadership on groups of ten- and eleven-year-old boys, recording outcomes such as productivity, the pros and cons of the style in question, and team dynamics. The results, which have not been without criticism for oversimplifying things and on methodological grounds, basically showed that, while autocratic leaders are the most efficient and productive, especially in times of crisis, their followers feel undervalued and micromanaged.[14] While democratic leadership enhances group morale, it can be an expensive luxury when faced by a major challenge or strict deadline, and it can complicate the identification of employees who are not carrying their weight. And, while talented, self-motivated followers can thrive with a laissez-faire leader, many become disengaged, which compromises team unity. Depending on the specific context, each identified style seemed to have advantages and drawbacks.

Perhaps as an example of the democratic leadership governing the leadership field, several other styles have been described since Lewin's groundbreaking work. All come with their own disciples and advocates, and none are ruled out a priori. They include transformational leadership, disruptive leadership, tipping point leadership, transactional leadership, situational leadership, visionary leadership, affiliative leadership, coaching leadership, pace-setting leadership, commanding leadership, charismatic leadership, bureaucratic leadership, sustainable leadership, and even servant leadership.[15] The last is defined as a decentralized organizational structure meant to "achieve authority rather than power" (whatever that means). And I may well have missed some leadership styles.

One arch-message from the plethora of styles is that, whoever you are and whatever your natural inclinations, don't you worry, because you will fit into a certifiable leadership category. Go ahead and apply. But another equally problematic arch-message from the leadership field is that a leader can change styles as needed, and relatively smoothly, depending on the situation. Rosy Callejas, a former manager at Salesforce, is typical of those who believe that you can change your leadership style on a dime. "You may find that you don't fit neatly into any one category," she writes. "The most successful leaders are those who jump between leadership styles. Pick and choose techniques that best fit the team or task at hand and adapt them along the way as needed. Effective leadership is, and always has been, about knowing what techniques to use and when."[16]

The idea of "jumping" between styles is also reflected in the "leadership compass" sometimes used to characterize leadership approaches.[17] Inspired by the Native American tradition of the Medicine Wheel and used in some development programs, the compass theory posits four main personality-based styles of leading that leaders fall under: North leaders are assertive, confident, get-it-done folks who will not let a "no" get in their way; South leaders are nurturing of those around them and exert control in a gentle and feelings-guided way; East leaders are visionaries who look to the future and think in terms of creative solutions, mission, and purpose; and West leaders weigh all sides of the issue in a data- and evidence-based manner that makes the most of available resources. Each style has associated downsides but no fatal or unresolvable flaws and no planetary alignment that would doom the leader, only weaknesses to work on. "All directions have profound strengths and potential weaknesses," we are told, "and every person is seen as capable of growing in each direction. Each person can learn the gifts associated with each direction—through practice and self-awareness." With the help of a coach or a development program, the North leader can be pulled south; the South leader north; the East leader west; and the West leader east. In this framework, character is malleable, and personality is not destiny. Your "natural" position on the compass will not ruin your leadership chances any more than your astrological sign will doom your love life.

The ancient compass motif may have inspired another popular leadership framework advocated by MIT Sloan School of Management professor Deborah Ancona and colleagues, and often taught in leadership classes. This framework distills leadership's necessary qualities to four essential capabilities, each representing one of four directions: visioning, sensemaking, relating, and inventing. What differentiates this compass is the invitation to move from visioning to relating to sensemaking to inventing as you go through your typical workday—and the accompanying assumption that one can learn to be nimble that way: "Leaders in business settings need all of these capabilities to be successful, and cycle through them on an ongoing basis."[18]

Unfortunately, neither compass points in the right direction when it comes to leadership. That personality can be creatively remolded like Play-Doh and its components "cycled through" or "jumped between" as needed would come as news to most psychology experts. Just like the idea that all personal styles can translate into leadership success is preposterous, so is the notion that we can pick up a smorgasbord of leadership capabilities and access them as situations warrant, when these capabilities are reflections of fundamentally different temperaments, DNA profiles, and ways of being and interacting with the world.

Not all personalities are fit to lead, including if leading means the ability to socialize effortlessly, elbow your way to the top, or improvise self-confidently about things you know little about just to project authority or power. Saying that not all personalities are fit to lead is not nearly as depressing as it sounds when we remember that individuals who lack these abilities can still excel—and be much happier for it—doing things other than leading. This was highlighted to me by Jeff, a soft-spoken thirty-two-year-old MBA student and former patient of mine. When I first met Jeff, he had started an MBA program with a leadership "track" after spending six months doing volunteer environmental research in sub-Saharan Africa. Jeff's goal, postgraduation, was to return to Africa, where he hoped to help budding entrepreneurs interested in green technology obtain US microloans.

Jeff's MBA and leadership curriculum progressed rather predictably, covering courses such as how to "Know and Lead the Organization," "Know and Lead Others," and "Know Yourself." Somehow, however, the latter course failed to "diagnose" Jeff as an introvert who was more comfortable in his own company or around people he knew well. Instead, Jeff's instructors suggested that, through practice, he could learn to be as comfortable as his socially extroverted classmates at pitching ideas to venture capital investors, attracting seed money, signing on collaborators, and chitchatting with followers. But Jeff wasn't "improving," and would sweat, tremble, and palpitate his way through required role-play interactions, including dry-run pitches that students were assigned to make on random startup ideas. This drove him to see me, in hopes of getting a medication that would "slow [his] heart down" as he went through the dreaded role-play.

Upon our meeting, Jeff shared that he had always been shy and never enjoyed public speaking. In class, he wouldn't raise his hand, even when he knew the answer to the teacher's question. In all his relationships, one-on-one was his preferred mode of interacting rather than group settings. This hadn't impacted his personal life very much—Jeff had two close long-term friends and was dating—but it was impacting business school. Role-playing; spontaneous, unrehearsed presentations; and "networking," such as one would have to do with potential venture capital investors, would be some of the most anxiety-producing situations for him and for many individuals on the shyness spectrum. Yet his school's curriculum did not seem to make room for shyness, promoting, instead, the idea that good leaders are "socially intelligent" creatures capable of dominating interpersonal situations and interactions—*and that he could become that person himself.* On the personality grid, Jeff would probably be considered low on extraversion and high on neuroticism. Like all personality combinations, this was a difficult-to-change one that his MBA program could not have been expected to identify and should not have assumed it could "cure."

As Jeff desperately tried to become the social animal he wasn't, the seemingly accessible ingredients considered essential to the consummate leader were leading to his personal breakdown. Increasingly, he sought in potentially addictive anxiety drugs the solution to his leadership block. "I read about Xanax and Valium—if I could have a prescription for those, I think I can get through this," he told me. "Another student in my program didn't have the schmooze gene, either. These medications seemed to help," he added. These medications, however, came with potentially serious side effects, not the least of which is to develop a dependency to them, and I wasn't prepared to prescribe them, at least not yet. And intensive psychotherapy, often considered the first-line treatment for this issue, was not an option for Jeff as he didn't feel like he could take enough time off from school to devote to it. So I recommended propranolol, a non-habit-forming medication in the beta blocker family that is sometimes used to treat performance anxiety and that I had used successfully in other patients, including an opera singer and a standup comedian with severe stage fright. But the beta blocker didn't work for Jeff, and neither did other relatively safe antianxiety options, including gabapentin (made him "foggy"), hydroxyzine (made him sleepy), buspirone (made him nauseous), and Zoloft (made him anorgasmic).

But over conversations between failed treatment attempts, it was becoming clearer to Jeff and me that perhaps the best course was not a medication but a change of some sort. It wasn't psychotherapy per se that we were doing, but it was close, and we would spend more time discussing his priorities and sacrifices than going over medication specifics. We debated if his MBA leadership curriculum, with its idealization of personality traits he did not possess and could not medicate himself into acquiring, was worth all the symptoms, diagnostic labels, medication "trial and error," and intolerable side effects. And what were we treating anyway? Shyness? And then, on the day he said he wanted to revisit the idea of prescribing Xanax or Valium, Jeff uncharacteristically no-showed for our appointment. He did not explain or reschedule or return messages checking on him.

Ten months later, a postcard arrived depicting an African savanna. The scene was so serene it could be used in one of those virtual reality simulations intended to encourage inner peace. Jeff had dropped out of his MBA program, relocated to Africa, and was finding success building a solar energy plant. "No anxiety, no regrets," he wrote. Jeff's temperament may not have lined up with today's concept of manager or boss, but this didn't mean he couldn't find happiness or meaning doing something that was more in line with who he was.

Jeff made the right choice if what he needed to succeed in his leadership curriculum was a personality transplant. Personality is rather fixed, research suggests, and not something we can easily learn to change or grow out of—with or without medications. One landmark study in the personality studies field tracked over 2,400 Hawaiian residents, first assessed in the 1950s and 1960s as elementary school children between six and twelve years of age.[19] At the time of that assessment, the students' teachers were handed sheets of paper, each of which had a particular trait (e.g., gregarious) printed at the top, and were instructed to rank students in their classroom from highest to lowest on that trait. The teachers did this for thirty-nine personality traits.

Nearly forty years later, the surviving students were reassessed to measure the stability of their personalities over time, after mapping the thirty-nine childhood characteristics to the corresponding Big Five personality traits. From elementary school through the hormonal upheaval of adolescence and well into adulthood, the personality profiles showed significant stability over time.

Another study assessed personality change across adulthood in a group of Harvard alumni who were first assessed after completing their college education at around age twenty-two, then again at around sixty-seven years of age.[20] Over the forty-five-year interval from early to late adulthood, the personality traits of neuroticism, extraversion, and openness showed significant stability.

A less scientific but also powerful demonstration of stability over time came to us courtesy of a British docuseries titled *Up*, which tracked the lives of ten males and four females from Britain over a fifty-six-year stretch, starting when they were seven in 1964, then every seven years up into their sixties.[21] What is remarkable watching the various installments is the relative consistency between who the protagonists became and who they were as kids. By and large, it doesn't take much extrapolation or projection or "correcting" for life events to recognize in the sixty-three-year-old some of that seven-year-old. At least personality-wise, "the child is father of the man," as a famous poet once wrote.[22]

The striking stability in people's personalities, as observed in several longitudinal research studies as well as clinically and anecdotally, led psychologists and leading personality researchers Paul Costa and Robert McCrae to this dramatic conclusion in their appropriately titled 1984 book, *Emerging Lives, Enduring Dispositions*:

> Many individuals will have undergone radical changes in their life structure. They may have married, divorced, remarried. They have probably moved their residence several times. Job changes, layoffs, promotions, and retirement are all likely to have happened

for many people. Close friends and confidants will have died or moved away or become alienated. Children will have been born, grown up, married, begun a family of their own. The individual will have aged biologically, with changes in appearance, health, vigor, memory, and sensory abilities. Internationally, wars, depressions, and social movements will have come and gone. Most subjects will have read dozens of books, seen hundreds of movies, watched thousands of hours of television. *And yet, most people will not have changed appreciably in any of the personality dispositions measured by these tests.*[23]

So strong were McCrae's and Costa's research conclusions about the fixity of personality over time that they felt a need to reassure their psychotherapist colleagues that psychotherapy was still worthwhile, even if changing people's dispositions was clearly an uphill battle. "Dwelling on the constancy of personality may be depressing to practitioners in the business of changing people and their lives, and brings to mind that most vexing of questions, the ultimate effectiveness of psychotherapy. . . . We emphatically do not view personality stability as a cause for despair and the abandonment of psychotherapy. But we do feel that it necessitates and justifies a different set of expectations and criteria for success."[24] Psychotherapy was still very valuable, the world's foremost personality experts seemed to be telling us, but please be realistic, manage your expectations, and don't ask for the moon!

Research, then, teaches us that personality is quite stable, stubborn, and sticky. It tends to "set" early on, with genetics playing a determining role. And while some personality change is possible, it unfolds hesitantly and over decades, not during a busy afternoon in the office. Given the genetic component, and unless executive coaches gain gene-editing powers, it is hard to imagine how they could succeed at totally transforming a leader's innate personality or natural position on the compass. Rather than be able to "jump" between styles or from one end of the compass to another as circumstances dictate, our leaders are more likely to chronically inhabit their one personality—let's hope it's a congenial one.

All this makes less believable the prospect of executive coaches serving as de facto therapists to pull off significant change in people's fundamental dispositions. It also makes more uncomfortable the infusion of leadership training with so much psychological and neuroscience jargon. There is a surfeit of superficial psychological references in what the leadership industry offers. Consider, for example, Blue Point, a leading purveyor of leadership training that, according to its website, counts clients like Microsoft, Salesforce, Starbucks, and Gap Inc. It offers a two-day, one-day, or half-day workshop called "The Leader Within," designed to "significantly accelerate (participants') development as leaders."[25] It "takes (them) on a deeper journey into their inner world where they will learn to tap the enormous power of their emotions and moods. . . . They will learn to recognize their own emotions in a wide variety of interpersonal circumstances, respond to these emotions in ways that enhance their leadership, become aware of the emotions of others, and be a positive, energizing force within their organization." Or consider the "NeuroLeadership" Institute and its podcast *Your Brain at Work*, whose very names suggest a certain mastery of the neuronal pathways involved in leadership.[26] A podcast or a two-day, one-day, or half-day event is likely to disappoint, almost by definition. Psychoanalysis, which attempted to effect fundamental change in individuals, was known to be a long-term process unsuitable for the commitment-phobic. A pair of studies from the New York Psychoanalytic Society and Institute in the mid-seventies and the late eighties found that the median duration of psychoanalytic treatment was five to six years of four to five sessions a week on the couch—"Sorry, Your Time Is Not Up" is how *New York Magazine* titled an article describing the research.[27] Freud himself had this to say about the frustratingly slow course of the treatment he pioneered: "To shorten . . . treatment is a justifiable wish. . . . Unfortunately, it is opposed by a very important factor, namely, the slowness with which deep-going changes in the mind are accomplished."[28] How conceivable is it, given the tectonic timescale of "deep-going changes in the mind," that a weekend workshop will send leaders on an inner-world journey that is deep enough to allow them to recognize their emotions and those of others across a wide range of circumstances? Indeed, offerings such as Blue Point's "Leadership Express Series" seem to this psychiatrist destined to fall short simply because, just like personality, there is nothing "express" about leadership.[29] Overall, the field appears to want to pay psychology and neuroscience lip service, using them to "look" psychologically attuned and neuroscientifically rooted, when true knowledge of psychology and neuroscience would suggest different conclusions than what a lot of the industry would want us to believe.

Not that even years of psychoanalysis are guaranteed to work. Paul was a married man in his forties when he came to see us for a "codependent relationship" with his mother that was pushing his wife and two teenage daughters away. In fact, when we met him, Paul's wife had just asked for divorce, citing his inability to "individuate" from his mother.

Paul's mother immigrated from Ireland with her only son, then four years old, to escape a violent alcoholic husband by joining her brother in California. She could not see a future for her son in that home environment and in a culture that seemed to want her to hide her husband's behavior rather than make him address it. Paul's mother would raise him as a single parent, working sixteen-hour shifts as a nurse aide to send him to a private Catholic school, then to college, where he studied civil engineering, eventually finding significant success as a builder of commercial real estate properties. Never having time to make friends and never remarrying, Paul's mother continued to make their relationship the center of her life. The usual milestones of graduating from college, financial independence, marriage, and fatherhood would not change that or make it any easier for her to "let go." She continued to want to weigh in.

And Paul continued to struggle with becoming his own independent man by allowing his roles as husband and father to supersede that of being the dutiful son. With every significant decision

pertaining to his career, but also his marriage and kids, Paul felt a
need to seek out his mother's advice and, more often than not, to
follow it. Nothing seemed doable without her benediction, causing
much tension with his wife and daughters. Paul did not defend his
behavior; he knew that his relationship with his mother was alienating his family and was desperate to establish boundaries with his
mother. But how to achieve this without "hurting her feelings,"
knowing how much she had sacrificed for him? To try to answer
this question and finally "individuate," Paul had spent nearly ten
years in therapy, accumulating an almost encyclopedic knowledge
of its flavors and shades, not to mention its shortcomings.

"Call me a professional therapy patient if you want, but you
name it, I've done it," Paul said of the many therapy schools he
had tried in search for answers. "I was in psychoanalysis for three
years. I then tried behavioral therapy, cognitive therapy, exposure
therapy, motivational therapy, acceptance and commitment therapy, client-centered therapy, and Gestalt therapy, but don't ask me
in what order. I even tried art therapy. However, when my last
therapist recommended something called DIRT therapy, I drew
the line and thought I would come here instead."

DIRT therapy stands for Danger Ideation Reduction Therapy.
It is a relatively new psychotherapy intervention that was developed for OCD and that is intended to reduce the fear of dangerous outcomes that patients feel when they do not perform certain
behaviors. It was, indeed, an unusual recommendation, given that
Paul did not suffer from OCD. Was it supposed to reduce the danger that had become attached in his mind to upsetting his mother
by pushing her away? I wasn't sure but at the same time could understand why a therapist who had seen Paul fail multiple types of
treatment might make an out-of-the-box recommendation.

"Multiple types of treatment," but also multiple delivery
forms. "I did one-on-one therapy, and I did group therapy," he explained. "I did in-person therapy, and I did online therapy. I did
individual therapy on my own, and I did couples therapy with my
wife. I saw a psychiatrist, two psychologists, a licensed clinical social worker, and a marriage and family therapist. I tried therapy

through my insurance plan, and I paid for private therapists out of pocket. Nothing seemed to help."

With Paul having almost exhausted therapy modalities and types of specialists, I was at a loss as to what to suggest next. I was not convinced about DIRT and hesitated to recommend revisiting an approach that had already failed. I also did not see medications as a legitimate answer, given the lack of specific symptoms we could target. Three things would eventually help break our stalemate. I recommended that Paul check whether his mother might consider therapy herself, using her heavy history of trauma as a "window" to convince her to give it a try, and she was surprisingly open to it. In parallel, Paul also started talking to his priest, who formulated Paul's issue as a case of "Irish Catholic guilt" around disappointing one's long-suffering mother, an interpretation that deeply resonated with Paul and that he wanted to explore further with his priest. Paul also found a valuable outlet in volunteering to talk to therapists in training about his insights from ten years of being what he called a "professional therapy patient." The trainees loved him, and he found great meaning in the experience of teaching them about the patient perspective. Slowly but surely, glimmers of a positive shift were starting to emerge, and things were looking tentatively up.

Although not a direct reference to leadership or somebody undergoing a successful personality change, Paul's case nonetheless speaks to the challenging work of therapy and its uncertain outcomes, even when using well-researched modalities and even when conducted by well-trained professional therapists. While a priest did seem to help him in the end where no one else appeared to succeed, I hesitate to generalize and still advocate that nonprofessional "therapists" from ecclesiasts to life coaches to executive coaches stay out of the work of therapy.

Two previous occupants of the highest office in the land, George W. Bush and Barack Obama, also help demonstrate how fixed personal style can be—how resistant to change, even when guided by the best advisers in the world—and how this can get in the way of great leadership. (I say this as citizen and taxpayer, not diagnostician; I cannot ethically diagnose someone I haven't evaluated and have no reason to suspect there is anything pathological to "diagnose.") The fact that both presidents seemed to represent polar opposites on the leadership style compass, and stayed in their respective "prison," may help further illustrate the point.

George W. Bush was a classic guy-next-door leader. His reported history of cocaine and alcohol use did not hurt—it humanized him.[30] The fact that he grew up in the shadow of a brother who was described as the parents' anointed one endeared him to many.[31] The black-sheep-among-Brahmin status may have caused him to seek refuge in an alternate identity, dropping his upper crust insignia, losing his Harvard Business School ring, and embracing brush-clearing on his Crawford, Texas, ranch, with a drawl to match. But none of it came across as totally fake or overly studied. There was an authenticity to this down-home persona, even if nothing in his family history or upbringing could have predicted it. Leaders would kill for that.

We know the rest of the story. The authenticity, down-home folksiness, and the "compassionate conservatism" he projected made it easy for many to assume best intentions as he led a disastrous war based on inauthentic evidence and what was described as an oedipal need to finish his father's work in Iraq.[32] His father, George H. W. Bush, you see, had led the first Iraq war in response to Iraqi dictator Saddam Hussein's invasion of Kuwait, his oil-rich, peaceable neighbor, in the summer of 1990. A highly well-regarded diplomatic charm offensive by Bush senior's administration ensued, leading to the formation of a large coalition that forced Saddam Hussein to retreat from Kuwait. "Retreat," but not relinquish his leadership of the country—which gave the son an opportunity to finish off the job, thereby outdoing a father who, legend has it, did not think highly of him. Outdoing the father did not turn out so simple.

"Inarticulate" was one of the adjectives hurled at George W. Bush.[33] Countless "Bushisms"—those verbal slip-ups, malapropisms, and syntactically challenged utterances—helped cement that reputation.[34] Although he would later receive much flak for it, one particular statement can be excused for its very intelligence. "I'm the decider, and I decide what's best."[35] He spoke these words in reference to his Secretary of Defense, Donald Rumsfeld, to address rumors that he would be let go. The former president put it succinctly and accurately. To be commander in chief is to be decider in chief, and a leader is someone who can make decisions clearly and unequivocally. Later, he would title his autobiography *Decision Points*.[36]

Never mind that the decisions might have been instinctive, from-the-gut, or lacking essential grounding. From the audience's perspective, for better or worse, a leader's ability to make a difficult decision efficiently and while communicating conviction can be more important than the content of the decision itself. In other words, Bush coming out forcefully and unequivocally in favor of maintaining Rumsfeld communicated a crucial leader-like clarity of purpose, even if you thought Rumsfeld was the devil in the form of secretary of defense.

Contrast that with the worry-it-to-death approach of some other leaders, whose caution and deliberation, after an eternity of waiting for them to make up their minds already, can be summed up as mental masturbation. To capture this paralyzing state of inaction, the French combine the word for navel, *nombril*, with the charged suffix "*-ism*" to come up with "*nombrilisme*." And in some ways, President Barack Obama may have done too much navel gazing for his own legacy and our collective good.

A critical example of what may be seen as Obama's overly deliberate style involved his handling of the famous "red line" on the issue of Syrian chemical weapons. Criticized for his they've-been-at-each-others'-throats-for-centuries reticence and his fear of entangling the US by doing "stupid shit," President Obama finally announced in a news conference in August 2012 a more muscular approach, in the face of mounting atrocities against civilians and an epic refugee crisis that was already destabilizing volatile neighboring countries and threatening to reach Europe.[37]

"We have been very clear to the Assad regime, but also to other players on the ground, that a red line for us is we start seeing

a whole bunch of chemical weapons moving around or being utilized," the president said. "That would change my calculus. That
would change my equation." Pretty strong rhetoric from a very
calibrated leader who weighed his words extremely carefully. Sure
enough, the red line was crossed, repeatedly, after that, including in August 2013 when, within three hours on one day, some
3,600 victims flooded Damascus hospitals showing telltale signs
of neurotoxin exposure, according to Doctors Without Borders.[38]
Obama's calculus remained the same, however. No new variable
seemed to disrupt the equation.

He would spend the remaining four years of his presidency
"monitoring the situation" and reaching for ever-more-difficult
explanations for the inaction, apparently against the advice of his
secretary of state, Hillary Clinton.[39] (Clinton would later have this
to say about her former boss's approach: "Great nations need organizing principles, and 'Don't do stupid stuff' is not an organizing
principle.")[40] Obama continued in a style of leadership—"leading from behind"—that was becoming attached to him since the
Libya debacle, even as the death toll from the war in Syria climbed
to 400,000; ISIS emerged from the chaos to spread globally; and
hundreds of thousands of Muslim refugees spilled across the Med-
iterranean, feeding a European populism that brought us Brexit,
threatened the foundations of the European Union, and contributed to the Trump takeover in the US.[41] Through his unwaver-
ing support for Assad, Vladimir Putin assured the survival of the
Syrian regime with little meaningful resistance from the US or
NATO; later he would be emboldened to embark on his Ukraine
adventure. In a sense, the disaster of George W. Bush's knee-jerk
war was mirrored by Barack Obama's overly intellectualized approach to a fight. A trigger-happy leader is a dangerous thing, but
so, too, can be a very gun-shy one.

"No-drama Obama" may have been a breath of fresh air after the reflexes of the previous administration, but it can be a fine
(red) line between a fixation on being drama-free and paralyzing
frigidity. Ultimately, the professorial president would come across
as more comfortable in his ivory tower than getting his hands

dirty leading. Seemingly detached from his followers, he would help precipitate a pendulum swing toward a presidency that was described as the epitome of raw, anticerebral populism—but more on that later.

It would be fair to say that Obama and Bush seemed to occupy opposite ends of the disposition compass. One lesson might be that being all-North, all-South, all-East, or all-West can compromise a leader's leadership. Another lesson is that leadership style, like personality style, is rather fixed, and this fact matters hugely. It would be hard to imagine Obama "pulling off" a Dubya if a particular situation required a spontaneous, "from the gut" decision—and vice versa. It would be hard to imagine either one switching from his natural compass position to the one much more comfortably occupied by his immediate predecessor/successor.

Bush and Obama seemed to leave office the same individuals they had entered it eight years prior, and seemed to lead in much the same way. For all the talk of growth, learning curves, experience gained, and "evolution," one remained an academic, the other more at home on a ranch. The most visible changes at the end of presidents' tenure are often physical and not related to their unique, personal "signature." They were not pulled in a direction diametrically opposed to the one they were inclined to occupy, and this would be very much in line with what, as psychiatrists and psychologists, we see in our practices day after day and case after case: personality is stubborn, and will fight you back when you try to bend it into something it is not.

And these resistant-to-change leaders are blessed with the best strategists, minders, image consultants, and coaches that money can buy, and with the best data (up-to-the-minute polling, endless focus-grouping, etc.) to track what works and what doesn't and to microtune their leadership style accordingly. If they seemed resistant to change, how much lasting impact and transformational change could a crash management course by an arguably less talented trainer produce?

And yet, much of leadership development today is about developing a "brand," one that often involves stamping out the personality "signature" the leader might have had. It adds up to a big paradox: On the one hand, we have the message that all personalities and leadership styles are essentially workable. On the other hand, there is emphasis on "branding," with one particular brand being valued above all others. What might it be?

When psychiatrists get together, we "process." This word refers to an exercise in self-reflection, outward analysis, reading between the lines, and tea leaf reading. But for most non–mental health professionals, to process—and its associated adjective, processed—is more likely to conjure up a mild taste in the mouth and a not particularly interesting texture. I am talking about Velveeta. In its reliable smoothness, Velveeta is the homogenized outcome of massive industrial food processors that turn batch after batch of individual components (none of which could rightly be called cheese) into overprocessed identical yellow bricks. Velveeta might well be the perfect metaphor for today's ultrapasteurized, "on brand" leader.

In an age that likes to think of itself as tolerant, there is a lot of intolerance at the very top, where strong forces conspire to stamp out individuality and make leaders more alike than different. Voices that dare to dissent and people who dare to have unique personalities constitute legal and other risks to the company, university, or other institution. The code of conduct acceptable for leaders has been compressed, with variations in behavior and temperament confined to a narrow range. Basically, keep your philosophy, political leanings, and life experiences to yourself—we are not interested, thank you—and lead without personality. Always *appear* responsive to followers' concerns, regardless of how unreasonable or provocative you might find them. Walk on eggshells. Be characterless. The blander you come across, the better. Call it brand "bland." But by not letting our leaders have their own personality, we do not let them "be," so how can we expect them to lead?

Consider Tom, an academic colleague with administrative responsibilities at a Midwestern university, who recently told me of a letter he received before the COVID-19 pandemic from three members of his large division, asking him to ban "ruminant meat" from their functions. Tom, a carnivore, worried that the beef-and lamb-free menu would make group lunches less appetizing to the majority, alienating meat eaters and negatively impacting attendance. Yet his executive coach, whom he was meeting with weekly at the request of his department, strongly recommended that Tom agree to the ban, as it would project sensitivity to the planetary havoc wreaked by cattle and sheep farming. Other carbon-footprint-reducing gestures that he proposed would not cut it, the coach argued, as they would not be "bold enough." Never mind that Tom found the whole thing ridiculous—hypocritically signaling responsiveness was the desired brand, and Tom felt he could not say no without being eco-shamed. The meat ban went in, and as Tom predicted, attendance significantly dropped. It took a pandemic for attendance to recover again, as people logged in from their homes—and their kitchens.

By ignoring his own insight into what his colleagues wanted and implementing what his career coach suggested, Tom inadvertently created the exact outcome he wanted to avoid: poorly attended meetings and fewer opportunities to discuss the challenges facing his division. Does that sound like good leadership?

This approach to leadership training has echoes in the tight embrace by Fortune 500 HR departments of mandatory "diversity training" despite evidence—summarized in a *Harvard Business Review* article by sociologists Frank Dobbin from Harvard and Alexandra Kalev from Tel Aviv University, based on three decades' worth of data from over 800 US firms and hundreds of interviews with managers and executives—that this approach unfortunately doesn't work in terms of increasing diversity in management and may in fact make some employees *less* sensitive to those who are different.[42] A new way is desperately needed, they conclude, if we want to truly improve things.

What seems to count more is the "optics" and the legal protections that come from "looking" sensitive to these issues should you get sued, not any incontrovertible proof that these interventions actually work. As such, leaders are pushed to push their employees to enroll in annual trainings whose efficacy is debatable—complete with tests at the end to ensure employees dropped their biases after an hour-long webinar—when other practices could go much further toward building a truly diverse, representative, and equitable workplace, and when the money might be better spent elsewhere, such as providing equal pay for equal work. You may not want to quote to your coach from another article by Dobbin and Kalev, in *Anthropology Now*, that "hundreds of studies dating back to the 1930s suggest that antibias training doesn't reduce bias, alter behavior, or change the workplace," and that "mandatory participation . . . will make participants feel that an external power is trying to control their behavior," which has been shown to reinforce bias.[43] You will probably not get too far if you suggest that real change doesn't mean checking the "D.E.I. training" box, but, instead, requires investing in aggressive recruitment from underrepresented communities, committed mentorship, and new ideas from creative visionaries.

By helping create a straitjacketed, homogenized pool of leaders, with little room for personal nuance, distinction, idiosyncrasy, or going against the grain, the leadership industry (and the larger culture) is depriving us of truly transcendent leaders. Professional speech writers often write their speeches, just to be sure, further muffling their personality and "voice." Leaders are increasingly forced to present a cookie-cutter façade, to be standard, and this "processing" into Velveeta leads to pent-up resentment among everyday men and women, which in turn can manifest itself in Trumpism and violently anti-PC movements—and leaders.

Much is lost by embracing a narrow leadership brand. The new CEO, forced into a blunted personality and affect, may be compared to a psychiatric patient who is in complete remission, that is, whose symptoms have been completely eradicated, but who, as happens in some cases, has seen the bothersome symptoms replaced by feeling "nothing."

SSRIs, for Selective Serotonin Reuptake Inhibitors, have brought about a true psychopharmacology revolution since their introduction in the 1980s. Generally safe and well tolerated, they have become the first-line medication intervention for unipolar depression and several anxiety disorders. An occasional SSRI side effect, though, is emotional numbness. These patients will describe how their lows are thankfully mostly gone, but their highs are also few and far between. They don't cry anymore, but they don't laugh, either. Their depression and anxiety "cure" had caused numbness to replace the symptoms they came in with. Hardly the sought-after effect, the right thing to do in this case is to decrease the dose or switch to another medication altogether or to therapy.

This was the case with David, a forty-eight-year-old married father of two who came to see me for a depressive episode that took away his ability to experience joy, made him irritable with his kids, and was associated with weight loss, insomnia, and a difficulty concentrating that forced him to go on medical leave from his accounting job. During his lowest points, David also wished he wouldn't wake up in the morning, although his two young kids prevented him from going too far in this disturbing line of thinking. We made the decision to treat his severe depression with the SSRI paroxetine and dosed it rather aggressively in an attempt to increase the chances of it working or working sooner. Four weeks into his paroxetine trial, a positive shift could already be discerned in David. Initially, he required some convincing to appreciate that he seemed more hopeful about his ability to come out of his depression and was not thinking about dying anymore. By week six, his sleep, appetite, and concentration were so close to their normal baseline that David was asking if it would be OK to stay on paroxetine for the rest of his life since he liked it so much. By week eight, David hit two further milestones: He was back at work and could once again help his kids with their homework. Around that time, however, it was also becoming obvious that there was a going-through-the-motions aspect to his recovery. While essentially fully functional and no longer depressed, David did not seem to be experiencing the usual highs of his normal mood cycle. When I asked him if he could describe his mood in a word, he said "flat." A side effect to paroxetine seemed to be the cause, and it took a 75 percent reduction in the dose to give David back his full emotional spectrum while fortunately maintaining his response.

Flatlining can be an example of overtreating, and history teaches us that we overtreat and overdiagnose—narrowing the scope of "normal" psychology—at our own risk. The greatest president in the history of the United States and the greatest prime minister in the history of Great Britain appear to have suffered from mental illness. Abraham Lincoln's "melancholy" is well documented.[44] As a young man, suicidal feelings found an outlet in passionate, dark verse:

> *Yes! I've resolved the deed to do*
> *And this is the place to do it:*
> *This heart I'll rush a dagger through*
> *Though I in hell should rue it!*[45]

What we might today call his major depressive disorder was hard to hide. "No element of Mr. Lincoln's character was so marked, obvious and ingrained as his mysterious and profound melancholy," wrote his colleague Henry Whitney.[46] "His melancholy dripped from him as he walked," declared his law partner, William Herndon.[47]

Similarly, were he to seek a psychiatric consultation today, it has been said that Winston Churchill would likely be diagnosed with bipolar affective disorder.[48] According to his friend Lord Beaverbrook, the man was always either "at the top of the wheel of confidence or at the bottom of an intense depression."[49] Combine his well-documented extravagance with money, lack of inhibitions (epic drinking, smoking 250,000 cigars over his ninety-year life, and holding meetings in his bathtub or in personally tailored, pale-pink silk underwear), abnormal energy (his workday began at 8:00 a.m. and ended after 2:00 a.m.), prolificness (more published words than Shakespeare and Dickens combined), and racing thoughts (of which US president Franklin D. Roosevelt would say: "He has a thousand ideas a day, four of which are good."), and you might arrive at a certain definition of mania.[50]

Likewise for what Churchill called his "black dog," or low periods that he suffered from on numerous occasions in the 1930s, 1920s, 1910s, and earlier, and during which he would be paralyzed by despair, oversleep, show little energy or interest in things, lose his appetite, and have difficulty concentrating.[51] These darker periods could last months and be accompanied by more ominous thoughts yet: "I don't like standing near the edge of a platform when an express train is passing through," he told Lord Moran, his personal doctor, who recorded it in his diaries before it was included in a book. "I like to stand back and, if possible, get a pillar between me and the train. I don't like to stand by the side of a ship and look down into the water. A second's action would end everything. A few drops of desperation."[52] This deep familiarity with "desperation" may have helped him relate to the devastation of war and the plight of its victims. On the "high" side of the bipolar wheel, it might have required a grandiose spirit touched by mania to imagine, when all the odds were against Britain, a path to victory and to inspire a nation to pursue it. Maybe he wasn't a great leader *despite* mental illness, but because of it.[53]

In an interview with the *Financial Times,* Alastair Campbell, the author and former director of communications and strategy to the UK prime minister, made the case that exceptional motivation, which is necessary for many people's success, often comes from chronic inner dissatisfaction or even mental illness.[54] According to Campbell, who attributes his own success to his struggle with depression, those who strive and achieve are not so much driven by the joy of winning as they are by the pathological fear of failure. This fundamental intrinsic "flaw," common to many great leaders, cannot be planted by a zealous coach or caught like a cold. It doesn't rub off on you. You either have it or you don't, and if you do, you shouldn't necessarily medicate it away.

Campbell's position and Churchill's and Lincoln's examples join Marcel Proust's appreciation for what those whom we consider to be on the abnormal spectrum of psychological health have to offer, including as leaders in their fields. In his masterpiece *Remembrance of Things Past*, Proust, one of the world's foremost novelists (and neurotics), had this to say: "All the greatest things we know have come to us from neurotics. It is they and they only who have founded religions and created great works of art. Never will the world be conscious of how much it owes to them, nor above all what they have suffered in order to bestow their gifts on it."[55] Anxiety, discomfort, even suffering, can sometimes find an outlet in great accomplishments. As such, we should be careful not to insist on a very narrow range of "normal" and not to process away all the idiosyncratic traits of people and emerging leaders—all that propels them to go against the current or makes them different or "risky" or have character. The annals of history are rich with individuals of great consequence who skewed deliciously from the ordinary, not just Lincoln and Churchill but Ludwig II, the "Mad King" fairy-tale castle builder who bankrupted Bavaria but gave Bavarians an identity and world-class architecture in the process, and King George III of England who despite bouts of madness held his country together during the tumult of the American Revolution, the French Revolution, and the Napoleonic wars. Or consider Abd al-Rahman III, the tenth-century emir and caliph of Spain's Cordoba, who enjoyed spectacular military success and is remembered as a humanist who built palaces, collected books, and turned his city into the most dazzling, cultured, and civilized destination in medieval Europe. Yet, taking stock of his life in a letter he wrote at the end of his reign, Abd al-Rahman arrives at this devastating accounting: "I have now reigned above fifty years in victory or peace; beloved by my subjects, dreaded by my enemies, and respected by my allies. Riches and honors, power and pleasure, have waited on my call, nor does any earthly blessing appear to have been wanting to my felicity. In this situation, I have diligently numbered the days of pure and genuine happiness which have fallen to my lot: They amount to fourteen."[56] An enviable legacy and countless pleasures and gratifications at his fingertips did not seem to improve his lot of only fourteen days of happiness.

On the modern business front, what has been nonclinically described as Steve Jobs's "paranoia" was, as we will see, a critical determinant of his success.[57] (In a comment he wrote for the cover of *Only the Paranoid Survive*, the book by Intel CEO Andy Grove about the need to stay on the lookout for competition coming out of left field and beating you at your game, Jobs said: "This book is about one super-important concept."[58]) More recently, Andy Dunn, cofounder and former CEO of the men's fashion brand Bonobos, chronicled in his book *Burn Rate* how his bipolar illness interacted with his executive role, sometimes impairing his decision-making and sometimes elevating it. "For me, controlled hypomania is when I am at my entrepreneurial best: able to work long days, with high levels of endurance; generating kinetic positive energy for recruiting, fundraising, and motivating the team; and having frequent sparks of ideas, perhaps even moments of vision," he said. "Everything is clicking, everything is making sense, life has purpose. Colors seem brighter; gratitude flows. This is the zone where creativity and productivity flourish."[59]

Dunn is not alone, as data suggests an overrepresentation of bipolar disorder among the entrepreneurial and executive class. One study from the Karolinska Institute in Sweden, for example, assessed a registry of nearly 70,000 individuals with bipolar disorder, and showed that persons with bipolar disorder were more likely than their matched controls to possess superior leadership skills. "These results can be read as support of a potential in persons with bipolar disorder . . . that should be safeguarded and utilized," Simon Kyaga, the study author said.[60]

None of this, it must be emphasized, is an invitation for sufferers of mental health problems to eschew treatment, nor a call to look in the ranks of patients with severe psychiatric illness for the leaders of tomorrow. Rather, it is to highlight this crucial concept: by pulling the outer reaches of the emotional and character spectrum closer to the bland center, by elevating the predictable "Brand Bland," we can rob ourselves of truly unique, larger-than-life figures and can cause "maverick" leaders to go extinct. Herb Kelleher, whose irreverence was, as we saw, part and parcel of his difficult-to-resist appeal, would have a hell of a time rising in today's corseted leadership culture—too unpredictable, risqué, and risky for most corporations and leadership minders to stomach.

Similarly, John McCain, who, for a generation of Washington, DC, politicians and voters, defined the maverick, independent-thinking politician who could not be pigeonholed or contained within his party affiliation, seems firmly ensconced in a bygone era. In McCain's case, to go against his party's dogma on climate change, immigration, and campaign finance reform, for example, and to do so with such panache, would be to break too many leadership rules today.[61] To our loss.

Today's leadership industry is deeply conflicted about personality and does not know quite what to do with it as it sends this crazy-making message: all personalities are welcome, and all personalities must go! The backlash to this personality vacuum has been nothing less than frightening.

PART II

WHY LEADERSHIP IS SO DAMN DIFFICULT

EVEN IF THE leadership industry were entirely scientific and fully in command of the process by which good leaders can be produced—and we have seen in Part One that it mostly is not—good leaders would still be difficult to come by for reasons that have nothing to do with the industry itself and everything to do with the cultural and historical moment we inhabit; a moment that poses unique challenges to the emergence and success of leaders.

Part Two will address the impossibility of leadership today—why it's so damn difficult. First, for better or worse, technology has turned us into a perfect democracy, where we are all equal—and equal to the speed of our internet connections. Natural hierarchies, such as between parent and child, professor and student, and doctor and patient, have been shaken, even inverted. New technologies have tricked us into feeling more informed and empowered than is often justified, and as a result, not easily willing to cede authority to a leader. This has resulted in a culture-wide allergy to hierarchy when peace with a certain degree of it is an absolute necessity for successful leadership. But this new "allergy" has not changed our DNA and how, like our wild relatives, we continue to crave the security of hunting in packs and of having a pack leader. This has given rise to a particular leadership style—call it paleo leadership—that dominates much of our political discourse. Perfectly suited to social media, it is characterized by exaggerated alpha displays, out-of-bounds narcissism, and overt aggression.

When it comes to democracy and governance, its effects have been devastating.

Part Two will also show that, historically, good leaders are people onto whom we can collectively project our aspirations and dreams. This requires that our leaders be, to some extent, mysterious and unknown, so their record and history do not contradict whatever goal or outcome we want to imagine them pursuing on our behalf. But in our current social media surveillance culture, it is virtually impossible for anyone, including leaders, to cultivate mystery or keep a secret. This section will show that leaders are now an open book rather than a blank slate, and in this difference lies a fundamental challenge to leadership today. The absence of privacy, a threat to healthy psychology as I have argued in my published research, is depriving us of the ability to imagine leaders in the best possible light or as champions of our personal causes. Simply too much is known—their biographies, foibles, idiosyncrasies, records, positions—to allow our imaginations to concoct best-case scenarios. Yet the ability to project such "best-case" scenarios on leaders is essential for us to give them a chance and to imagine them as defenders and representatives of what we hold dear.

The final section of Part Two examines other complicating factors to leadership, including the ingrained and fundamentally untenable view that, in America at least, everyone can be a leader (this idea starts as early as kindergarten, when we are taught that any one of us can be president), as well as biases against women in leadership roles, which shrinks by half the pool of potential leadership candidates. Like the overly inclusive message that all are natural leaders, prejudice that excludes large swaths of society is another obstacle to good leadership that is explored in this section. This section also highlights how the cosmetic approach that leadership culture has chosen to "solve" this deeply rooted and serious problem—namely the broad and uncritical reliance on "DEI" (diversity, equity, and inclusion) initiatives as a cure-all—itself speaks of a massive leadership failure.

5

OUT OF THE WILD AND INTO THE SOCIAL MEDIA SWAMP

Equality, Democracy, and Paleo Leaders

WHAT HAPPENS WHEN a society feels so empowered by new technologies that it can no longer "do" hierarchy and its students think they can lead on teaching, its children on parenting, and its patients on doctoring? Now consider what happens when this society's DNA is still pulling it in the direction of submission to a leader? This is the leadership conundrum we are currently living out in all its frustrations, contradictions, and conflicts. On the one hand, we feel emancipated from leaders and just as fit to lead as the next person and, therefore, see no real reason to submit. On the other hand, we unconsciously ache for a leader who will keep us safe and take care of our needs, just like it used to be in older, simpler cave times. Our digitally fortified, virtual selves don't have patience for leaders and hierarchy, yet we still fall for the X (formerly known as Twitter) version of that most primitive type of leader our species has known. Social media are serving as a shortcut right back to the cave, technology-mediated "progress" and rosy internet predictions be damned.

In trying to dissect our particular moment to see what it is about it—about us, really—that complicates leadership today, we must start with a defining characteristic of our time—the internet and our online selves. By giving users a not-always-warranted sense of empowerment and by attracting and magnifying certain personality traits in leaders and followers, the internet has acted on followers and leaders alike to complicate their relationship and burden it with new and unfamiliar "baggage." In the political arena, the baggage has been heavy enough to cause entire democracies to crater under its weight.

WITHOUT EQUAL VOTING rights, equal opportunities, and equality under the law, it would be easier to reduce democracies into what French philosopher Alexis de Tocqueville called the "tyranny of the majority."[1] In many ways, the internet and internet-related technologies have flattened the playing field among people online to where we could be excused if we closed our eyes and, for a brief second, felt like we were living in a more equitable society. The normal accoutrements of power that, offline, identify people as belonging to a particular class, profession, or age group do not exist online or do not exist nearly to the same degree. Our income, physical strength, and demographic characteristics are not as deterministic a force as the speed of our internet connection or the number of likes and retweets under our belt. This would have constituted a historic advance for humanity if it had brought with it true equality or realized the dreams of early World Wide Web utopists and visionaries, some of whom called the internet an "Athens without slaves"—basically, an improved upon and perfected form of that first democracy that we have been trying to recapture since the fifth century BCE.[2] By ensuring a more or less equal voice to every online citizen, the vision went, the internet would become a powerful societal leveler and democracy enabler, spreading "one person, one vote" principles to all online users, and pulling off a feat that Athens itself could not pull off at the dawn of Western civilization. This hot air balloon has deflated at a rate that is directly proportional to the growth of our internet bandwidth, to where saying, today, that the internet has been a "Net" benefit to democracy feels as quaint as a dial-up connection over a landline. Instead of the "great equalizer," we got a compression of hierarchies and pseudo-equality. Instead of a voice, we got a soapbox. This has direct implications to leaders, leadership, and democracy.

Internet-related technologies have created a more horizontal society where the built-in hierarchies that used to separate people—by educational level, professional qualifications, life experience, and so on—no longer matter in the same way. Experts' opinions don't count for much when any question you can think of can likely be answered by hopping on Wikipedia or doing a quick Google search. Students no longer look to their teachers as the unique gatekeepers of precious repositories of knowledge. In a strange reversal of the typical knowledge flow from parent to child, parents now often rely on their kids to learn all things tech, putting kids in the driver's seat on issues crucial to functioning today. In the medical arena, many patients now self-diagnose on Dr. Google, seeking real doctors only for a "second opinion" or to obtain specific medications and treatment interventions that their online research has convinced them will help.

What does the rattling of these traditional hierarchies have to do with leadership? The "democratization" of our culture, as enabled by internet-related technologies, to where everybody can feel equal regardless of age, experience, and CV, has created conditions that make it increasingly difficult for a true leader to emerge. In a sense, technology has made us feel too equal and too empowered to consent to be led or to be patient with leaders. We feel we know better or can easily figure it out. Just as naturally unequal relationships, such as between parent and child or teacher and student, have been reconfigured by new technologies, the relationship between leader and follower has been similarly reconfigured, making it difficult, if not impossible, for many people to tolerate the inferiority implied in occupying the lower position in that dynamic. We feel we can lead in the same way we feel we can parent and teach. The very foundation of the leadership pyramid is on newly shaky grounds, making it less stable when it comes to supporting a leader on top.

EDUCATION IS A prerequisite to equality and to a functioning democracy. The educated citizen who is informed about the issues and who votes on them is the cement that holds democracy together. Otherwise, it is apt to veer in ugly directions. So what are some ways in which the bounty of online information is transforming education? And is the result necessarily a boon for education, democracy, and leadership culture?

Long before the COVID-19 pandemic and the forced switch to remote learning, a colleague who was a senior physician at a medical school in the Midwest was complaining about dwindling attendance at his lectures. Out of a class of ninety or so medical students, only seven or eight would show up, the rest supposedly studying the material on their own at their own pace with their school's blessing. My colleague felt disrespected—like he wasn't worth his students' in-person engagement—and had a hard time writing the required evaluations at the end of the semester on students he had essentially never met. But what was worse was that the patients that he would invite to discuss their personal experiences with a particular disease also felt disrespected, especially when they had battled serious symptoms to make it to class, some even showing up in a wheelchair or with an oxygen tank to share their life story in front of an empty lecture hall.

I would describe my colleague as happily "old school." Having taught generations of medical students, he felt like he knew what worked, had the framed teaching awards on his office walls to prove it, and was not eager to mess with the tried and true. He also still wore a bow tie to class. His was not the profile of someone who would take kindly to his medical school administration's decision to experiment with the attendance-optional pedagogic model for its didactic lectures, as many other medical schools had already done. So many, in fact, that, according to a 2017 Association of

American Medical Colleges survey, less than half (47.3%) of all second-year medical students in the US still went to lectures at all.[3] (The "hands-on" clinical portion of the medical education that takes place in hospitals and clinics has, thankfully, remained "in person.")

The reasons behind what may seem like a surprising trend in teaching our future doctors are numerous and include some research showing that lecture attendance does not always correlate with better exam performance. Students now demand more "flexibility" in the curriculum, paralleling employees who want more room to navigate a better balance between the office and family responsibilities. Students also feel like they have sufficiently proven their discipline and self-motivation by getting into medical school in the first place and should not be "treated like children" at this stage. Then there is the adoption by the larger educational field of a more "learner-centric" philosophy where students are encouraged to interact directly with educational material as the instructor recedes to a more passive role. And there is schools' constant tinkering with pedagogic models to see if the learning experience can be improved upon and to try to distinguish themselves. But the biggest reason is that new technologies have made this possible: Lectures can be recorded and streamed at the student's convenience. Online libraries can be accessed wherever and whenever. Search engines can answer any question a student might have. All these developments have conspired to make the bow-tied lecturer an optional relic that might fit better in a history of medicine museum alongside primordial skull drills and medieval arrow removers than the modern cloud-based lecture hall.

But my colleague wasn't buying any of it and didn't understand how students could learn adequately, attending class on an entirely voluntary basis. Besides not retaining important facts, he wondered how they could learn professionalism and other "intangibles" that needed to be modeled to be transmitted. Pushing against his school's policy, he wrote to the class directly, imploring them to start attending in person and explaining what he felt was being lost with their reliance on remote learning. He also guilt-tripped them a bit, bringing up how the guest patients he was inviting for their education were feeling ignored. To his surprise, more than two-thirds of the class obliged, and, two-thirds of the way into the semester, he got to meet for the first time dozens of students who he had been supposedly teaching all along and who he was supposed to write evaluations for but had never seen once in class.

Things, unfortunately, did not substantively improve. While attendance grew appreciably, he could not help noticing how distracted many students seemed to be by their gadgets. They were present, but not really. No longer streaming his lectures, they seemed to be streaming other content—in class. He felt he would need to ban smartphones next, something he wasn't prepared to do, precisely because he didn't want to "treat them like children." In an honest exchange about gadgets, remote learning, attention span, and attendance-optional teaching after lecture one day, he was struck by one student's reaction: "With all due respect, Professor, we haven't learned anything that we cannot learn online." My colleague retired at the end of the semester.

His honesty might have been brutal, but the student was technically right. No information nugget we teach in medical school cannot be found online or be engaged with in some manner on a digital platform. It's all there, somewhere in the 120 zettabytes that make up the internet.[4] But there are several assumptions implied in the student's statement: We can trust Google with prioritizing accurate information in its yields. A megabyte downloaded is a megabyte learned. Learning is about knowing how to search the online haystacks, not building your internal library. Learning does not include "softer" skills that we pick up from teachers and mentors and that are not amenable to digital platforms. And there is nothing lost when we can no longer concede that someone knows more than Google about a particular topic.

In a way, it can be said that it was an act of democratizing education that pushed my colleague into an earlier-than-planned retirement. His services were no longer appreciated by students who felt they could learn on their own and who no longer saw him as holding the key to information that was crucial to their development as young doctors. Technologically enabled, his students felt almost like his knowledge equals. His students' resistance to a hierarchical relationship with him, one based on an acknowledged differential in experience levels, is one example of how the new equality is playing out online. My colleague was not a "leader" in any real sense, but the same exaggerated empowerment that complicated his students' relationship with him can complicate their relationship with any leader they may have to "submit to" down the road, since following a leader also implies accepting that the leader has experience they do not have, information they do not possess, or talents they lack.

Other examples from the field of education speak to the same issue. Thanks to a surfeit of online content to inspire them, term paper assignments no longer need strike the same terror into the hearts of high school and college students. A visit to Wikipedia is a given, but there is also Googling "term paper," which yields 10,000,000 entries and counting, with samples covering every possible term paper topic. If information is power, these resources, unimaginable a generation ago, can contribute positively to a student's perceived writing potency and homework effectiveness. Unfortunately, they have also contributed to a plagiarism epidemic that has spawned an industry of AI-enabled plagiarism detection software meant to scan homework essays against publicly available material. Already by 2011, more than half of 1,055 college presidents surveyed by the Pew Research Center were reporting a significant rise in cheating over the preceding decade, blaming it on the internet.[5] By pushing learning and homework more fully online, the pandemic exacerbated this trend; according to a study of 80,000 papers from 51,000 students by the plagiarism software maker Copyleaks, the average amount of copy-pasted content in plagiarism events rose from 35 percent pre-pandemic to 45 percent just a few months later.[6] Indeed, Copyleaks or similar software (Unicheck, Scribbr, Grammarly, Plagramme, etc.) is the new must-have teacher accessory besides the red pen, and in some cases comes with a "plagiarism score" that can be incorporated into the paper score. (Some software makers also market directly to students, as though encouraging them to plagiarize until just below the detection level!)

Not to mention ChatGPT, the OpenAI bot that burst onto the scene in 2022 and that can write decent original essays and poems from scratch, no copying needed. "With ChatGPT, a student can turn in a passable assignment without reading a book, writing a word or having a thought," fretted Johann Neem, professor of history at Western Washington University, in an interview with *Inside Higher Ed* about a tool that is essentially replacing thinking.[7] Can students be inspired by online information and sophisticated software in a way that enhances and expands what is taught in the classroom? Without a doubt. Has all the available information fed a sense of empowerment that is exaggerated or in some cases flat-out deceptive? Absolutely. The 10,000,000 entries awaiting the person who Googles "term paper" are, on the surface, an exercise in democratizing access to learning in that they dethrone the teacher as main guide, arbiter, and wordsmith, and emancipate students by putting directly into their hands a trove of valuable material. But the reality is not so sanguine for education and, by extension, leadership culture. Similar forces to those that "emancipated" these students from their teachers are also "emancipating" them from their leaders.

But the biggest—literally "massive"—flirtation with using technology to democratize education so far was our adventure with MOOCs, for "Massive Open Online Courses." Theoretically open to all comers, MOOCs brought together star educators, user-friendly online platforms, and no or low participation costs.[8] They typically included a combination of recorded and live video lectures, online readings, interactive forums, and some sort of assessment module (often peer-to-peer or auto-graded). In 2011, Stanford launched the MOOC *Introduction to AI*, quickly enrolling 160,000 students from 190 countries.[9] This encouraged its instructor, Sebastian Thrun, to cofound the MOOC company Udacity, and to predict that in fifty years there would be only ten universities remaining in the world, with Udacity having a realistic "shot" at being one of them.[10]

Meanwhile, the *New York Times* was declaring 2012 "the year of the MOOC."[11]

Jerry Brown, California's technophile thirty-fourth and thirty-ninth governor, was besotted. At the dawn of his second governorship, could he have finally stumbled upon the solution to California's two most entrenched education problems—making college more affordable and more accessible? In January 2013, he signed an agreement with Udacity and San Jose State University to "democratize education" by offering affordable MOOCs. "We've got to invest in learning, in teaching, in education," he said. "And we do that not by just the way we did it 100 years ago. We keep changing."[12] The change started with three low-cost, for-credit pilot MOOCs, each offered to about 100 students.[13] Disheartening does not begin to describe the results, as nearly 57 percent of San Jose State students and 73 percent of students from outside the university failed the MOOCs.[14] Further, those who succeeded tended to be the most privileged students, not the underserved ones that the initiative was hoping to help. Other MOOC data (that I, along with colleagues at Stanford and the University of York, compiled for a review of MOOCs for the journal *Educause*) was similarly bad, including a University of Pennsylvania study of a million MOOC users, only 4 percent of whom actually completed the MOOC course they registered for.[15]

It didn't take long for the world to be thoroughly MOOC'd out. By July 2013, San Jose State had suspended its partnership with Udacity. Explaining in *Inside Higher Ed* the enterprise's failure, education commentator John Warner said: "[Udacity] believed that the platform itself could deliver 'education,' rather than recognizing that education is not a product but a process, one that happens (or not) inside of those being educated. Udacity seems to view learning like a virus. As long as you're in close enough proximity to an educational product, you will learn."[16]

The story here is of the sorry outcomes that our culture has repeatedly run into when it assumed that internet-related technologies are, by definition, instruments of democracy. When, in the name of democratizing education, we reduce the role of the lecturer to a streamed presence and essentially expect students to control the learning process, 96 percent of students seem to quit. Signing up for a MOOC couldn't be easier, but so is dropping out. Easy come, easy go. A real, grounded, and, yes, hierarchical relationship is essential for learning to happen, but hierarchy is not something we do well anymore. To the extent that hierarchy is built into leadership, this is relevant way beyond the virtual classroom and attendance-optional lecture.

Internet-related technologies, then, have failed to truly democratize education, flattening the teacher-student relationship by encouraging excessive self-confidence in some students, and, in the case of ChatGPT and MOOCs, blowing up the educational paradigm altogether. Another hierarchical relationship that has seen itself interestingly "democratized" by internet-related technologies is parenting. The transmission of knowledge and the modeling of behavior, typically a rather one-way street from mother or father to child, finds itself reconfigured, with the child taking the role of technology teacher and the parent settling into the student seat. The very natural parent-child know-how disequilibrium has been shaken by new technologies, and, if you consider the degree to which these new technologies permeate and control our lives, this is at least a magnitude 7.0 on the Richter scale.

According to a 2019 survey of 1,135 US parents with young children, 65 percent of kids under thirteen have a personal cellphone, and 40 percent were six and under when they first used one.[17] Weaned on new technologies, children are almost by definition more adept at using them than their parents. Parents, however, are just as enamored with these tools, which creates a situation in which they often have to rely on their young kids to add bells and whistles to their Instagram pages, be initiated into TikTok, master a videogame, learn how to communicate with Alexa, or transfer content from an iPhone on the fritz to a shiny new device.

Not to mention today's quintessential parenting task of activating parental controls on a kid's account! Concerned about her teenage son's use of a social media platform and some overly sexualized messages that were circulating around his student group, one of my patients decided, after a long debate in therapy on balancing her son's privacy versus his safety, to take action by turning on the parental controls offered by the platform. But there was a small problem in that this non-tech-savvy parent did not know quite how to do it, so she did what she always does in these situations, which is to call on her live-in "IT support"—her own son—to make it happen. He was happy to offer his services and, for a change, did not need to be bribed. Only the quality of his work on this particular task left something to be desired and was a far cry from his seamless execution on other IT tasks she had requested of him. Perhaps unsurprisingly, my patient's son opted for the least restrictive parental oversight possible over his account, which allowed him to continue operating essentially unmonitored, including apparently sending inappropriate messages to a classmate whose mother eventually approached my patient to complain. As my patient put it, if she had found her tech help on Yelp or TaskRabbit, she would have given him a bad review, but she found him in her basement.

Parents relying on children for tech-related help is not new. A 2014 study of 242 child-parent sets showed that up to 40 percent of parents were taught how to use technology products by their children.[18] This "bottom-up" educational process was true for computers, mobile technology, and social media use. Before and since, in successive waves of the internet revolution, children and teenagers have led the way, with parents following in lockstep behind, even as, in many cases, they complained about the effects on their kids of the technology in question. Teens were at the forefront of the texting craze, for example. A 2012 Pew Research Center survey of teen texting found that the average number of texts had risen from fifty a day in 2009 to sixty three years later, causing alarm among many parents. More than a decade later, many parents' texting logs put these numbers to shame.[19]

Similarly, teens may have received much of the early negative attention linked to "sexting," or the texting of sexually explicit messages, photos, or videos. Yet by 2015, a full 88 percent of adults between eighteen and eighty-eight were sexting, according to a 2015 survey from Drexel University.[20] Yikes. Further, teens and "digital natives" got much of the flack for video game addiction in the aughts, but today's gamer prototype is no longer the nerdy fourteen-year-old boy playing by himself. As many as 64 percent of US adults now play video games regularly, with the average gamer more likely to own a house and have kids and with 55 percent of parents regularly playing with their children.[21]

Besides texting, sexting, and gaming, there is evidence that the same process is unfolding when it comes to social media use. Parents and older adults have continued to flock there, gradually raising the average user's age, when—it couldn't have been more unfair—this was for some time considered the domain of teenage girls. *Saturday Night Live* nailed the sociological consequences of the parental invasion, offering along the way an answer to the vexing question of "Oh no! My mom wants to friend me on Facebook. What should I do?"[22] Well, download SNL's "Damn it, my mom is on Facebook" app, of course, and watch it transform problematic content like a bong gif into something innocuous or even parentally desirable, like a saxophone! (There was no mention of another badly needed app—"Damn it, my boss is on Facebook.") While a younger demographic continues to dominate newer social media platforms like Snapchat and Instagram, we can, if internet history is any guide, expect parents to eagerly follow suit. Brace yourselves for more embarrassing mom dancing videos on TikTok!

None of this is necessarily bad; bonding is bonding, whether it occurs around the dinner table, the campfire, the gaming console, or on social media. Still, the child-to-adult transmission of online skills, knowledge, and hobbies represents an inversion of sorts of the parent-child relationship and an example of children "leading the way" on technology. Given that technology is probably the most important force shaping society today, this is no minor "leadership role."

Medicine has not been spared the technology-mediated flattening taking place in other formerly hierarchical relationships like parenting and education. Medical professionals have felt a loss of control within the doctor-patient relationship on a variety of levels. In many ways, this process has been empowering to patients in the best sense of the word. Patients may be, however, asking Dr. Google questions that far exceed its training and its abilities to advise on. At times, this has resulted in "cyberchondria." Casually defined as excessive anxiety about one's physical health that comes from one too many medical searches, it is caught on health information sites, spreads on social media, and has no cure short of logging off. Its rates seem to be on the rise.

Another negative consequence of "Dr. Google" has been to misinform some patients and send them on clinical wild-goose chases, even as endless medical online resources have given them the reassurance and self-confidence that they can finally take their health care into their own hands. The National Institutes of Health provides a useful guide for evaluating the accuracy of health information online, but, in my experience, very few patients methodically ask the questions that the NIH wants them to ask of the sites that they visit in search of medical answers:

- Who runs or created the site or app? Can you trust them?
- What is the site or app promising or offering? Do its claims seem too good to be true?
- When was its information written or reviewed? Is it up-to-date?
- Where does the information come from? Is it based on scientific research?
- Why does the site or app exist? Is it selling something?
- Is the information reviewed by experts?[23]

As such, like many doctors, I have seen my share of patients who had self-diagnosed and felt rather certain about the self-diagnosis, only for it to turn out to be a mis-self-diagnosis and lead to serious consequences. One patient was convinced she was a hoarder from the excessive shopping she was doing and insisted on receiving a particular medication, sertraline, as she had read it was effective for OCD and knew that hoarding was a condition in the obsessive-compulsive spectrum. The patient turned out to be in the manic phase of bipolar illness, with telltale symptoms that included decreased need for sleep, high irritability, pressured speech, and racing thoughts. Her over-shopping, clutter, and "hoarding" were the consequences of overspending by someone who was touched by mania and whose mania convinced her that she had more financial means than was the case. Sertraline and medications in its family can actually trigger mania in someone with bipolar illness or can make it a lot worse. It was the absolute last thing she needed, but my patient would not take no for an answer and ended up obtaining sertraline from a relative. Predictably, her mania worsened. Only my patient wasn't "hoarding" clothes and books anymore. . . . Within two weeks of self-prescribing the medication, as her mania became more acute, she had bought an electric car and had made an offer on a house. Undoing the damage done online took a long time, but it was the necessary first step before she would agree to stopping sertraline and starting a bipolar-type medicine. By the time we got to that point, however, she was having to declare bankruptcy.

To my knowledge, my patient did not leave me a scathing review on Vitals.com, Healthgrades, or RateMDs for declining to prescribe the medication she was so intent on taking. When the manic episode subsided, she actually expressed gratitude for my insistence on the treatment course I had sketched out and flushed the sertraline down the drain. But my colleague, an addictionologist, had not been so lucky. He is many doctors' go-to specialist for severe addiction-related problems, so I was more than a little surprised when a patient I was trying to refer to his practice refused to see him, citing the horrible online reviews. Incredulous, I checked the site she consulted, and, indeed, saw withering review after withering review. It was like reading about a different doctor than the one I had known since medical school. Seeking clarification, and maybe even wanting to suggest a little online reputational damage control, I asked him about it. To my surprise, he was quite unfazed. As he saw it, his job was to safely wean people off the benzodiazepines, sleep aids, and opiates that they had become addicted to. He explained how he was clear with patients at the beginning of treatment that he would not be renewing these medications open-endedly. Rather, the goal was to get them off drugs that might have sounded like a good idea for anxiety, insomnia, or pain at some point, but that had since turned into full-blown addictions. This "tough love" hard line, however, is not always appreciated by patients, especially if they are in the throes of severe drug dependence, not on board with quitting, or mostly seeking someone to rubber-stamp refills, and it rarely generates fawning online reviews.

My colleague may be among the best addiction specialists in his field, but, given the online reviews, it is a miracle anyone seeks him out. I should not have been surprised: Only 2 percent of the physicians with the best online reviews actually make Consumer-Medical's list of top performers in their field when assessed based on scientifically validated performance criteria and quality metrics.[24] My colleague will survive, though, and the bad reviews have not proven nearly as devastating to his practice (or his wait list) as the undeserved dress down left by a "hangry" customer (because a pandemic-related driver shortage caused his delivery to arrive late and cold) was to a beloved local Vietnamese deli's business. Eighty percent of consumers, studies show, trust online reviews as much as personal recommendations, and even one negative review can cause a business to lose up to 22 percent of its customers.[25] For our local deli, this meant a business shrinkage that it could not afford, causing it to shut down just as the lockdown was starting to ease up and restaurant business was starting to look up again.

But, faced by an unjust review, a restaurant, hotel, or spa has an ability that a medical professional does not have: it can fight back. These establishments can provide context, offer details, post pictures, show receipts, link to other reviews, and even name names in their own defense. Not so for the disparaged doctor or other health care provider. HIPAA (Health Insurance Portability and Accountability Act), the federal patient privacy law, prevents us from disclosing any patient information, which means that a negative review must go unaddressed because addressing it would involve disclosing treatment or symptom details. The doctor cannot even acknowledge having seen the reviewer, as this would divulge that they have indeed been a patient, which would breach their confidentiality. Still, one dentist could not resist responding to a patient who had accused him on Yelp of misdiagnosing her: "I looked very closely at your radiographs and it was obvious that you have cavities and gum disease that your other dentist has overlooked. . . . You can live in a world of denial and simply believe what you want to hear from your other dentist or make an educated and informed decision." Ouch. Another dentist did not quite get away with responding to a negative review she saw as unfair, triggering, instead, a formal complaint against her from the US Department of Health and Human Services, which enforces HIPAA.[26] Double ouch.

"Damned if you do, damned if you don't" seems to be the mantra for many health care providers being Yelped about. Their sense of helplessness is a novel emotion that they are still learning to navigate, and a far cry from the old, privileged position they long occupied in the doctor-patient relationship. Few situations may feel as vulnerable as sitting in a dentist's chair as she leans over and puts her hands, drill, sickle probe, mirror, and suction device in your mouth, seemingly simultaneously. Yelp has shifted the power dynamic away from this inherent submission. Many patients who feel they have been wronged and have had enough no longer have to take it and are making it known, as soon as the anesthetic wears off, that we are now operating in a new era where they are the ones who call the shots. Will they "submit" more easily within a leadership dyad than they do with their dentist? That is the question as far as this book is concerned.

Beyond the classroom, the living room, and the medical exam room, a similar "flattening" is playing out in the professional realm more broadly. It started in the early nineties when increasingly portable computers and novel communication technologies made remote work possible; came alive with Uber and the gig economy; and reached its apotheosis with the Great Resignation. In his 1992 travelogue *Exploring the Internet*, Carl Malamud introduced the "digital nomad" who "travels the world with a laptop, setting up FidoNet nodes."[27] FidoNet was a worldwide computer network that involved communication between bulletin board systems in a "store-and-forward" mechanism, with information sent to an intermediate station, or node, to be stored, before being sent at a later time to its final destination or to another node. No esoteric knowledge of nodes or "store-and-forward" code is required in 2024, where anyone can be a digital nomad, working over WiFi networks from hotels, coworking spaces, coffee shops, libraries, or the beach, anywhere in the world.[28] Previously unimaginable services are here to support the beach office. Health insurance plans through companies like World Nomads ("Explore Your Boundaries") and SafetyWing ("Insurance for Nomads by Nomads"), for example, follow you wherever your adventure takes you, helping give you peace of mind as you work hard and explore harder.[29] Along the way, Earth Class Mail, a virtual mail service, allows you to maintain a fixed physical address and will store and forward your mail to you wherever you are and for however long you are gone.[30]

Entire countries, not just a few select startups, are rolling out the red carpet. Greece offers a tax break to "digital migrants." Estonia has a business-friendly "digital nomad visa." Barbados has a "Welcome Stamp" program. The island of Madeira, a Portuguese region off the coast of Morocco, is also beckoning. In what seems like a much more inviting version of the seriously sullied WeWork space, the island converted the infrastructure of one of its coastal towns to launch the first European Union "digital nomad village."[31] "Like summer camp for grown-ups" is how *The Washington Post* described the exotic locales where digital nomadism is playing out, with "playing" being the operative verb, since much of the mythology of this lifestyle is in its contrast with Drab Town, USA, and the boring work office back home that is a few doors down from the office snitch who has the CEO's ear.[32]

But you do not need to jet anywhere to take a "location-independent" approach to your career. Forty-seven million—forty-seven million!—American employees quit their jobs voluntarily in 2021 alone in what was dubbed the "Great Resignation."[33] According to a Pew Research Center survey from 2022, majorities said low pay (63%), lack of advancement opportunities (63%), and feeling disrespected (57%) were reasons for quitting.[34] Forty-five percent cited lack of flexibility. Consequently, rigid bosses were forced to flexibilize, disrespectful ones had to show some R.E.S.P.E.C.T., and stingy ones had no choice but to open the purse strings as majorities of employees who quit seemed to work out better deals for themselves in what was also dubbed the "Great Renegotiation" and the "Great Reshuffle."[35]

Among the newly negotiated must-have perks employees have been insisting on is a "remote-first" model. *I might also consider a "hybrid-first" model, but I'll have to think about it.* Tempting as it might be, they don't necessarily want to relocate to an island off the coast of Morocco—they just don't want to return to the office. There were seeds of this movement already in the pre-pandemic trend toward a "gig economy," where people were leaving traditional companies to essentially be their own bosses. Many were becoming free agents, not just the Uber drivers who were making taxis obsolete, but also the Airbnb hosts competing with local hotels and the home chefs advertising popups in their living rooms and attracting customers from established restaurants. Writing for *Forbes* in 2016 on the future of work, Brian Rashid highlighted the changing reaction to the idea of the independent contractor or "freelancer:" "Once stigmatized as laziness or unemployed, the word 'freelancer' is starting to shed these negative connotations." The internet was allowing a sky-is-the-limit expansion of work possibilities and newer freedoms for employees away from the office. "Who says you can't drive an Uber in the morning, design websites all afternoon, and cater your own food company at night?" he asked. "The old economy would lead you to believe that you should pick one job, work hard for the next 40 years at that company, and then retire. Not the new economy." By 2020, he predicted, one in every two workers would be a freelancer to some degree.[36] Then COVID-19 happened, and droves of workers left the traditional office and, with it, the traditional boss, making even this dramatic prediction from 2016 feel like something of an underestimation.

Speaking to CNBC, the organizational psychologist Anthony Klotz, who is credited with coining the term "Great Resignation," said: "The pandemic brought the future of work into the present of work." The move to remote work might have taken several decades, but the crisis hastened it. "Because these work arrangements give us more flexibility and control over our lives, and more autonomy and freedom in how we structure our lives, I don't think most people are willing to go back to a traditional work environment. The new changes are here to stay."[37]

Working out of their kitchens or "Zoom rooms," these domestic digital nomads are forcing bosses who insist on a return-to-office date (or RTO, as it has been known) to eat their words or at least make serious concessions. Apple, Google, and McKinsey are only a few of the mighty employers who have had to publicly back down in this huge game of chicken that employees have been decisively winning.[38] By the end of the first quarter of 2022, even as they eagerly filled restaurants, crammed into airplanes, and sent their kids back to in-person schooling, only a third of office workers in the US had returned to full in-person work. The same pattern held true in the rest of the world: only 26 percent in Britain, 28 percent in Australia, 32 percent in Germany, and 35 percent in France had done so.[39]

"A Full Return to the Office? Does 'Never' Work for You?" is how the *New York Times* titled an article on the phenomenon, quoting the population of homebound workers in an imagined exchange with the once-omnipotent CEO. Behind a screen, deprived of the insignia of leadership and power, geographically removed from direct reports, the CEO has been reduced to being just another Zoomer.[40] If he insists anyway, his employees might just all move to Airbnb: after announcing in May 2022 that its workers could live and work anywhere, including abroad, on a permanent basis, Airbnb reported more than 800,000 visits to its careers page.[41]

The boss was to the traditional office what the sun is to the solar system—the heliocentric focus around which everything revolved. The Zoom-enabled dispersal of workers in space has liberated them from their orbit around the C-suite, freeing them to explore other stars. Copernicus, Kepler, and Galileo may have devised mathematical models to measure planets' fixed paths around the sun, but nothing is stopping today's workers from defying their "normal" position on the galactical map as they break away from the CEO's hold to seek out other cosmoses. For workers, the Great Resignation and "pandemic epiphanies" to never fully return to the office can be seen as proof positive that the centrifugal forces unleashed by COVID-19 are, to a significant degree, here to stay, like a nonclinical, chronic symptom of "long COVID." For CEOs, the unfamiliar feeling of no longer being the center of the universe is epoch-marking as far as corporate leadership history goes and definitely therapy-worthy. Many did not become leaders to rule virtually, abstractly, or "in theory," as it can feel running a company over Zoom or Microsoft Teams. To feel the full extent of the power many of them crave and many of them became CEOs to exercise, they will have to find a way to concretize things again by bringing employees back to the office, thereby bringing themselves back to the center of the universe. How this push and pull of power hunger, personality theory, economic conditions, and gravity will interact in years to come to drive this dynamic has all the makings of a psychological office thriller.

I shed no tears for the newly humbled boss. It is hard not to sympathize with employees voting with their feet as they escape stressful work environments or disrespectful, ungenerous CEOs who took them for granted because they could. If the rise of remote work does prove fatal to traditional top-down office "org charts," this would not necessarily be a bad thing. Too many patients have shared with me—reluctantly, guiltily, and in hushed tones—how working from home has significantly enhanced their well-being and helped them achieve, finally, that elusive work-life balance. As a result, they view the pandemic as an unquestionable plus in their lives, even if, for fear of social opprobrium, they, for the longest time, could not verbalize it that way. One patient had been in therapy for two long years for severe anxiety caused by difficulty managing two critical relationships in her life: a mercurial, moody boss at the law firm where she practices law, and a teenage son with special needs whom she is raising alone as a single mom. The time and energy she invested in the former took her away from the focus she wanted to devote to the latter, adding guilt to severe anxiety. Courtesy of COVID-19, however, she reached an "aha moment" of sorts that no therapy pearl, insight, or tool had helped her reach. She called it "quiet quitting," a term she introduced me to and that refers to lower engagement with one's work and a new attitude, made possible in her case by working remotely, not to go above and beyond the job description and not to allow work to take one away from other life priorities. By "quiet quitting" and working from home, she became better able to juggle things. Sensing she might be "half out" by insisting on working from home, her boss started showing more appreciation and less unpredictability. Benefiting from his mom's increased presence in his life, her son's grades improved, and he seemed to blossom socially as well. Who needs a shrink when one can quiet quit?

There is much to like about the internet-enabled "democratization" of concentrated power, whether between employee and boss, patient and provider, child and parent, or student and teacher. Bosses, doctors, teachers, and even parents may have been taking advantage of their privileged position at the top of the hierarchy a bit too much, leaving those at the bottom with little say and recourse, and a lot of resentment. But even as we celebrate this new internet-mediated equality, we should ask ourselves what this means for our relationship with leaders and leadership, more generally. We have to consider that a hidden cost of internet-related technologies may be a society that is fundamentally allergic to hierarchies of any kind. The forces and possibilities unleashed online may represent the last nail in the coffin of that all-powerful leader who enjoys great control over our schedules, incomes, career progress, war and peace decisions, and so forth. We simply have too many options or know too much, or so we think. And therein lies a serious threat to leadership today. Leadership can be democratic—up to a point.

Charles de Gaulle, who led the French resistance against Germany in World War II before becoming a two-term president, is said to have complained about the impossibility of governing a country with 246 kinds of cheese.[42] This was understood as a reference to the challenge of uniting people around a common purpose or shared agenda when there are too many diverging preferences and priorities. It was bad enough in the early '60s when de Gaulle was managing recovery from World War II, the Algerian War, and Cold War pressures from the US and Russia, but, to push the metaphor further, the number of *fromages* has only increased since—to about 400 today, even 1,000 if you count subvarieties.[43] By the camembert yardstick, the French may have become positively ungovernable. But they are not alone in being unleadable. For a democracy to work and for chaos to be kept at bay, citizens still have to coalesce under one "Big Cheese," and that has become more difficult to do. To resurrect the leadership styles taught in leadership school and covered earlier, one could say that the "democratic leadership" style can be seen as carrying within it the seeds of its own demise. There cannot be leadership without followership, and if followers feel too empowered to follow or too imbued with leadership qualities themselves to play second fiddle, they will not tolerate for long somebody bossing them around, deciding on their behalf, pretending to know more than they do, or claiming to have superior capabilities. If leadership implies somebody positioned atop or out front, we no longer easily tolerate that positioning and are no longer comfortable with that configuration. A pyramid with a leader at the apex has become an unstable structure, an edifice for pharaonic times—in other words, a thing of the past. If we don't exercise the "muscle" of following in basic relationships at home, in school, in the workplace, and in our interactions with experts, there is no reason to assume we will cede any more easily to a leader or entrust that person with power over us.

And yet, if society and the economy have become more democratized, how do we reconcile that with a leadership that as humans we seem to instinctively crave and that, by definition, involves accepting a certain lower status for those who are led vis à vis those who lead? For humans are tribal animals by nature. We hunt in packs. In the wild, packs have leaders. Leaderless packs are vulnerable. They cannot hunt and secure food effectively. Their young do not survive to assure the continuation of the species. In that sense, grandiose or not, we are still "designed" to seek leadership, a characteristic we share with our wilder relatives, from lions to hyenas, elephants, meerkats, wild African dogs, gorillas, bonobos, and chimpanzees, all of which show evidence of organizing under a leader in their natural environments. In an age where many of us are touched by the grandiosity of feeling freer and more knowledgeable than is perhaps warranted, this can lead to disappointment and frustration, and herein lies our conundrum.

The previously mentioned hierarchy that has been observed within wolf packs has influenced decades of "pack theory"–influenced training practices for dogs, who share 99.9 percent of their DNA with wolves.[44] Our own DNA is almost 99 percent shared with chimpanzees, our closest evolutionary relative, and chimp groups display leader-follower dynamics.[45] According to Erna Walraven, zoologist, senior curator at Taronga Zoo in Sydney, Australia, and author of *Wild Leadership*, chimp leaders lead through a combination of brute strength and intimidation, emotional intelligence, and political strategizing.[46] A good "dominance display" seems like a prerequisite, but a successful chimp leader will also groom those he seeks to influence and play with babies to impress their mothers. He will build alliances with other male chimps—grooming with them, for example—to limit competition and retain power. Sound familiar?

The very long list of leadership styles that have been described—democratic, but also transactional, transformational, disruptive, servant, and so on—seems to be missing one that is quite popular: paleo leadership. If the popular "paleo diet" represents the foods that primates and cave people ate during the Paleolithic era from around 2.5 million to 10,000 years ago, paleo leadership may represent the way they were led.[47] To the extent that paleo leaders may have exercised leadership with a primitiveness befit an unadulterated state of nature, we have the counterpart of that ecosystem immediately visible to us today on X (Twitter). For this is where paleo leadership in all its alpha male characteristics now plays out, and this is where we still display our continued weakness before such manifestations of leadership, *as empowered and emancipated as we may otherwise feel.* The scene simply moved out of the wild and into the social media swamp. The internet may have changed our psychology, cognition, and just about everything else, but it has not changed our DNA, which may be why, even as our wired selves rebel against hierarchies, we still go for "dominance displays," if not in the wild, then on social media. We still very much respond to today's equivalent of a primate displaying enlarged canines, a bear opening his jaw wide in proximity to another bear, two elephant seals posturing chest to chest, and two male snakes flipping and entwining until a rival is subdued. It's just that, instead of the tundra or other wilderness, it is a pixelated habitat that is now the medium for primordial chest-thumping and omnipotence—and for our enthrallment.

The lessons that Walraven learned in the wild led her to describe the pull of leaders as "hardwired" and often driven by security concerns. "Wild animals will follow a leader they can trust to keep them safe, a leader that has their back at all times, a leader that acts with the best interest of the group at heart," she writes. "We have the same expectations of our leaders. We want our leaders to demonstrate the kind of behaviours that deliver on these hardwired expectations of leadership." From her perch as a zoologist who has observed animal societies in the wild and in human custody for over three decades, we, like all our evolutionary relatives, are preprogrammed to seek a leader. From my perch as a psychiatrist who is interested in the psychology of leadership, this preprogramming is playing out in two interesting ways. First, it is coming in conflict with our newfound vision of a less hierarchical society and the allergy we have developed to hierarchy, causing us to simultaneously bristle at leaders and crave them in a no-win, confusing double bind. Second, it is not making us any more immune to leaders who prey on original fears and insecurities. Whatever the hardwired role that DNA plays in falling for a leader, the choice is momentous, if we are to believe Walraven and the lessons she learned from decades of embedding herself among our animal brethren: "I've watched generations of animals live their lives with the intrigue and the ups and downs of all communities. My conclusion is that animal societies, and the individuals within these, thrive or fail by the quality of its leadership." God help us.

We carry those genes and live with that DNA. If society has become more "level" and if we feel more empowered, this can lead to impatience with leaders who don't deliver as quickly as we would like, and an almost "genetic" weakness for those who show maximal dominance displays. In politics, this helps explain why societies seem just as vulnerable to the lure of "strongmen" who present themselves as protectors against lurking predators, from Vladimir Putin in Russia to Viktor Orbán in Hungary to Recep Tayyip Erdoğan in Turkey to Jair Bolsonaro in Brazil to Narendra Modi in India to Trump in the US.

Over a decade ago, before most of these "populist" leaders rose to dominance, I argued in my book *Virtually You* that the internet, while seeming, on the surface, to promote democracy and the myth of an Athens without slaves, actually had all the ingredients necessary to produce a specific kind of leader, one who could undo democracy.[48] We saw, in the educational sphere, for example, how democracy and the internet are not easy bedfellows, in that the equality that we are promised online is not the equality we actually get—and how the flattening that results can affect our concept of leadership. Here, we discuss the internet's specific effects on personality, and how this can help select for leaders who are not the best suited for our democratic system of governance or for leading, period. A series of relevant online psychological transformations, and the forces that make them possible, are important to review in order to explain the process and what it means for leadership. This is as relevant outside the political arena as it is inside. After all, leaders of all stripes increasingly hang around social media, trying to advance professional goals, humanize themselves, develop their brand, and "own" their message. Whereas only 39 percent of Fortune 500 CEOs had a public social media presence in 2015, 62 percent of them utilized at least one platform by 2020, according to data from Influential Executive, a marketing agency that helps leaders "develop an authentic social media presence."[49] So what do you get when you cross internet with personality, and what does it mean for leadership and democracy?

We may not like to think of these personality traits as "authentic" when they manifest online, but, as I argued in *Virtually You*, the aggression and narcissism we witness on social media from leaders and nonleaders couldn't be more so, if by authentic we mean "straight from the gut" (or cave), unvarnished by civilization, education, moral grooming, or spiritual sprucing up.[50] Why do these traits assert themselves so seamlessly on social media? Online anonymity has been offered as an explanation—"On the Internet, nobody knows you're a dog," went the famous Peter Steiner *New Yorker* cartoon from 1993, showing a dog sitting at a computer, talking to another dog.[51] Anonymity, however, is far from the only answer. A lot of our texts, emails, and posts are more violent than they ought to be but carry our signatures or personalized Bitmojis and, as such, are hardly anonymous. Another explanation for the emergence of these negative personality traits, then, is invisibility. If we cannot see the person we are interacting with eye-to-eye, we do not get to experience his pain or how our comment is landing, which can make us underestimate the seriousness of our behavior. In the infamous "I Love You, Now Die" case from 2014, Michelle Carter, a then seventeen-year-old girl, was found guilty of involuntary manslaughter for instructing her eighteen-year-old boyfriend, Conrad Roy III, to gas himself over text.[52] Reading the texts that the verdict rested on, it is almost impossible to imagine how, if their exchanges had been face-to-face, she could have reprimanded him the way she did for failing to make good on previous suicidal threats; how she could have made him promise that he would follow through this time; how she could have told him to do it away from home so nobody would interrupt the process; and how she could have sent him research on various methods before settling on carbon monoxide poisoning. "And u can't break a promise. And just go in a quiet parking lot or something," she texted, in one of thousands of missives that would be almost unimaginable if she could have seen his eyes while saying it.[53]

A third reason for the emergence of negative personality traits online is the lack of hierarchy. Hierarchy helps contain behavior insofar as people are more concerned about consequences when there is an authority of some sort that they feel answerable to. As we have seen, there is a constitutional hypersensitivity to hierarchy in many online-facilitated dealings. This, combined with anonymity and invisibility, results in the free-for-all that is often social media. The effect is to reproduce what Freud called the id, that instinct-driven, aggressive part of our personality that seeks instant gratification with no regard for morals, rules, or etiquette. Calling it "a chaos, a cauldron full of seething excitations," whose only objective is to "bring about the satisfaction of the instinctual needs subject to the observance of the pleasure principle," much of psychological development becomes about taming and channeling the id.[54] Social media have meant that the id has found a shortcut to rise straight back up to the surface, undoing psychological development and facilitating the emergence of negative personality traits that we would have been better off leaving "repressed."

Violence is chief among these traits. One does not go online to become moderate. Instead of a moderating influence, internet culture often nurtures violent or extreme views by connecting those who harbor them with like-minded voices that echo and reinforce them. This means a more divided society, where it is easier to demonize the other, whether it's immigrants, "shithole countries," "coastal elites," "deplorables," or "cancellation" targets.[55] The result is a hyperpolarized environment of siloed groups and echo chambers that is a far cry from the happy "global village" once imagined. It is also a place where leaders get to live out their violent fantasies, and where followers get to violently agree with them and violently disagree with their opponents.

Another personality trait that is nurtured online and that could not be more relevant to leadership culture is narcissism. As the Greek myth went, Narcissus was a hunter known for his beauty. The object of many people's desires, he, however, was stingy with his affection and loved nobody back. One spurned soul prayed to the goddess of revenge, Nemesis herself, that "he who loves not others love himself."[56] Nemesis answered her prayer: Narcissus saw his own reflection in the river and instantly fell head over heels, staring at his image for the remainder of his life and eventually dying of self-infatuation.

The story of Narcissus and Nemesis was well known to the Greeks living in that first democracy, so it wouldn't be fair to blame Instagram for inventing narcissism. Instagram can, however, be fairly blamed for magnifying and perfecting it—can anyone say "selfie"? Narcissists love a stage, and X (Twitter), if nothing else, is that. Through edited biographies, enhanced pictures, and superficial relationships that suggest popularity, social media encourage narcissistic expressions. The likes, friends, and follower counters are there to promote self-love with every incremental heart and thumbs-up we collect, until, that is, they start doing the opposite when we fail at these most important of races. An old Yahoo campaign rings truer than ever: "Now the Internet has a new personality. Yours!"; "The Internet is under new management. Yours!"; "There's a new master of the digital universe. It's You."[57] The internet and new technologies are, in other words, ours and all about us. In this context, it is only slightly shocking to hear that Adam Neumann, the fallen WeWork CEO and cofounder, apparently trademarked the word "We," then sold it to his company for $5.9 million.[58]

Internet-related technologies put us in the driver's seat, and, just like that, the sky becomes the limit, and the world becomes our oyster. If this doesn't tickle one's ego, that ego may be terminally frigid and simply un-tickle-able. If, like many leaders, someone feels uniquely endowed, loves an audience, loves to be loved, and is not above manipulating others to feel the love, that person will gravitate to X (Twitter) like a moth to a flame.

A look at the criteria used by the *Diagnostic and Statistical Manual of Mental Disorders* (DSM) to define narcissistic personality disorder shows how the internet might interact with personality to magnify existing narcissistic traits or help them emerge. The criteria include:

- a desire for unwarranted admiration;
- a display of arrogant, egotistical behaviors or attitudes;
- exaggerated self-importance;
- preoccupation with fantasies of infinite success, power, beauty, or ideal love;
- a belief that one is extraordinary and can only be understood by, or should connect with, other extraordinary people or institutions;
- a sense of entitlement;
- interpersonally exploitative behavior;
- lack of empathy;
- and resentment of others or a conviction that others are resentful of the person.[59]

Each of these criteria that, together, define narcissistic personality disorder would seem like a fecund touch point for the internet to act on and stimulate.

It would probably not be wrong to describe the forty-something CEO I *almost* saw in my practice as perfectionistic, although a more honest description might be that he thought he was perfection. The entitlement began early and strong. For starters, he asked to jump the clinic wait list, saying he was accustomed to "concierge service" and a "boutique" approach from his other providers. Somehow, he was accommodated. He then asked that no trainees be involved in his care, despite knowing that ours was a teaching institution, and training was at the center of its mission. Somehow, he was accommodated again. Next came inquiries about my credentials. Somehow, I was convinced to send him highlights of some scientific articles I had published. After I passed the credentials test and met his other requests, he reassured me that nothing was really wrong with him and that he was only seeing me at the insistence of his wife who felt he had "very high standards." Oh, and all along these "negotiations," he kept referring to me by my first name, like his long-lost buddy.

Treating patients who do not believe they need help is rarely productive, and maybe I should have known better than to offer him an appointment. Maybe I should have asked him instead to come back when and if he is ready. For, after making us jump through all sorts of hoops to make it happen, my "buddy" did not show up for his appointment. No expression of regret was deemed necessary for usurping a slot that another patient could have benefited from or wasting our time.

In processing what happened afterward, more than the entitled requests, it was how we seemed to bend over backward to accommodate them that really bothered me. But when you combine lack of shame in making unreasonable demands with stratospheric self-regard, people can feel like they cannot push back and have no option but to acquiesce. Who am I to tell him off? By virtue of seeing himself as a VIP, he made us see him as one.

A week later, as I was still trying to forget about this, I was surprised by a social media "friend" request from him. I declined the opportunity but could not resist checking his profile, which turned out to be an experience in post-traumatic stress. Basically, take our offline interaction and multiply it by his large number of followers, and you can start to get a sense of the self-adulation, adulation by others, and disregard that were on display. I never got to diagnose him in person, but a rather safe diagnostic bet would seem to be narcissistic personality disorder.

If social media encourage narcissistic tendencies in users, they can be expected to interact particularly toxically with leaders' psychologies, since research suggests that narcissism is overrepresented among leaders. Yes, our lot as followers is not only to contend with an overrepresentation of psychopathy or antisocial personality disorder among our leaders as we have seen, but, also, with an abundance of cases of narcissistic personality disorder. Studies have shown that narcissistic individuals are more likely to seek leadership positions and more likely to be rewarded with them when they apply. Search committees and company boards, it turns out, are quite susceptible to the charms of overly confident individuals who believe they are stars and carry themselves like ones. As a result, narcissists progress to CEO-level jobs much more quickly than their equally talented but non-narcissistic colleagues.

One study from 2021 by researchers Paola Rovelli and Camilla Curnis brings this home rather dramatically.[60] The researchers recruited a sample of 172 Italian CEOs, making them complete the Narcissistic Personality Inventory (NPI), a scale that measures narcissistic traits, and carefully recreated their detailed professional and educational histories, including all previous assignments and positions leading up to their current CEO position. The researchers then carried out a series of statistical analyses to determine the probability of the subjects ascending to CEO-level positions at any given point in their careers. The results showed that narcissism was very strongly correlated with the likelihood of making it to CEO at any given time point. In fact, an increase in narcissism of one standard deviation above the mean was linked to a 29 percent increase in the likelihood of becoming CEO. Even an increase in two standard deviations above the mean—a very high level of narcissism that one might expect would cause overt symptoms that could derail someone's career—still increased the odds of becoming CEO. According to the study authors, these findings are quite concerning insofar as narcissism has also been associated with less collaborative workplace cultures, interpersonal exploitation, and white-collar crime such as tax evasion. Importantly, these findings were also true when the firm was a family business, suggesting that even family members—whom one would expect to be very familiar with the narcissists in question and to perhaps know better than to prematurely approve their promotion—cannot resist them. If their mothers, siblings, and cousins fall for them, wouldn't we expect voters or other followers to do the same?

Still, it is important not to naïvely signal that self-interest can never be a big part of the equation for good leaders. If, instead of pure altruism, it is the quest for personal fame, fortune, and legacy that motivates a leader to do good deeds that attract followers, we'll take it! This is not the "narcissist" we fear and are warning about, but rather we are sounding the alarm about the self-infatuated one who manipulates others and compromises values on the way up, significantly limiting the chances of good deeds happening. The opposite of a narcissist need not be Mother Teresa.

In the realm of political leadership, narcissistic traits make social media appealing, and social media in turn magnify the self-love and bring out the violent, straight-out-of-the-id messaging. The two online personality traits—violence and narcissism—then combine to attract and rile up a potentially limitless number of followers. When it comes to "strongmen" and implications for our system of governance, one more ingredient completes the online trifecta threatening democracy: the internet is inconsistent with deep analysis. With its 280-character limit, there is only so much context one can provide or find on X (Twitter). Quite tellingly, a very common co-occurring condition with internet addiction is attention deficit disorder, showing the cost to our attention spans of a heavily online life.[61] Among other places, there is evidence for this in our online reading patterns, which were described by an early British Library study as "horizontal, bouncing . . . in nature" and "promiscuous, diverse and volatile."[62] Even the articles we retweet, supposedly because we like them so much that we cannot wait to share them, are articles we largely haven't bothered to read, as research into the online magazine *Slate* has shown.[63] We are too distracted to focus, read attentively, explore context, delve into stories, and sift the fake from the real, which is a real problem if you consider that democracy requires an educated citizenry that understands the issues and votes accordingly and informedly. An impatient, distracted audience that does not do its homework is the perfect prey for a populist leader's narcissistic persona and aggressive social media messaging. Then, with a bazillion not-so-informed followers who are in thrall to the star power and who "bought into" the aggressive, paleo-style messaging about predators, the populist can claim to represent the voice of "true people" that no rule of law, institution, or media freedom should be allowed to stand against. And this, ladies and gentlemen, is how democracy is being undone by leaders' "authentic" online personalities.

If, despite rejecting hierarchies, we are still hardwired to seek protectors who wear their braggadocio like a visible canine and stir up paranoia, we are, by a similar logic, also still attracted to the regalia and power semiotics of would-be monarchs. France, whose cornerstone historic achievement is a revolution that brought about liberty, equality, and fraternity, seems to have been living in absolutist nostalgia ever since, and could not rid itself fast enough of a recent president who called himself "Monsieur Normal" in favor of Emmanuel Macron, a president with a self-described "Jupiterian" style—Jupiter being the Roman god of the skies, thunder, and lightning; the king of the gods.[64] The French had no use for a chatty "buddy" in the presidential palace, so they replaced him with a Jupiter, a remote leader they wished would function above the political mayhem as he issued thunderbolt judgments and laid down dictates. In line with his view of himself and of his leadership style, Macron moved summits and meetings to the grandiose setting of the Palace of Versailles, the historic residence of the kings of France built in the seventeenth century by Louis XIV, the Sun King himself.[65] He even underwent a physical transformation that turned the already handsome thirty-nine-year-old into a transfixing Boy King: cropped hair, tight jaw, no smile, blue eyes lost in distant meditation—and $30,000 in makeup products in his first three months in office to better look the part.[66]

As a powdered marquis with royal aspirations, Macron couldn't be further from "Normal," but the French were still unimpressed, as suggested by his chronically tenuous approval ratings and the number of times that he or his party lost an election or flirted with losing.[67] While citizens may unconsciously crave a Jupiter, they feel too smart, too emancipated, and too in possession of Jupiterian qualities themselves to put up with one for too long. In this psychological double bind lies a momentous challenge to leadership today—*leaders, can't live with them, can't live without them!*

The innate search for a leader may also explain the blind eye we turn to figures like Bernie Madoff, the financier who helped launch the Nasdaq stock market and seemed magically capable of generating endless high returns for his awestruck clients. When we think we have leadership qualities, or can easily acquire them, it takes spectacular promises by leaders to catch our attention. In Madoff's case, it was his promise to churn out consistent 15 percent annual returns on investments despite wild fluctuations in the market.[68] Leaders' promises now almost *have* to be too good to be true, or we risk thinking we can pull off the job ourselves. (*Too Good to Be True* was also the title of Erin Arvedlund's book on the Madoff story, having drawn early attention to his unrealistic model in an article in *Barron's*.)[69] As such, Madoff's closest friends and family, famous and not-so-famous clients, and hundreds of university endowments, charities, and pension funds, suspended disbelief as he took fresh infusions from new investors to pay off old ones in a giant Ponzi scheme that dwarfed the original turn-of-the-twentieth-century one by Charles Ponzi himself. When the economic crisis rocked the system's foundations in 2008, the structure came crumbling down, and investors were cheated out of $65 billion.[70] The godlike figure died in prison serving a 150-year prison sentence after being charged with eleven counts of fraud, money laundering, perjury, and theft.[71] Stable, true pyramidal structures have given way to horizontality and . . . pyramid schemes!

Not every overpromising leader is running a criminal operation that results in a prison sentence, of course, but there is often still some bad outcome attached to overpromising, if only the disappointment followers feel when leaders underdeliver. The more we doubt our leaders because we feel empowered, the more they overpromise to get our attention and get us to follow. And the more they overpromise, the more they underdeliver, which only feeds the doubts we have about them and about leadership—and only leads to more overpromising.

It is a cycle that is not easy to escape; one that is particularly vicious if the leader in question happens to be a narcissist as many, as we have seen, tend to be. Narcissists are particularly good at overpromising, because they genuinely believe that they are capable of things that the rest of us are not capable of, and because they are not necessarily morally offended by lying in describing their unrealistic goals or by disappointing us when they fall short. The *Harvard Business Review* has the following recommendations for the "overconfident, chronically certain leader" with the tendency to overpromise: orchestrate debate and invite dissent by explicitly soliciting different views; assemble people with the courage to challenge you, not "yes people" who don't dare disagree; and invite outside voices that might bring new perspectives.[72] But there is a problem with this common-sense approach if the leader doing the overpromising happens to be a narcissist, as an "overconfident, chronically certain leader" has a high chance of being. Dissenters, people who say "no," and diverging voices go against every neuron in a narcissist's psychology, insofar as narcissists often think they have a monopoly on vision, strategy, and execution. It would be like preaching to a know-it-all leader about the importance of lifelong learning for leaders—it just doesn't work! More realistic recommendations would seem in order: better awareness on the part of followers of how narcissism and leadership interact, a system that does a better job weeding out narcissists on the rise, and a healthy suspicion of leaders who get off on exercising their star power and self-love on social media.

In summary, compromised hierarchies are contributing to a fake sense of equality and to overconfident followers who, even as they reject leaders, remain vulnerable to figures who want to dominate and promise them the moon. The internet and new technologies act at all these touch points, reactivating the id, nurturing narcissism, and taking us out of the wild and straight into a social media swamp that no one seems capable of draining. Along the way, and among other damage, entire democracies are being compromised.

When I wrote in *Virtually You* about the internet's fatal threats to personality, society, and democracy, and warned about the rise of populists, the *New York Times* called me the "internet's Hobbes," Hobbes being philosophy's incorrigible pessimist.[73] Much of that early pessimism has sadly come to pass. "Flat as a pancake" is how a patient recently described her depression, and there is something depressing about all this technology-enabled flatness. Maybe it's the thought that true democracy has not been served by our artificial online empowerment and pseudo-equality. Maybe it's the dystopia of an upside-down world where students lead on education, children lead on parenting, and patients lead on doctoring. Maybe it's watching the Salesforce Tower, which opened in 2018 as the tallest building in San Francisco and was designed to withstand high-magnitude earthquakes, being brought down, not by a geological event, but by the seismic decision of its workers not to return to their offices.[74] Or maybe it's the realization that a non-paleo leader who might help us do something about our online, offline, and democracy problems would have a hell of a time rising from all this horizontality.

6

MAGICAL THINKING

Leading in a Post-Privacy Age

WE NOW LIVE in a post-privacy age, yet another technology-mediated change with direct implications on how we elevate and imagine leaders—and their ultimate success. A comment in 1999, a more innocent time internet light years away, by Scott McNeally, the cofounder and CEO of Sun Microsystems, to a *Wired* magazine reporter was a preview of our current dilemma: "You have zero privacy anyway. . . . Get over it!" In case this was not clear enough, he further called consumer privacy issues a "red herring."[1]

McNeally's insensitive remarks have proven brilliantly prescient, for we now inhabit a world where facial recognition technology is being used to track the frequency of mall visits for marketing purposes, scan crowds in concerts for promotional metrics, surveil people at antigovernment protests, and solve shoplifting cases.[2] It is also a world where behavioral biometric data such as typing cadence, finger movements on trackpads, and how we engage with apps and websites have become an electronic signature of sorts that can be used to digitally identify us.[3] McNeally may not have been thinking about his own rise as CEO and Silicon Valley éminence grise, but among the many tragedies of living in a post-privacy age—or the many "red herrings" as he may or may not still prefer to call them—is that the lack of privacy complicates the process by which leaders emerge, insofar as myth and even secrecy are essential ingredients to the process. Alas, courtesy of Silicon Valley éminences, these ingredients have become rare as a unicorn, understood in the dual sense of the word: the mythical creature of legend and the startup that reaches a valuation of $1 billion. The role of myth in leaders' success was dramatically illustrated by President Obama's rapid rise—and a certain early prize he was awarded.

Minutes before a Nobel prize is announced, winners are contacted by the Royal Swedish Academy of Sciences or, depending on the specific prize, another Nobel committee to inform and congratulate them. For many winners in North America, the middle-of-the-night call from Sweden is a prank until proven otherwise. But how can the callers "prove" they are who they say they are? I imagine endlessly entertaining exchanges resulting from this combination of half-asleep incredulity, royal decorum, and impossibly high stakes, but the transcripts of these conversations are not made public, so we only have winners' recollections of "the" phone call to go by. George Smoot, a University of California at Berkeley physics professor and astrophysicist who won the Nobel for physics in 2006 for his contributions to the Big Bang Theory, required some convincing from someone he recognized. "A member of the Nobel Committee called me at around 2:45 AM, he had a Swedish accent and told me that John Mather and I were sharing the Nobel Prize in physics," he recalled. "I soon talked to someone I knew personally and by the time the phone call had ended I was convinced it was legitimate."[4]

Abdulrazak Gurnah, the Tanzanian-born British novelist who won the Nobel for literature in 2021 for his work exploring colonialism and refugee issues, had to be persuaded. "These days you get these cold calls, and I thought this is another one of them," he recalled. "This guy said, 'Hello, you have won the Nobel Prize for Literature.' And I said, 'Come on, get out of here. Leave me alone.' He talked me out of that, and gradually persuaded me."[5]

For Angus Deaton, the Princeton University–based British-born winner of the 2015 Nobel in economics for research into poverty and data collection, no amount of prior "shortlisting" for the prize could have made the odds feel likely. "I was not lying in bed at six o'clock this morning thinking 'oh that phone call should come,'" he told a news conference. "There was a very Swedish voice . . . who said, 'I would like to speak to professor Angus Deaton, there is a very important telephone call for him from Stockholm,'" he said. "Then they were very keen to make sure I did not think it was a prank. . . . And of course as soon as they said that I thought, 'Oh my gosh, maybe this is a prank.'"[6]

Unlike the physics, economics, literature, and other Nobels, the committee awarding the peace prize is based in Norway, not Sweden. But Norway did not call the Obama White House in 2009 to inform the president he had won that year's peace prize. According to coverage from the time, the Nobel committee makes exceptions for presidents: "Waking up a president in the middle of the night isn't really something you do," its chairman said.[7] So the call to Obama did not come in a Norwegian "voice" or a Scandinavian "accent," but, rather, very American ones, since it was White House press secretary Robert Gibbs who reportedly woke the president up shortly before 6:00 a.m. to inform him. Gibbs had received a 5:09 a.m. email from the White House Situation Room, which monitors world events around the clock, telling him about the announcement and carrying a rather incredulous title: "item of interest."

Vetted by the Situation Room, there was no reason for the president and his staff to think this was a prank, but they seemed to wish it had been one. Nine months into Obama's presidency, the freshman president had not yet had a chance to accomplish much, much less win a Nobel prize for it. Other American and foreign presidents who had won the top award before him included Theodore Roosevelt in 1906, for negotiating the end to the Russo-Japanese War, which killed more than 150,000 people on both sides and 20,000 Chinese civilians in Manchuria; Woodrow Wilson in 1919, for negotiating the Treaty of Versailles that ended World War I and for leading the formation of the League of Nations, the United Nations' precursor; Mikhail S. Gorbachev in 1990, for his role in ending the Cold War; and Nelson Mandela in 1993, for his role in ending apartheid and laying the foundations for a democratic South Africa.[8] Acknowledging the awkwardness of the president's admission, rather prematurely, into this club, the White House's response was muted and restrained, with the president himself downplaying the affair: "To be honest, I do not feel that I deserve to be in the company of so many of the transformative figures who've been honored by this prize, men and women who've inspired me and inspired the entire world through their courageous pursuit of peace. . . . And that is why I will accept this award as a call to action, a call for all nations to confront the common challenges of the 21st century."[9]

For his Republican opponents, Obama had won more for his charisma, star power, and oratorical skills than for tangible accomplishments. But the committee actually cited "extraordinary efforts to strengthen international diplomacy and cooperation between peoples." In explaining their surprising choice, the Nobel committee chairman said: "The question we have to ask is who has done the most in the previous year to enhance peace in the world. And who has done more than Barack Obama?"[10] They were presumably referring to the hope, engendered by his campaign, of healing and coming together again, and contrasting that with the sharp divisions between the Western and Muslim worlds and even among previously friendly nations that accompanied the Bush-Cheney years and that administration's disastrous decision to invade Iraq. Still, barely nine months into the Obama presidency, much of the world was not buying that the new president was Nobel material, at least not at that stage of his leadership and his career.[11] What was the committee seeing that many citizens, critics, and Nobel historians around the globe were not?

What they were seeing was the limitless potential made possible by Obama being a relative unknown; someone onto whom Norway and Sweden, but also Germany, where he wowed a crowd of tens of thousands in 2008 and closed down a main Berlin thoroughfare, and Egypt, where he spoke to a standing ovation and chants of "We love you" in 2009, could project whatever their hearts desired.[12] His intense charisma and command of the stage, combined with being a newcomer with a relatively thin record, made it much easier for him to embody in his audience's mind whatever they wanted him to embody. That mystery can be very helpful to leaders. When they are not on the record regarding a follower's particular interest or a voter's pet project, and never had to address it in public, it becomes easier to assume they will crusade for it like it was their own.

This process was also echoed in Obama's winning presidential campaign slogan "Yes We Can!"[13] Voters could complete it with whatever they wanted to project onto his presidency—Yes We Can offer health care for all, Yes We Can close Guantanamo, Yes We Can dig ourselves out of the Great Recession, Yes We Can jail the CEOs who brought us the Great Recession, Yes We Can legalize same-sex marriage, Yes We Can pull the troops out of Iraq, Yes We Can pull the troops out of Afghanistan, and so on. The slogan's catchy Spanish translation—*Si se puede*—only increased its one-size-fits-all appeal. To succeed, a leader has to be able to make followers dream, even unrealistically so, and has to leave something to their imaginations. This process is aided when the leader is a touch unknown, mysterious, or, like that slogan, incomplete, giving followers the opportunity to fill in the blanks. In this age of Big Data and decades' worth of Instagrammed meals, vacations, birthdays, and company Christmas parties, hyper-granular knowledge of a leader's "course of life"—the Latin-to-English translation of *curriculum vitae*—impedes things by impeding mystery. Obama's history-making presidency could not have possibly achieved all these projected goals, and many progressives would indeed end up looking back on his presidency as a rather conventional one.[14] But, as far as leadership lessons go, this is secondary. The main "take home" may be that he allowed people to plant their dreams on him, and they soared with his soaring oratory.

* * *

CANDIDATE HILLARY CLINTON may have been a tragic counter-example; someone so well known that she essentially functioned as a dream blocker. The woman who, by many accounts, was the "most qualified person" ever to run for president suffered, fatally, from also being the best-known person ever to run. By the time she ran her 2016 presidential campaign against Donald Trump, Hillary Clinton had served as secretary of state for four years under Obama, was the junior senator from New York for eight years, had run in two very competitive Democratic primaries, had led Bill Clinton's push for health care reform as first lady, and, having lived in the White House for eight years during her husband's presidency, had more direct knowledge of the inner workings and demands of the presidency than just about anyone one could think of.[15] Her "course of life" seemed to destine her to be president. How could all this competency and experience have lost, much less to someone whose CV did not suggest anything remotely presidential? What happened?

What Happened, conveniently, is the title she gave to her 2017 memoir of the traumatic loss. In it, she provided a long list of factors that she believed brought about the shocking outcome: FBI director James Comey; Russian president Vladimir Putin; Senate majority leader Mitch McConnell; Democratic primaries opponent Bernie Sanders; Green Party candidate Jill Stein; President Barack Obama; the American media as a whole; the *New York Times*; WikiLeaks; sexism; and white resentment.[16] She also blamed herself, specifically her comments describing Trump supporters as a "basket of deplorables" and how government policies would put "coal miners out of business." She even acknowledged that she just did not click with many voters. "I have come to terms with the fact that a lot of people—millions and millions of people—decided they just didn't like me," she wrote, essentially admitting to a charisma deficit. "Imagine what that feels like."

But the list is not as exhaustive as it might appear because one important reason goes unmentioned: there was no mystery there. A couldn't-be-more-experienced candidate, she was also an all-too-familiar one, something that can be a serious obstacle to leaders of all kinds. There was no way for voters' imaginations to run wild, attaching all sorts of unreasonable wish lists onto her candidacy, and molding her in their minds into whatever version of President Hillary they wanted to see in the Oval Office. "What You See Is What You Get" has served as an effective tool for salespeople peddling all sorts of products. To successfully "sell" leaders, however, we need to believe that what we will get is more than what we see. For that to happen, we can't afford to think that we've seen it all. In Hillary Clinton's case, many voters thought there was nothing left to be revealed. Her position on every issue imaginable had been encyclopedically recorded, her private pain exhaustively chronicled, and her miles traveled as secretary of state obsessively counted (956,733—a record!).[17] Several articles even dedicated themselves to painstakingly tracking her evolving hairstyles.[18]

And Hillary seemed to have understood the cost—to her person and her leadership—of having too much data "out there," which may be why she still tried to create a bubble of confidentiality where none existed. Much was made during the 2016 election of her deadly fear of press leaks—"Snitches get stitches" was a campaign mantra, according to *Politico*—and the disastrous home-brewed email server "solution" that would come back to haunt her.[19] Many have ascribed ill motives to her decision to use a private server for government business and to hold off on sharing with the State Department emails she deemed "personal"—obscuring the inner workings of her team; shielding the "Benghazi emails" related to Christopher Stevens, the US ambassador killed in the attack on US government facilities in Benghazi, Libya; camouflaging the web of Clinton Foundation donors and relationships; and so on.[20] But, without excusing it, I like to think of the behavior as a desperate defense of a private, inviolate zone by a public figure who was under the glaring light of an unforgiving microscope, uncomfortable, as we insisted on reading every email she ever sent and received, including about her daughter's wedding, her mother's funeral arrangements, and her Pilates routine.[21]

Try as she might, however, we weren't about to let her have it. Our culture has become as allergic to privacy as it has to hierarchy. She may control the "snitches" on her campaign's payroll, but how about the rest of humanity idly gossip mongering on social media? In the name of "Information is power," we can't stop Googling and "information-seeking," ignoring, sometimes to our own detriment, the slang wisdom of "TMI" (for "Too Much Information"). And so, two weeks before the presidential election, after the home server investigation had supposedly closed with no criminal behavior identified, we were chasing Hillary's emails all over again, this time all the way down the dark hole that is Anthony Weiner's hard drive.[22] According to FBI director James Comey, an unrelated investigation into illicit text messages between Weiner, who was married to Hillary's top aide, Huma Abedin, and a fifteen-year-old girl, had yielded emails sent or received by Abedin that were pertinent to Hillary's closed investigation. Nothing good could have come out of this one. "Drip-drip-drip" is how Hillary would later describe the many lives of this scandal and the unquenchable thirst for ever-more data about her.[23] Try as she might to maintain a modicum of privacy, we got to read every missive in her Inbox, Sent, Junk, Drafts, and Trash folders. Imagine what that feels like.

The Senate floor where US Supreme Court nominees are confirmed is far from the Brandenburg Gate where Obama transfixed Europe or Chappaqua, New York, where Hillary installed her private server, but something similar is at play as potential justices try to inject mystery and best-case-scenario projections into their views by giving vacuous nonanswers to very specific questions. Commenting on US Supreme Court nominee Neil Gorsuch's ability to duck questions at his 2017 hearing, Senate Minority Leader Chuck Schumer said he "avoided answers like the plague."[24] In that respect, Gorsuch was following in the footsteps of many predecessors. Here is the late Justice Ruth Bader Ginsburg's evasion tactics from her confirmation hearing in 1993, as described by none other than Elena Kagan in a 1995 law review article, before she became a Supreme Court Justice nominee herself: "When asked a specific question on a constitutional issue, Ginsburg replied that an answer might forecast a vote and thus contravene the norm of judicial impartiality. . . . But when asked a more general question, Ginsburg replied that a judge could deal in specifics only; abstractions, even hypotheticals, took the good judge beyond her calling."[25]

Come her own confirmation hearing in 2010, however, Kagan seemed to eat her words as she demonstrated a newfound appreciation for the nonanswer. Reflecting back in her hearing on that inconvenient law review article, Kagan would say: "I skewed it too much toward saying answering is appropriate even when it would provide some hints" about how a potential justice might rule in a specific case. "I think that that was wrong. I think that, in particular, it wouldn't be appropriate for me to talk about what I think about past cases—you know, to grade cases—because those cases themselves might again come before the court." Her successful avoidance moves and masterful dancing around questions caused a senator to joke about giving her the "Arthur Murray award," Murray being the American ballroom dancer and businessman with the eponymous global dance studio chain.[26]

Elena Kagan, like Ruth Bader Ginsburg and Neil Gorsuch, can be said to have understood the danger of being an open book and the importance of being a blank canvas. The former means you are on the record and can be attacked or disagreed with on your positions, while the latter leaves room for others to imagine you having the position they want you to have and sharing their ideologies, causes, and priorities. The former invites criticism, the latter allows for hope and optimistic speculation. As extremely divided, politically speaking, as Gorsuch on the one hand and Kagan and Bader Ginsburg on the other would turn out to be, and as bitterly polarized and broken as the Supreme Court has become, this might be the only remaining point of consensus, the only common denominator. *Vive la* bipartisanship!

IN THE CORPORATE world, the hiring practices of companies can be seen to illustrate the same point. Despite the billions spent by corporations on coaching and developing their management bench, despite all the investment in up-and-comers and high-performing employees, they often overlook internal candidates in favor of outsiders, much to the consternation of staff members hoping to move up the ranks and eyeing a promotion. According to an article in the *Harvard Business Review*, from the end of World War II through the 1970s, corporations filled approximately 90 percent of their vacancies through internal promotions and lateral assignments.[27] In 2019, the figure was a third less. While internal candidates should have the considerable advantage of knowing the company well and not needing to research its mission, values, goals, and culture; while they should not face a steep "learning curve," they suffer from the considerable disadvantage of being a known entity, someone on whom self-serving, contradictory, and unreasonable expectations cannot be easily projected. In the experience versus mystique showdown, mystique often wins. And that can be a steep challenge for successful employees who have their eyes on leadership positions within their companies. They have valuable institutional knowledge and would be much quicker to hire and cheaper to onboard. You don't need recruiters to source them or have to pay moving costs or invest in as many incentives to lure them. You are familiar with their performance history, work style, preferred work environment, and whether they are a good fit for the senior position. But, unfortunately for them, the better we know them, the less attractive they can become because of how much more difficult it gets to project wild aspirations for how they will fare as leaders. From the search committee's perspective, it can be easier to let their imagination loose and not be bound by realism intruding on the process if they make an offer to an unknown outsider candidate.

The fact is, people want and need to be able to project their hopes and dreams onto their leaders, but this is only possible if our leaders are able to maintain a certain mystique about their history, biography, and character; if they are more like external than internal candidates; if, in short, they are capable of keeping a few secrets from us. But we now live in an open-book culture in which our ever-expanding digital footprint tells all. Not even a fig leaf of illusion is possible to maintain in a post-privacy age. Some of this is self-inflicted: old information and pictures, voluntarily posted and shared by us, that then sit there, somewhere, impossible to delete and waiting to be Googled. Some of it is inflicted upon us: friends, families, and colleagues who post on our behalf, and large databases that collect information and compile data, then make it conveniently and cheaply available to anyone looking. Regardless of the source, the effect is to make potential leaders more known than is perhaps healthy for followers trying to project their highest possible hopes on them. JFK and Winston Churchill would not have been who they were in their followers' minds, and their legacy would not be what it is today, if leaked evidence of the former's reported womanizing and the latter's penchant for lounging in pale-pink silk undies was regularly going viral. Yet in today's culture, every impurity is immediately tweetable and forever chronicled, with the degree of impurity directly correlated with its likelihood of achieving virality.[28]

Queen Elizabeth II, who hosted President Kennedy at Buckingham Palace in 1961 as one of thirteen US presidents she met, and for whom Winston Churchill served as the first of fifteen UK prime ministers, spent ninety-six years in the harsh spotlight and reigned for seventy years that witnessed Britain's retreat from the empire, wars hot and cold, and the introduction of both TV and the internet, while managing to remain totally unknown.[29] The level of scrutiny she faced during her nearly century-long existence was only matched by her inscrutability. Besides her love of horses and corgis, we seemed to know nothing about her beliefs or inner life. "Have you come far?" was a favorite and often only question she would ask people she met—she had to say *something*!—but don't expect her to have opined on Brexit, whether she was more Tory or Labor at heart, or how she *really* felt about Margaret Thatcher, Queen-of-Hearts Diana, or Meghan Markle.[30] Those opinions remained as guarded as the contents of the iconic handbag that never left her, and as opaque as the reason for why she needed a handbag for walking around the palace in the first place. The constancy of character, style, and ritual in the midst of a rapidly evolving world inspired stability and a sense that this, too, shall pass, and the daffodils will return. The payoff was immense in that she became a rock of unity since both the right and the left could claim her; she kept the monarchy going at a time when it could have been easy to dismiss it as an irrelevant anachronism of history; she accumulated unsurpassed global "soft power" as world leaders also united around her persona; and she caused many a Sottish secessionist and English antimonarchist to bow their heads, hold back authentic tears, and curtsy to her coffin as her funeral cortege made its way through the streets of Edinburgh and London.

Today's leaders, in contrast, *want* to be scrutable, and often confuse oversharing with authenticity. They have convinced themselves that by posting about personal things, tweeting on every issue under the sun, and baring their souls on TikTok, they are being genuine and "owning their story." Unless they fix this, they will not "come far." Somebody should remind them that social media is not a personal diary or a therapist, and that they are not Kim Kardashian, a reality TV star whose mega empire has rested on busting her own privacy. Until she knew better, that is. Indeed, if a generational divide prevents today's leaders from learning from Queen Elizabeth, why not take advice from Kim? Speaking at an information technology conference in 2019, she had this to say: "I think at the beginning, I didn't know what the word 'privacy' really meant. I was very okay with people knowing every detail of my life." She then explained how, over time, she found a balance so she could still share with fans and still maintain "some privacy." "I figured out a really good balance of sharing what I want to share."[31]

Many tweeting CEOs are not as smart as Ms. Kardashian. If she overshares, it is because this is her business model. If they do, it is a side gig that can divert from their true business and that can diminish them in the eyes of their followers. Elon Musk is an extreme example. Even if the Tesla electric vehicle he brought us ends up saving the planet from the apocalyptic effects of the internal combustion engine; even if the SpaceX rockets he is sending into space end up colonizing Mars and "making humanity multi-planetary," as the company's mission states; even if his Neuralink implantable interface ends up seamlessly fusing man and machine; his reputation may never recover from his X (Twitter) stream-of-consciousness, his overexposure, and how he has saturated our lives with details we would just as soon forget.[32] He will not come far. We need leaders to maintain a modicum of mystery and a measure of opacity, but they can't stop posting. And we, of course, can't stop following. As of this writing, Mr. Musk has 103.1 million followers and counting. This only encourages the outpourings and diminishes the leadership.

THE INFORMATIONAL BOUNTY about leaders' tastes, views, politics, and personal and professional lives has the unintended consequence of complicating their leadership. One modern business leader who seemed to understand the pitfalls of this approach and the importance of mystery is Steve Jobs. Among contemporary business leaders, few would contest demigod status for the Apple cofounder. Three factors helped sustain his mythical reputation: a wonderful comeback story of someone who cofounded his company in 1976, was ousted from it in 1985, then returned to rescue it from near bankruptcy in 1997; an early death in 2011 at the height of our love affair with his brainchild, the iPhone, which froze our image of him at his productive best; and, perhaps most of all, his legendary secrecy.[33] For Jobs, more than any contemporary leader, understood the importance of surprise in cultivating a following.

Engineers working on a 9.7-inch display, for example, had no idea that it was intended for what would become the iPad. Until Jobs strode on stage in his branded black turtleneck and blue jeans to introduce the new product to the world, his engineers thought they had been working on a big iPhone or a small laptop. Other teams working on other iPad components were similarly siloed. Indeed, anticipation of what products Apple might unveil at its annual Macworld conference was one of its most effective marketing tools. Apple also told analysts far less about its operations than most companies did and raised to state-secret-status low-level decisions, often leaving its directors out of the loop.[34] According to Leander Kahney, author of *Inside Steve's Brain* and *The Cult of Mac*, Jobs was "incredibly secretive and private. You'd be hard-pressed to find a picture of him and his kids, hard-pressed to hear him talk about anything but Apple products." Because little was known about his personal life and views also meant that Jobs could never disappoint his fans' preconceived ideas of him. "People could project their own ideas on to him, and he could be a lot of things for a lot of people," according to Kahney.[35]

Scientific research lends some legitimacy to this notion. In 2011, Maia Young, Associate Professor of Organization and Management at the University of California in Irvine, published a study with colleagues from Columbia University and California State University, Long Beach, in which she showed that the more her study subjects found Jobs to be mysterious, the more they thought of him as a visionary in tasks and talents far afield, from predicting government spending to GDP to stock market trends to the future of interest rates.[36] "The more people saw him as having mystique, the more they ascribed to him the ability to predict those things," she told the BBC. When mysterious people are successful, she said, we perceive them "as if they have a special something endowed to them that most of us don't have access to." She called this process of engaging in fanciful, unrealistic assessments of a leader's abilities that some leaders inspire in followers "magical thinking," borrowing a term from psychiatry that has been linked to psychotic disorders, among other serious psychiatric conditions.[37]

To his credit, Steve Jobs did not want to hog this crucial secret of his success to himself. He was happy to share it. At a *Wall Street Journal* conference in 2010, three years after the first iPhone came out, he discussed the responsibility that tech companies owed users regarding their privacy, saying all the right things and mincing no words in front of an audience that included Mark Zuckerberg, the Facebook CEO. "Privacy means people know what they're signing up for, in plain English, and repeatedly. That's what it means. I'm an optimist, I believe people are smart. And some people want to share more data than other people do. Ask them. Ask them every time. Make them tell you to stop asking them if they get tired of you asking them. Let them know precisely what you're gonna do with their data. . . . A lot of people think we're old-fashioned, maybe we are, but we still worry about stuff like this."[38]

We are far here from "red herring" and "get over it" territory. In 2024, his words ring truer than ever and make him a visionary on a topic he was not given credit to have "led" on in his lifetime. We can say he is leading from the grave on a defining issue for our era, a feat that is the utmost in what a leader can hope to pull off. This is what legacy is about. Writing in 2018, Ben Lovejoy, the British technology writer, had three reactions to Jobs's early embrace of privacy in tech:

> First, how prescient a comment it was at a time when privacy was not the hot button issue it is today. It was a concern to some degree, of course, but the greater focus then was on the excitement of what could be done with data. Few imagined just how massive an issue tech privacy would become in the wider world outside of Silicon Valley. Steve may or may not have predicted that tech privacy would grow into a mass-media topic, but he did know that it was an important issue on which Apple needed a very clear statement of its principles.
>
> Second, that Steve knew the heart of the matter is consent. You can offer people any deal you like: collecting masses of data, collecting modest amounts of data, collecting no data at all. The important thing is that users get to make the call.
>
> Third, . . . that Steve already knew that you can't necessarily trust tech companies to do the right thing. You have to put in place protections that guard against sketchy behavior, be they technical or legal.[39]

Of course, as things panned out, the iPhone has been far from the guarantor of privacy or cultural gift that its creator may have envisioned, and Apple has been accused of weaponizing secrecy in a way that stifled internal company debate about wages, work hours, and employee harassment.[40] In fawning over Jobs's privacy views, I could easily be accused of engaging in some serious magical thinking myself, through an influence posthumously exerted on me by the man himself. Still, Jobs's words on privacy seem to mirror the life he lived and the priorities he espoused. He talked the talk in his public life and walked the walk in his private and professional life in a way that is still adding to his legacy. His refusal to overshare guaranteed that the mystique of Apple products, but also of its leader, was preserved, and that his fans continue to admire his person, his accomplishments, and his leadership trajectory to this day. The high premium he put on privacy was an essential ingredient of his success and continues to feed his legend. It is also incredibly difficult to pull off today.

We might better respect a leader's choice to fight for privacy if we respected it enough in our own lives, but we entertain a very conflicted relationship with privacy. We have privacy "issues." Serious ones. Unlike Jobs, we talk the talk, but don't walk the walk. On the one hand, study after study show a high level of concern among users about privacy. For example, in a 2019 Pew Research survey of US adults, 81 percent believed that they have very little or no control over the data that companies collect on them.[41] Eighty-one percent also believed that the potential risks of companies collecting data on them outweighed the potential benefits. Big majorities also expressed concern when the government was doing the collecting. This points to a healthy level of anxiety over a defining topic of the digital era, and might prompt one to think that it has significantly changed users' behavior or led them to exert significant pressure on elected officials to enshrine privacy protections into the law or on Big Tech to drastically change its ways with our data, but none of these things is true.

Unfortunately, only relatively small proportions of people take full advantage of the built-in protections offered by smartphones, such as limiting tracking and targeted marketing based on collected personal data. According to another Pew Research survey, more than a quarter of smartphone owners say they do not use a screen lock or other security features to access their device, with 40 percent saying they update their apps and operating system only when it's convenient for them to do so.[42] What might explain this contradiction—the high level of voiced concern about privacy accompanied by insufficient privacy-protecting actions? One can think of at least five reasons. First, they don't make it easy. Before Facebook consolidated its mobile privacy and security settings in response to the Cambridge Analytica scandal, they were spread across twenty screens. A second possibility is that money trumps privacy.[43] We have willingly entered into a devil's bargain with social media companies whereby, in exchange for keeping their sites free, we accept that they will use our information as their business model—that they essentially turn us into their product. A third possibility is that we don't have a choice. To be a functional member of society today; to be attractive to friends, mates, and employers; lest you should look abnormal, you must have a sizeable digital footprint with a complex web of interconnections, and this comes with privacy risks. A fourth possibility is that we don't know how much they know. Many of us don't know, for example, the extent to which ad trackers follow us from page to page as we traipse across the web, attaching unique identifiers to us and building out our profile to where they know us better than we know ourselves and better than our therapists know us. Finally, the fifth possibility is that we have "gotten over it." We have taken Scott McNeally's dictum to heart and have given up. His "zero privacy" world has become normalized to where we have stopped trying. This helplessness also seems to be the lesson from a 2012 Finnish study in which researchers explored the long-term effects of ubiquitous surveillance. Deploying a whole array of sophisticated audiovisual sensors, microphones, cameras, and smartphone spyware in ten households over six months, they collected thirty-two terabytes of data that covered phone call recordings, text message exchanges, GPS locations, mouse clicks, keystrokes, desktop screenshots, browsing histories, and credit card usage. What they found was that, while the study subjects initially changed their behavior in response to being watched and eavesdropped on—for example, dressing in areas not covered by the cameras, moving personal conversations outside the home where there are no microphones, and manipulating the sensors—most subjects reported decreasing anxiety over the course of the study, describing their response to ubiquitous surveillance over the study time as "normalizing" and "getting used to it." The study authors concluded that "people can gradually become accustomed to surveillance even if they oppose it."[44]

Psychologically speaking, this would be tragic. "Protecting Privacy to Protect Mental Health: The New Ethical Imperative" is the title I gave to a 2019 article I published in the *Journal of Medical Ethics,* in which I tried to present a "sanity defense" of privacy and of not "giving up" on it.[45] After all, research has shown that crucial psychological functions and needs, including one's sense of autonomy, the ability to recover from setbacks, the ability to contemplate, and the ability to achieve emotional release through catharsis, all require privacy protections to function properly.[46] To the extent that privacy is compromised, these crucial psychological functions are also compromised, with serious consequences at all levels of culture. The surveillance society we are inching our way toward is one where we cannot feel autonomous because we do not control the personal information that defines who we are; where it is hard to move on from trauma and open a clean chapter because much online "documentation" reminds us of it and pulls us back; and where we are too distracted to contemplate what all this means for us.

When it comes to leadership, the consequences are at least twofold. First, followers who have stopped caring about their own privacy will react negatively when leaders insist on protecting theirs and will demand to know everything there is to know about them. Nothing short of thirty-two terabytes on a leader will suffice! Yet, as we saw, leaders who divulge too much, overshare in the name of authenticity, or bare it all for whatever reason are engaging in a process that complicates their rise and success as leaders, because they are blocking their followers' ability to see all the potential they can imagine in them. A second effect still might be on leaders' own mental health. Do we really want leaders who are psychologically compromised in their ability to recover from setbacks, contemplate issues, attain catharsis, and achieve autonomy?

I teach an annual course, Technology vs. Psychology, at UC Berkeley, in which I devote at least two lectures to discussing with my class of Gen Z digital natives the implications to psychology of having so little privacy. Theirs is probably the generation whose mothers inaugurated the practice of sharing pictures of their pregnancy ultrasounds with friends on Facebook. Do they care that their digital footprint extends to their uterine lives? Does it matter to them that they've been collecting likes on social media since literally before they were born? I got a thought-provoking answer to this question the last time I taught the course from a student whom I will call Tim. All semester long, Tim had distinguished himself through his hard work, his ability to listen patiently and answer confidently, his superior communications skills, how he assumed responsibility for a project's outcome when group tasks were assigned, and how he encouraged others to excel in their respective roles. In many ways, Tim came across as an effective classroom leader and seemed to have all the markings of a successful future one as well. This might explain why I was so struck by his reaction to the lecture I gave inspired by a piece I had written for *The Hill* on the growing use of facial recognition tools despite the lack of meaningful legal protections and despite the documented sex, age, and racial biases in the technology.[47] "If everything is public, people won't lie anymore," Tim said, confident as always. "That would be a good thing."

Tim did get an A+, although not necessarily for this rather troubling answer. A major problem with privacy today, is that, unlike other big issues of our time, nobody seems to want to lead on it, and a lot of work needs to be done to educate future leaders like Tim, who may have never truly experienced it, that it is worth fighting for and leading on. If we do not find those leaders, the consequences could be civilizational, insofar as progress has gone hand in hand with fortifying the individual's right to privacy protection against the tribe, religion, state, and so forth. In medicine, privacy protection has been a duty of physicians at least since Hippocrates wrote: "What I may see or hear in the course of treatment . . . in regard to the life of men . . . I will keep to myself, holding such things to be shameful to be spoken about."[48] The right to privacy was also alluded to in the Fourth Amendment to the US Constitution in 1789, which stressed "the right of the people to be secure in their persons, houses, papers, and effects, against unreasonable searches and seizures, shall not be violated."[49] In 1948, Article 12 of the United Nations Universal Declaration of Human Rights spelled it out even more: "No one shall be subjected to arbitrary interference with his privacy, family, home or correspondence, nor to attacks upon his honor and reputation."[50] And, in 2009, the European Union Charter of Fundamental Rights brought us fully into the digital era, stating that "everyone has the right to the protection of personal data concerning him or her."[51] This progress in the individual's right to privacy is being threatened by a runaway tech revolution that is dissolving the individual into a bunch of bytes that can be scaled, shared, bought, and sold in a bazaar of Big Data. This amounts to evolution in reverse, and it will take true leadership by a privacy-conscious leader to correct the course. However, despite being up there with ozone damage in its potential for making life unlivable, privacy protection has found very few champions.

On the evening of Steve Jobs's death, I decided I would drive home from work past his house, a mere ten minutes from my office. I felt a journalistic need to observe firsthand and maybe describe in a piece I might write how his legions of Silicon Valley followers were reacting to the news. All day long at Stanford, one could feel a certain heaviness, and no conversation seemed whole if it didn't bring up "the news." So, it was with an expectation of hordes of superfans unleashed by the death of their superhero that I made my way to his block. What I witnessed was far more powerful. A small scattering of people quietly filed by to pay their respects, contributing to a makeshift memorial of flowers, notes, and bit-into apples that referenced the famous logo. There was no gawking or spectating or intruding on the family inside. There were no hordes. He wanted his privacy, and people were letting him have it.

7

LEADERS AND THE UNCONSCIOUS

The Challenge of Ingrained Bias

THERE'S THE OCCASIONAL, rather innocent putting your foot in your mouth and saying something stupid or insensitive, and then there's the repetitive verbal aggression that suggests a deeper problem of the "-*ism*" variety. Don Lemon, former CNN lead anchor, might be guilty of the latter, as suggested by a series of on-air skirmishes with cohosts and guests that culminated one February 2023 morning in a sexist, ageist rant on his show while discussing the presidential candidacy of Nikki Haley, the fifty-one-year-old former South Carolina governor who had suggested a day earlier that politicians over age seventy-five should be subjected to mandatory mental competency tests. Lemon considered Haley too old for a female leader, insisting that women past their "20s and 30s and maybe 40s" were no longer in their "prime." How "prime" should be defined, he asserted, was a matter for Google to decide. When his visibly stunned cohosts—one thirty, one forty, both female—tried to push back, Lemon doubled down, prompting a swift, harsh, and multidirectional backlash. What's a CEO to do with a troubling pattern, an unmitigated meltdown, aggrieved coworkers, irate viewers, and a show that, with Lemon, became the network's lowest-rated morning show in nearly a decade? Solve the problem by sending Lemon to sensitivity bootcamp, of course! After missing only three broadcasts, one of which he spent being photographed soaking up the sun on a Florida beach, Lemon was back at his desk with his coanchors, CEO Chris Licht having reassured us that Lemon had "agreed to participate in formal training."[1]

It didn't work. Barely two months later, Lemon would get into another cringeworthy confrontation, this one with the presidential candidate Vivek Ramaswamy, in which Lemon seemed to put down his Indian American guest's race ("whatever ethnicity you are"). It took that, and the apparent refusal of guests to come on his show, for CNN to finally terminate his contract.[2] Real change is hard, Mr. Licht—just ask any therapist.

Sensitivity training has become an all-purpose fix that is invoked whenever society's prejudices threaten the course of business, when a business wants to show its commitment to diversifying its C-suite, or when a leader wants to project sensitivity around these issues. Unfortunately, this has happened without the necessary evidence that these interventions work and despite some suggestions that they might actually make things worse—a possibility we cannot afford. Prejudice is often unconscious, implicit, and deep. People are socialized into it and don't necessarily choose it or make a conscious decision to embrace it. Psychoanalysis warned of the power of the unconscious in dictating behavior, and of the need to bring its content into the light of conscious awareness, lest it continues to dominate our lives and lest we continue to act it out. Psychoanalysis also taught us how arduous and time-intensive that process can be. To the extent that prejudice is an unconscious force, nothing short of a complex and committed journey that makes people's unconscious biases conscious can fix it. A cruise through an online training module as you simultaneously check email or an after-hours workshop won't cut it. The fact that rather simplistic DEI-style trainings have become leaders' go-to solution when it comes to the serious problem of bias speaks to a massive leadership failure. The results of this failure are two-pronged: society remains just as divided, and the leadership class remains just as homogeneous. To successfully address our biases and genuinely diversify leadership, look past DEI to psychology and the unconscious.

Some deeply ingrained prejudices conspire to make good leadership increasingly rare. Besides the cultural shift toward an open-book society and the technology-enabled pseudo-equality, another societal characteristic that complicates the rise of good leaders is ingrained bias, including against women. Often unconscious, such bias represents an extra hurdle for women, discouraging many from seeking positions of leadership and punishing those who do. "What would happen if women ruled the world?" is a question we commonly hear asked. It might be a long time before we find out, but even if the answer turns out to be "not much," logic suggests that if we allowed them an equal opportunity to lead, the pool of talent from which we choose our leaders would essentially double, increasing the chances of good leaders emerging.

It's as American as apple pie, but utterly peculiar to foreigners looking in, that beginning in kindergarten, kids here are told that anyone can become president. In an Instagram video that went viral after the 2020 presidential election, Vice President Kamala Harris is seen taking a break from awaiting election results to have a conversation with her grandniece, Amara Ajagu. In the video, the adorable four-year-old could be seen sitting in her aunt's lap as the little girl discussed the possibility of becoming president someday. She either says, "I know I'm going to be president" or "I couldn't be president"—the sound quality isn't very clear—to which Harris immediately replies, "You could be president," before adding a qualifier, "But not right now, you have to be over the age of thirty-five." Ajagu's ambitious response to her auntie: "I know I could be an astronaut president."[3]

Would that age were the only obstacle keeping women from becoming president, and that learning to spacewalk, pilot supersonic aircrafts, and control robotic arms were guarantors of a career in space. Some outliers in the animal kingdom seem to have decomplexified female leadership. University of Wisconsin animal behavior professor Jennifer Smith and colleagues identified six mammalian species for which female leadership appears to be the norm, when leaders are defined as those who have a disproportionate influence on collective decisions within a group. Killer whales, lions, spotted hyenas, bonobos, lemurs, and elephants are members of an exclusive club where female bosses are not constantly challenged, tripped, and held to unrealistic standards.[4] For us *Homo sapiens*, though, unconscious bias continues to conspire to make leadership more difficult to attain for many women and, for those who get there, uniquely challenging. Much of this bias and many of these challenges also apply to other minority groups that are underrepresented within leadership ranks, making a look at the situation of women in top posts informative beyond this one group.

The statistics speak for themselves. Despite women now surpassing men in the number of PhD degrees earned and in the number of acceptances into medical school, and despite unprecedented participation in the workforce, there remains one male bastion that seems relatively off-limits—the very pinnacle of corporate, academic, and government life.[5] According to 2021 data from the Women Business Collaborative, women made up only 5.4 percent of CEOs in S&P 500 companies and 8.2 percent of CEOs in Fortune 500 companies. Among the S&P 500 companies' top earners, only 11 percent were women. Further, 49 percent of private company boards still had no women on them at all.[6]

Women also have to wait longer and gain more experience before they are offered the top job. In a 2017 study by the Korn Ferry Institute, fifty-seven women who had become CEO of a Fortune 1000 or similarly sized company were compared to a representative sample of male CEOs. Relative to their male colleagues, women were four years older when they were named to their first CEO job (50.9 versus 46.8 years) and had worked in a greater number of senior roles, functions, companies, and industries. Indeed, it took companies a third longer to hire a female than a male CEO, suggesting greater deliberation, wavering, cold feet, and overall reluctance by the boards of directors making this decision when it came to women.[7]

Once they do make it to CEO, women tend to have a shorter tenure. According to data compiled between 2017 and 2022 of companies in the Russell 3000 Index, female CEOs have shorter tenures and are more likely to be forced out than male CEOs: On average, women in the role step down after 6.6 years, compared with 9.9 years for men.[8] This would include ouster at the hands of activist investors—large shareholders who use their clout to tell the CEO what to do and occasionally to get the CEO fired, and who, data suggests, target as many as a quarter of all female CEOs.[9] "Indra K. Nooyi. Marissa Mayer. Ellen J. Kullman. Irene B. Rosenfeld. Meg Whitman. Mary T. Barra. What do these women have in common?" asked a 2015 *New York Times* article, before supplying the answer: they were the female CEOs of some of the nation's largest corporations—PepsiCo, Yahoo, DuPont, Mondelez, Hewlett-Packard, General Motors—whose companies were targeted over a short period of time by activist investors seeking to make changes. This generated questions such as "Does Nelson Peltz have a problem with women?," in reference to a longtime activist investor who reportedly sought to replace Ms. Nooyi of PepsiCo, Ms. Kullman of DuPont, and Ms. Rosenfeld of Mondelez.[10]

Do governments do better by women leaders than corporations? When it came to serving as a head of state or government in 2021, the United Nations could count only twenty-six women worldwide.[11] Projecting forward based on the current growth rate, gender parity in the highest governmental position would not be achieved for another 130 years! That the United Nations, a worldwide organization, is predicting it will take more than a century to approach sex parity at the pinnacle of government should not come as a surprise, based on global research performed in the 1980s and 1990s into the so-called "Think manager, think male" effect.[12] At every step and across all decisions involved in the making and unmaking of a leader, the unconscious "Think manager, think male" mentality seems to operate, whereby characteristics that people tend to associate with leaders, like assertiveness, decisiveness, competitiveness, and even heroism, are also characteristics that they stereotypically associate with males. By contrast, superior communication skills may be the only stereotypically female characteristic that people tend to link with leaders. In the studies investigating "Think manager, think male," students studying management in the US, the UK, Germany, China, and Japan were asked to pick from a long list of qualities those that they associated with managers; those that they associated with men; and those that they associated with women. In country after country, researchers found significant overlap between the qualities that the management students chose for men and those that they chose for managers. In one rather representative finding from the Chinese sample, male and female subjects agreed that analytical ability, self-confidence, competitiveness, firmness, ambition, creativity, and vigor were qualities of both managers and men. Despite innumerable cultural, social, historical, political, and workplace differences among these five countries, the view of women as less likely than men to possess management characteristics was a commonly held belief among the management students studied. The global nature of managerial sex typing should be of concern also because, as the management students become the managers and decision-makers of the future, their stereotypical attitudes toward female leadership would be expected to prevent women's access to advanced opportunities internationally well into the future. With any luck, it will be less than 130 years.

There is, it turns out, one leadership niche where women seem overrepresented—so-called "glass cliff" positions. The term originated in reaction to a 2003 article in *The Times* by British journalist Elizabeth Judge.[13] In it, she cited data from the UK that correlated the presence of women on company boards with lower company share prices. "So much for smashing the glass ceiling and using their unique skills to enhance the performance of Britain's biggest companies," she wrote. "The march of women into the country's boardrooms is not always triumphant—at least in terms of share price performance. Analysis of shares of companies in The Financial Times Stock Exchange 100 Index shows that companies that decline to embrace political correctness by installing women on the board perform better than those that actively promote sexual equality at the very top." In response to the rather incendiary re-mark, researchers Michelle Ryan and Alexander Haslam from the University of Exeter set out to formally explore that correlation, publishing their results in a 2005 paper that peeked past the glass ceiling to identify a "glass cliff."[14]

In their paper, Ryan and Haslam examined the performance of FTSE 100 companies before and after the appointment of male and female board members. The study showed that the stock of companies that appointed women to their boards was more likely to have performed consistently badly in the preceding five months than that of companies that appointed men. In other words, women were more likely to have been promoted to the top-most position in situations where one was more likely to fail. While this can be seen as an opportunity to turn things around and get sig-nificant credit for it, it can also mean putting them in a no-win position. For many women in the study, instead of a sure-footed tenure at the helm, women found themselves teetering at the edge of a glass cliff.

Subsequent experimental research has lent further credence to this phenomenon. One study examined the views of eighty British political science undergraduate students on selecting a candidate to run for a seat that was either safe (held by the candidate's own party with a large margin) or risky (held by an opposition party with a large margin). Results indicated that a male candidate was more likely than a female candidate to be selected to run for the safe seat, whereas a female candidate was strongly favored for the hard-to-win seat.[15] Another line of research involved presenting identical CVs of male and female candidates, with the candidate's sex being the only differing variable between them. Results showed that, in times of crisis and upheaval, women were preferred over men.[16] And so are people belonging to other groups that are underrepre-sented in leadership: in the NCAA, for example, minority coaches are much more likely to be promoted to losing teams. A study that analyzed data from 1,504 coaches in 344 Division I NCAA schools with a men's basketball program showed that a minority individ-ual was more likely to be named head coach to a program with a losing record than a white individual. (In another parallel to female leaders, once appointed head coach, the minority individual was likely to have a shorter tenure—4.83 vs. 5.75 years.)[17]

The list is long of high-profile women CEOs who were hired to rescue sinking or at least lost-at-sea ships, with things often not going as expected due to what has been described as glass cliff scenarios.[18] Carly Fiorina was appointed CEO of Hewlett-Packard in 1999, the first woman to lead a Fortune Top 20 company, just as the dot-com bubble was about to burst and decimate $5 trillion in market capitalization, highly complicating her tenure and forcing her to resign in 2005.[19] Carol Bartz was appointed CEO at Yahoo in January 2009 at the height of the Great Recession for a four-year contract, only to be fired over the phone by the chairman of the board just two and a half years later.[20] Mary Barra, who would later thrive as General Motors CEO and make crucial decisions on electric vehicles, was appointed in 2014, just as GM was recalling 28 million cars for faulty ignition and other serious defects that had been linked to ninety-seven deaths.[21] Jill Abramson was hired as the *New York Times*'s first female executive editor in 2011, a time of plunging advertising revenues and tremendous uncertainty about the digital newsroom, but was met with fierce criticism and fired less than four years later.[22] And Marissa Mayer was recruited from Google by a floundering Yahoo in 2012 and resigned after five very rocky years. (OK, maybe she really *was* that bad, if you believe the profiles of her in *Forbes,* including one titled: "Marissa Mayer: A Case Study in Poor Leadership.")[23] But the mother of all glass cliffs might have been Brexit and the leader promoted to pull it off.

The Tower of London houses a windowless prison cell known as the Little Ease; a space so small, it was impossible for a prisoner to stand, sit, or lie down in, and for the duration of Theresa May's brief tenure as prime minister, it was "getting tighter and tighter." This is how a former minister described to the *New Yorker* the wiggle room and margin of error that the UK prime minister had in negotiating the country's decision to exit the European Union.[24] The seeds of the meltdown were sown in February 2016 when her immediate predecessor, prime minister David Cameron, called for an "in/out" referendum on EU membership to be held later that year.[25] Following a few months of vociferous campaigning, the UK voted on June 23, 52 percent to 48 percent, to exit the EU. A day later, Cameron, who had campaigned to remain in the EU, resigned, citing the need for "fresh leadership," and essentially washing his hands of any responsibility to see the process he set in motion through. One after another, Brexit's male architects also exited the stage or stood down from leadership roles, from Nigel Farage, founding member of the UK Independence Party and leader of the Brexit Party who had earned the nickname Brexit "puppet master"; to Michael Gove, UK justice secretary, whose "Mr. Brexit" moniker would not have suggested he would easily go away; to Boris Johnson, prominent Leave campaigner who also disappeared before reemerging as prime minster himself, vowing to deliver Brexit "Do or Die."[26] Quite unlike them, the boys were dropping like flies, their skyward egos that had so dominated the Brexit campaign falling back to earth, domino-style. No one would have predicted it, but, ultimately, the race came down to two women: Theresa May and Andrea Leadsom.[27] And so, on July 13, 2016, May, a minister who had voted against Brexit, was bequeathed a hot mess by her party in the form of the top job. *The good news, ma'am, you have been chosen prime minister. The bad news, you have to deliver Brexit.*

It was a thankless job if ever there was one and a setup for failure if ever there was one. No country had ever attempted to exit the EU, which had grown into a supranational, hyperenmeshed, ultrabureaucratic behemoth, where, Hotel-California-style but minus the love, it was impossible to really leave, try as you may to check out. In practice, May's mandate amounted to taking the UK out of the EU so she could fulfill her people's decision, while keeping the UK inside the EU so her people could continue to enjoy the benefits of membership. To the extent that one definition of tragedy involves a choice between two radically incompatible but equally undesirable outcomes, this was a Greek tragedy unfolding on the Thames. Oh, and the fact that, with her every Brexit move, Scotland threatened to secede, and Northern Ireland made noises about reuniting with Ireland. Breaking up Great Britain and taking the "United" out of the United Kingdom was just a side distraction, the tragedy within the tragedy.

Why did she take the job, one might reasonably ask. One reason could be that barriers of the glass ceiling variety would have prevented her from acceding to prime minister in normal times and under normal circumstances. She might not have had another reasonable shot at the top job until true parity established itself, which, as we have seen, feels more aspirational right now than an achievable short- or medium-term goal. Another reason might be that Theresa May was no stranger to challenges and really believed she could rise to this one and pull it off.[28] In her midtwenties, her father was killed in a car accident. A few months later, her mother died of complications from multiple sclerosis. She herself is a type 1 diabetic who has to inject herself with insulin before each meal. She rose above these and other hurdles, making it into Parliament, then becoming the UK's longest-serving home secretary in modern times, before ascending to prime minister and Conservative Party leader. She even survived an incredibly awkward state visit by Donald Trump, hosted between barbs and insults hurled at her from across the pond at the lowest point in the history of the bilateral relationship between the two longtime friendly countries.[29] Theresa May, it would seem, had more than proven her mettle and earned her stripes, but nothing could have prepared her for this. And the task ultimately broke her, as it probably would have anyone, and culminated in a tearful goodbye in June 2019, when she was forced to resign over stalled Brexit negotiations with the EU. "I have done my best," May told her people, her voice cracking, and "I have done everything I can."[30]

Another reason May might have accepted the job and given it her all is a sense of duty toward future female leaders; a calling to serve as role model. If a member of a group that is underrepresented in leadership manages to become a leader, it can be hard not to feel the weight of representing your entire group, not to feel that your success or failure also belongs to them and will reverberate well beyond your own CV. Although they may hesitate to attract attention to their minority status to protect against suggestions that they have come into leadership for something other than their leadership abilities, many still feel this responsibility in their hearts and will occasionally address its symbolism to the larger community. Theresa May, who never wore her gender on her sleeve, still ended her resignation speech by bringing up the historic dimension of her political journey for future women leaders: "I will shortly leave the job that it has been the honor of my life to hold," she said. "The second female prime minister, but certainly not the last."[31] A similar concern for what a woman leader's legacy for other women is going to be was communicated by Hillary Clinton during her 2016 presidential run. Having run an essentially genderless campaign against Barack Obama in 2008, she seemed to strongly emphasize gender during her campaign against Donald Trump eight years later.[32] To accept the Democratic Party nomination at the beginning of the campaign, she wore a white pantsuit, in a direct reference to suffragists and the women's movement, whose unofficial color was white.[33] For what was supposed to be her victory speech on election night, the—almost—first US female president was again to wear white, and many women in her audience were to wear white pantsuits over T-shirts emblazoned with "The Future Is Female." This breaking of the ultimate glass ceiling was to be held in New York's Jacob Javits Convention Center, a building made entirely of glass. This is where being a little superstitious can be advantageous: a literal glass ceiling over the figurative one you are trying to shatter could not have been a good idea, and Donald Trump was delivered as the president that night in a huge upset. Hillary would return to a very different stage the following day to give a somber concession speech in which, not wearing white, she directly and overtly referenced gender. "To all the women, and especially the young women, who put their faith in this campaign and in me: I want you to know that nothing has made me prouder than to be your champion," she said. "And to all of the little girls who are watching this, never doubt that you are valuable and powerful and deserving of every chance and opportunity in the world to pursue and achieve your own dreams."[34]

If these represented some reasons why women accept a challenging leadership position such as a glass cliff, what explains the observation that women leaders seem favored in precarious times? In times of crisis such as poor performance or a major scandal, those hiring a new leader may feel that stereotypically female characteristics, like teamwork and being communal, loyal, democratic, and better at communicating, are more important in a leader. A second explanation is wanting to signal boldness by making a bold choice. A company or country facing dramatic failure or an impossible pickle might need to communicate a strong commitment to changing its ways and upending business as usual, and what more powerful way to do this than picking a leader who channels outside-the-box thinking by looking nothing like her predecessor?

But there is a more insidious explanation, too. Writing for the *Guardian* about May's departure, management writer Stefan Stern said: "This image of the apparently broken, tearful female prime minister seemed to be demanded by the macho Westminster village, and now it has been granted."[35] A need to "prove" that women can't cut it at the top goes hand in hand with the "Think manager, think male" bias and is almost a requirement to continue to "justify" it. Stern references Hamlet's "Frailty, thy name is woman" line, one of the most quoted and problematic in all of Shakespeare, as though to say that these English men who memorized Hamlet as schoolboys may harbor a misogynistic need to find a latter-day Gertrude, Hamlet's mother whom he considered frail of character for marrying his uncle soon after his father's death, or even a latter-day Ophelia, Hamlet's rejected lover whom he drove to madness, and who ultimately fell off a willow branch and drowned in a brook.

It was a glass cliff that Theresa May fell off, but the fall feels just as final, because, in order for the bias to feel even more "justified," we now needed a male replacement to step in and clean up the mess, as, you know, only a man can do. Indeed, this phenomenon was described in 2013 by researchers Alison Cook and Christy

Glass of the Jon M. Huntsman School of Business at Utah State University, who dubbed it the "savior effect."[36] Using a dataset of all CEO transitions in Fortune 500 companies over a fifteen-year period, Cook and Glass found that occupational minorities—women but also people of color—were likely to be replaced by white men when firm performance declined during their tenure. In Theresa May's case, it was a triumphant Boris Johnson who became prime minister on a promise to "get Brexit done," before undoing himself in another tragedy of self-immolation that unfolded over several acts and multiple scenes and ultimately brought about his own resignation.[37] Other "saviors" who stepped in to fix a glass cliff–type failure include Scott Thompson, who replaced Carol Bartz at Yahoo; Robert Wayman, who replaced Carly Fiorina at HP; Dean Baquet, who replaced Jill Abramson at the *New York Times*; and Thomas J. McInerney, who replaced Marissa Mayer at Yahoo.[38]

And we are not done yet. The final step, after the female leader's fall and the calling upon of a male messiah, is to make sure that the fallen woman leader doesn't rise again. When women CEOs fail, they do not tend to have comeback stories at the same rate that men do. I am not sure what Theresa May is up to besides representing the town she has represented since 1997, and which carries the rather unfortunate—for our purposes—name of Maidenhead, but it is hard to imagine her getting a second chance that is of a scale anywhere resembling Adam Neumann's. The thoroughly disgraced WeWork CEO—perhaps the baddest of bad boy leaders, the one who presided over a $44 billion collapse and resigned in 2019 in one of the most spectacular CEO flameouts in recent memory—resurfaced rather effortlessly a mere three years later at the head of Flow, a brand-new, very buzzy startup.[39] Somehow, he had managed to secure a $350 million investment from the influential Silicon Valley venture capital firm Andreessen Horowitz, immediately putting Flow's valuation at over $1 billion—"unicorn" territory in Silicon Valley parlance—even before the business had begun operating or anyone, seemingly besides Neumann and Marc Andreessen, fully understood its model (something about offering a "branded rental-housing experience" in Southern city apartment complexes).[40] Neumann's alleged "tequila-fueled leadership style," "gross mismanagement," "toxic work culture," and "shady antics that included [as noted earlier] buying the trademark 'We' and selling it back to his company for $6 million"?[41] Water under the bridge!

The same goes for Travis Kalanick. It didn't take long after his embarrassing exit from Uber for him to reemerge at the helm of CloudKitchens, a startup that converts warehouses into massive kitchens that prepare takeout food for multiple restaurants. No lesser investor than Microsoft would take a second risk on him and give him its vote of confidence, helping drive the company valuation to $15 billion by 2022.[42]

One could imagine how, had he outlived his 150-year prison sentence, even Bernie Madoff might have been reintegrated back into the Wall Street fold as a comeback kid who paid his dues to society and had a lot of generational wisdom to impart . . . We love a good comeback story, but maybe not in a gender-neutral manner.

Antifemale bias is hardly exclusively male, unfortunately, making it even more entrenched and making the battle to eradicate it even more uphill. Andrea Leadsom, who, after the boys vanished, became Theresa May's main rival for the prime minister post, was a relatively inexperienced, pro-Brexit energy minister. In arguing why she should be chosen over May for the top post, she told the *Times of London* that "being a mum" gave her the edge in the leadership race.[43] (May has shared that she and her husband tried but were unable to have children.)[44] This sexist comment by Andrea Leadsom shows that antiwoman bias, in the form of sexism and discrimination, can also be a woman-on-woman problem.

In the "Think manager, think male" studies discussed, the sex-typing that linked manager characteristics with stereotypically male characteristics was true for male and female subjects in a big majority of countries studied.[45] In other words, in most studies, women and men were both more likely to imagine a stereotypical male fulfilling a manager's role. Uncomfortable to accept as this may be, it is still important to consider as it shows the pervasiveness of antifemale bias in leadership. Not only are women discriminated against as they struggle against the glass ceiling, offered glass cliff leadership jobs where they are likely to fail, often replaced by "savior" men when they fail, and rarely given second chances if they fail, but these obstacles are not exclusively male in origin.

Another manifestation of the unconscious bias against women in leadership has been described as coming from a surprising source—women leaders—and given the unfortunate label of "queen bee syndrome" in a 1974 article in *Psychology Today*.[46] The designation was inspired by honeybee queens who take their throne in a decidedly bloody manner. After worker bees create about a dozen candidate queens by feeding regular female workers a special diet, they let the prospective queens battle it out in a series of one-on-one showdowns that each ends in a lethal sting or in victory. According to the "queen bee syndrome," female leaders assimilate into male-dominated organizations in part by distancing themselves from junior women and legitimizing gender inequality in their organization, thus complicating the rise of other women leaders. As such, according to this process, some women leaders will end up reinforcing gender hierarchies, stereotyping other women, minimizing the existence of discrimination, and resisting efforts to fight it.

Recent studies have identified versions of this phenomenon across different cultures and high-level occupations: female executives and senior managers in the US and South Africa; female business leaders in Switzerland, the Netherlands, Albania, and Indonesia; female professors in Italy and Spain; and senior policewomen in the Netherlands.[47] Madeleine Albright, the first woman to become US secretary of state, may have been alluding to something related by pointing to "a special place in hell for women who don't help other women" in a 2006 speech celebrating the WNBA All-Decade team.[48] Still, it is important not to blame this phenomenon on some intrinsic feature of the "female character" or "the way women are," or explain it away as women being their own worst enemies. Instead, research suggests that this form of discrimination is the direct result of women suffering career discrimination. The message they internalize, according to a comprehensive review from 2020, is that "survival of women in a male-dominated work environment entails a form of individual mobility, in the sense that they have to prove to themselves and others that they are unlike other women in order to be successful."[49] Being "unlike" other women then involves taking on stereotypically male attributes that unfortunately can include antifemale bias. The message that culture sends women, and that some seem to internalize, is that to succeed in a man's world, you have to be just as "male" as the next guy. This, alas, would seem to include some career sex typing and sex-based discrimination.

It is, then, a complex process that the "queen bee" label oversimplifies by unfairly communicating that women are to blame when context and discrimination are at its roots. Even Carol Tavris, who was part of the original research team that coined "queen bee syndrome" in 1974, has lived to regret it.[50] Speaking to *The Atlantic* in 2017, she lamented how the team's findings had been weaponized into a tool for bashing women: "If women are their own worst enemies, after all, why should people push for women's workplace advancement?" Not to mention that "queen bee" also plays into culture-wide catfight fetishism. To that end, the newer concept of "self-group distancing," while decidedly less catchy, seems more appropriate.[51] It refers to one member of a group (e.g., a woman leader) distancing herself from the larger group she is affiliated with (e.g., junior or middle management women in the company) as a result of discrimination she faces. So, while "queen bee" should be retired in favor of "self-group distancing," the debate and research around it should not be silenced, lest we end up underestimating the totality of obstacles faced by rising female and other minority leaders and the pervasive and systemic nature of the unconscious bias headwinds. Dismissing the entire phenomenon as phantasmagorical or artifactual misses the point; doesn't do women leaders, women followers, or anyone else any favors; and ends up minimizing the total discrimination burden—from all directions. This would be just as true of the "self-group distancing" identified by research studies in other marginalized leadership groups as well.[52]

Accumulating over a lifetime of exposure to stereotypes, unconscious or implicit bias of this kind is particularly insidious in that it can go unrecognized by the person harboring it, yet still influence actions, judgments, and decisions. Here's a more common example from *The Stanford Encyclopedia of Philosophy*: "Imagine Frank, who explicitly believes that women and men are equally suited for careers outside the home. Despite his explicitly egalitarian belief, Frank might nevertheless behave in any number of biased ways, from distrusting feedback from female co-workers to hiring equally qualified men over women."[53] What we explicitly hold dear is often contradicted by what we implicitly believe, making this problem more challenging to diagnose and address. Often triggered by primary features like sex, race, age, and name, examples run the gamut from the micro to the very macro. Implicit bias encompasses even vocal cords: research has shown that potential followers favor male voices over female voices, even when leaders read from the same exact script.[54] It is also what makes well-meaning bosses more likely to describe female employees as "abrasive" in annual reviews, while lauding the same trait as "self-confidence" or "competitiveness" in male employees.[55] It is what makes a boy who is ten years old and Black more likely to be mistaken as older than his white counterpart and more likely to be perceived as guilty and face police violence if accused of a crime.[56] It is what makes fictitious Anglo-sounding names like "Frank" receive 50 percent more interview callbacks than African American–sounding ones like "Jamal."[57] It is what makes a doctor address comments about an older patient to the patient's younger companion.

Pervasive, systemic, multidirectional, and often unconscious, bias ends up limiting the pool of eligible leaders in a way that robs us of potentially transformative figures and hurts organizations and culture at large. Leaders are called upon to resolve this problem—both to open up leadership ranks to all qualified people in a way that increases the odds of good leaders breaking through, but also for the health of the workplace and the greater society.

Research has shown that discrimination hurts those on the receiving end in their psychological and physical health. In the wake of several high-profile racist attacks against African Americans in 2020, including the George Floyd tragedy, Sandra L. Shullman, president of the American Psychological Association, issued the following statement: "Racism is associated with a host of psychological consequences, including depression, anxiety and other serious, sometimes debilitating conditions, including post-traumatic stress disorder and substance use disorders. Moreover, the stress caused by racism can contribute to the development of cardiovascular and other physical diseases."[58] Leaders who successfully fight racism, prejudice, and discrimination are, then, also helping keep us healthy. They are also helping their companies' bottom line insofar as diverse workplaces have been shown to improve decision-making, problem solving, creativity, innovation, and flexibility, and to reduce harmful groupthink.[59] By how much might diversity improve the bottom line? Very significantly, according to a 2018 study into leadership diversity that involved 1,700 different companies with varying industries and sizes and across eight different countries. The study, from the Boston Consulting Group, found that, compared to companies with lower-than-average diversity on their leadership team, those with above-average diversity had 19 percent higher revenue due to improved innovation.[60]

Perhaps most importantly, if leaders get confronting unconscious bias right, there are dividends at the level of culture as a whole. We might, for instance, finally be able to answer "Yes" to the question of "Can we all just get along?" Rodney King, the Black man brutally beaten by police officers in Los Angeles in 1991, had put the question to us following the wide unrest that accompanied his assailants' acquittal by an all-white jury in 1992, and it has reverberated, unanswered, ever since.[61] Unfortunately, a look at how our leaders have not risen to the challenge of confronting unconscious bias suggests that these issues will continue reverberating for some time to come. For, handed a problem that is pervasive, multidirectional, ocean-deep, and unconscious, many of our leaders have reached for DEI—or answers that are skin-level, cosmetic, and tokenistic, and that, by and large, have amounted to little more than lip service served with a dose of hypocrisy.

DEI is many leaders' new best friend. Standing, as noted earlier, for diversity, equity, and inclusion, it no longer needs an introduction, having realized an acronym's biggest hope—to become a household "name." This, in no small measure, is due to many leaders promoting it through mandatory DEI trainings and development activities that target their millions of employees, and through a new class of hires that they have appointed with DEI at the center of their portfolios and titles. "They're everywhere," said Pamela Newkirk, author of the book *Diversity, Inc: The Failed Promise of a Billion-Dollar Business*, of the ubiquitous sensitivity workshops. "Every major company . . . every major institution whether it's academia or fashion—that seems to be the go-to strategy for dealing with the lack of diversity."[62]

They may be very fashionable, but, as we have seen, many rigorous academic studies have unfortunately failed to establish their efficacy. For example, the research mentioned earlier by Harvard sociologist Frank Dobbin and Tel Aviv University coresearcher Alexandra Kalev, involving over 800 American firms and spanning over three decades, showed that, five years after training became mandatory for managers, companies saw no increase in the proportion of minority groups in management, and, in fact, the percentage of Black women and Asian Americans at that level actually dropped. "On average, the typical all-hands-on-deck, 'everybody has to have diversity training'—that typical format in big companies—doesn't have any positive effects on any historically underrepresented groups like black men or women, Hispanic men or women, Asian-American men or women or white women," Dobbin told the BBC.[63] "Even the best programs have short-lived effects on stereotypes and no discernible effect on discriminatory behavior," Dobbin and Kalev wrote in *The Economist*.[64] Dobbin's theory is that managers and employees don't like to feel like they are being controlled and tend to react negatively when they do.[65] The fact that 80 percent of corporations in the

US do mandate these trainings, then, may inadvertently end up reinforcing employee bias—a possibility we can ill afford.[66] And people from minority groups seem to know it: research summarized by Brenda Major from the University of California in Santa Barbara and Cheryl Kaiser from the University of Washington in the *Harvard Business Review* shows that members of minority groups are far from convinced that companies with diversity initiatives would treat them any more fairly or be truly more inclusive, better to work for, or less likely to discriminate against them than companies without such initiatives.[67] With their colleagues, these researchers also showed that one particular demographic—young white men—felt threatened by companies that advertised diversity initiatives; performed worse on interviews at those companies compared to other companies; and were more stressed during those interviews, based on cardiovascular response data that the researchers collected.

The fact that, in the absence of solid evidence that mandatory DEI trainings work and in the presence of some suggestions that they may make things worse, leaders still insist on them as the go-to solution and pay enough for them to have turned DEI into a huge industry, raises the question as to whether this may have more to do with leaders' personal need to look sensitive and protect against cultural ostracism. Rather than a truly diverse, equitable, and inclusive environment, many seem more motivated by fear of being "de-platformed" and by being able to pull off a "diversity defense" when needed. *"Racially insensitive? Me? I just spent $1.5 million putting my organization through DEI training!"*—$1.5 million per year being the estimated annual budget of these efforts at Fortune 1000 companies.[68] This also points to a very un-leader-like quality: Rather than leading us to serious fixes to a serious problem, many are blindly following "solutions" that they know aren't any such thing. An early study found that only about a third of 765 human resources experts actually think that their diversity training has positive effects, so why are they putting their workforce through it and spending money on programs that don't deliver?[69] Leaders, who are not typically into following, are doing a remarkable job toeing the "party line" on DEI. Mentioning DEI in every company-wide meeting, specifying their pronouns under their email signature, and celebrating the twelve heritage months while ignoring an obvious problem, namely that there are many more groups in our workforces and within our communities that we should want to honor than the Gregorian calendar affords— none of this, on its own, will solve the diversity crisis or begin to address the significant problems that bias causes in the leadership class, the organization, and society as a whole. The result of delegating this to the DEI industry has been that minorities don't necessarily feel any more welcome, the culture still can't get along, and the C-suite seems as homogeneous as ever. But it *is* good optics, and many leaders are prioritizing that over real solutions and real leadership. In an echo to the easy acronyms sponsored by the leadership industry, acronymizing a complex reality doesn't solve the problem. We may have wanted DEI, but we ended up with "Diversity, Inc."

Other experts have taken on another aspect of the cosmetic approach to the entrenched diversity problem. DEI consultant Sangeeta Gupta wrote in *Forbes* in 2021,

> If you're looking for someone to lead your diversity, equity, and inclusion efforts, do not simply reach for the nearest Black, indigenous, person of color (BIPOC) individual. Over the past year, many organizations have done this. You would not hire a chief financial officer (CFO) based on their skin color. You hire for expertise. The same is true for the person leading your DEI efforts. The ability to create and implement an effective DEI strategy for your organization is an expertise that comes from education and years of experience. It does not come from being a woman or being a BIPOC individual or someone who attended a weekend seminar on DEI and got a certificate. It does not come from having a passion for DEI. I have a passion for art. That does not mean I can lead an art class.[70]

Her criticism brings up a psychological reality that goes unacknowledged by some of the oversimplification surrounding DEI. People are now often *automatically* considered all good or all bad for a particular post or position, based on one aspect of their complex identity. In order to address the pandemic of sexism and racism eating at our culture, we have come to minimize the notion that people are complex creatures who are all the unique product of their own signature mix of sex, race, heritage, biology, personality, sexual orientation, gender identity, trauma, privilege, experience, education, passions, politics, family, and the endlessly diverse panoply of exposures that life has brought their way. We each sit at the pinpoint intersection of all the many circles to which we have ever belonged, and, in that sense, we are all "intersectional." Reducing us to one circle of this concentric multitude oversimplifies identity, psychology, and humanity—and sells us short as complex, multifaceted human beings with many allegiances, belongings, and points of reference.

Yet this is how the tokenistic solutions favored by many leaders today work to increase diversity in the leadership ranks and the organization overall, sometimes with psychological costs that don't get talked about. Michael, a patient I saw, helped me better appreciate those costs. He was a fifty-year-old gay Black man who started out as the only child of a single mom who worked at a laundromat in a "deep South" state and ended up as a VP of marketing in the Bay Area, by way of a top East Coast college and a top West Coast grad school. He had been at his current company for about four years when I met him, one of which as VP. Michael had come to see me several months after the end of a ten-year relationship. He couldn't imagine himself successfully dating again at fifty, which, as he put it, was "like seventy-five in gay years." Just a few weeks into our work, however, Michael was able to take the big step of going on a dating app for the first time in his life, building for himself a relatively detailed profile that highlighted his hobbies, hinted at his accomplishments, and contained several attractive pictures. Rather quickly, the marketing executive became a hit on the dating market, receiving more interest from people who wanted to meet him than his social calendar could accommodate.

He was also already developing something of a crush on someone he met in his first days on the app, making him wonder whether this might be a "rebound" situation, which it seemed to be. I fully expected Michael to move on, having proven to himself, quite spectacularly, that he was fully capable of a romantic renaissance, even when he's fifty and gay! But as often happens in therapy, what brings patients in is not what keeps them in or what they *really* wanted to discuss coming in. More than his dating prospects or the definition of a rebound relationship, what was on Michael's mind was his self-definition and very identity.

Michael was in internal turmoil about the diversity politics of his company seniors and wondering who he was to them. "I am confident enough about my CV that, if the fact that I was Black and gay might have tipped the scale in my direction, I was fine with it," he said, referring to the interview cycle he went through before the VP promotion and how his hiring might have been an "inter-sectional" win for a company seeking to introduce diversity in its very straight, very white, and very male leadership class. What he was not OK with were the automatic assumptions that seemed to go with this win—that he would represent the "woke" voice in the C-suite; that he would be the ambassador to marginalized groups within the company; that he wanted to be responsible for the DEI portfolio instead of the marketing overhaul he was interested in and focused on in his interviews; that he wasn't a Republican; and so on. "I know what racism is; my grandma witnessed a lynching," he explained. "I spent my life wanting others to see beyond my skin color and sexual orientation; to make these nonissues. I thought I had succeeded. But when I got promoted, my Black identity seemed like my main value-added, the main thing I had to bring to the table. And it wasn't even my personal Black identity, but one that didn't really match me, which made everything so much worse."

Michael was reacting to a certain approach to diversity that essentializes identity: "look" Black (or any marginalized group), and you will essentially fulfill your role, because the organization can now check the diversity box. And, if you're Black, you will "naturally" be woke and be so on board with the current approach to DEI that you will surely want to lead it at the expense of other passions. What this strategy ignores, and what Michael was experiencing, is the imbalance any of us would experience if one of the many components that define us suddenly became the only one that the world wanted to see, skewing our sense of ourselves, and shortchanging other affiliations that are equally defining to us and equally dear. The fact that, as his company zeroed in on his skin color, it made assumptions about his views and politics around race, amounted to doubling down on essentialism. Reductionism squared.

When tokenism is used to increase diversity in leadership, the skin-deep approach often ignores the diversity *within* individuals, sacrificing psychological and other complexity along the way. To increase diversity in the C-suite, we sometimes pretend that a particular minority is not diverse, which is as inaccurate as it is offensive. Incomprehensible as it might seem, Donald Trump got more votes from minorities in 2020 than he did in 2016, gaining six percentage points among Black men, for example, and five percentage points among Hispanic women.[71] But these statistics are often ignored as we opt for oversimplification and an approach that, in the name of DEI, seems to invite us to think that there is only one way to "be" Black, Latinx, female, or a member of any other group.

Another illustration might be this story shared by Ken, a physician friend at an East Coast medical center whose division chief was under pressure from the hospital board to add a female physician to his all-male group. To accomplish that, he hired a candidate who, in the eyes of the search committee that Ken served on, was not necessarily more qualified than male applicants they had interviewed. A year into the position, however, the new division member came out as transgender, asked to be referred to with male pronouns, and began a physical transformation to look more and more traditionally male. The division chief, who had now lost his only female physician, prioritized finding another female candidate when the next position opened. The new search, which Ken also participated in, identified an applicant who was female and with a much better CV than the male applicants interviewed. Minimizing her impressive credentials, however, the division chief seemed to have only one burning (and inappropriate) question to the search committee: "Is she locked in as a woman?"

Or consider my other friend, a gay Asian woman who was a senior sales associate at a Southern California firm, and who surprised me when she shared that she was interviewing for new jobs. Until then, my friend had only talked about how much she liked her company and how lucky she was to have finally settled there. After a highly successful but rather mobile career course, this job was supposed to be a "keeper" and the one she eventually retired from. When I questioned the about-face, my friend explained that she had a very slim chance of being promoted to the new managerial sales position that just opened, even though she had the best track record of all internal candidates. My friend wasn't sure that she would like the job nearly as much under a new boss, so she felt she had to get out. When I expressed confusion, she explained that it was communicated to her, through the thick grapevine and as though they were doing her a favor, that senior administrators really wanted a minority candidate and that she shouldn't pass up other promising opportunities should they present themselves. When I expressed more confusion, given that she is gay, Asian, and female, she explained that the company felt that they had these profiles represented in management but lacked other profiles. And so, as my friend reluctantly explored other outside possibilities, besides researching obvious things such as company business model, culture, location, and stock performance, she found herself spending more and more time trying to glean what she could from social media accounts about the racial, sexual orientation, and gender identity demographics of the senior staff, in hopes of seeing how her personal minority status "ranked up." The Don Lemon story and the possibility it raises that being a member of two marginalized groups (Black and gay) may have somehow softened the blow of attacking two other marginalized groups (women and older adults) have echoes of this. If this played into the decision by CNN's CEO not to fire him immediately, it would represent a further failure of leadership beyond the original failure of assuming that training can solve such a problem.

Outlying cases, perhaps, but the point is that tokenism cannot be a solution to the serious diversity crisis and can inadvertently pit one underrepresented group against another in a zero-sum "equity" game from hell where one group's win is necessarily another's loss and where we risk hierarchizing minority groups and therefore people. The growing use of designations such as "white-adjacent," "model minority," Latinx, BIPOC (for "Black/Indigenous Person of Color"), "white ally," and TERF (for "Trans Exclusionary Radical Feminist"), some of which have come under strong criticism from the very communities they are supposed to give voice to, is a symptom of this new reality.[72] We no longer view things in majority and minority terms but have entire gradations, complex nomenclatures, and ever-narrower boxes into which we have to try to fit people. The result can be to further trap us in separate identity enclosures even as the aim is to level the playing field and bring people together. Can we all just get along?

Writing about these stories, with their hyperfocus on one aspect of identity that comes to define the person, caused me to flash back to an experience I had repressed, and did not necessarily care to resurrect, from a brief stint moonlighting in a prison shortly after completing my residency training. The prison had a staff of psychiatrists, psychotherapists, and clinical social workers who were there to serve the mental health needs of inmates. Each day, a group of patients would be brought out of their cells for appointments in our prison-based clinic, according to a carefully choreographed protocol that was designed to preserve safety and decrease elopement risk. Two weeks into working there, I couldn't help noticing a strange coincidence: on any given clinic day, all the prisoners I saw seemed to belong to the same race, with the race changing every day. This was no coincidence at all, it turned out, as the prison had an unofficial policy of scheduling appointments as a function of patients' skin color. As such, Monday and Tuesday were each designated for one of the two most common races that inmates in that prison belonged to, and Wednesday was designated for "Others." The disturbing explanation I was later given was that grouping patients that way decreased the risk of intergroup and gang violence and minimized clashes during transport from prison cell to prison clinic.

On the surface of it, there couldn't have been a bigger difference between a free gay Asian female sales associate who was passed up for a managerial job because she belonged to a minority that was no longer of hiring interest to her company and an incarcerated psychiatric patient who should have ideally been seen on Monday but had to wait until Wednesday because this was the day "designated" for his race. On a deeper level, though, my Proustian flashback and the unconscious connection I made between the two made some uncomfortable sense, since both situations seemed to reduce people to one "essence" when they had many more; when so much more besides gender, sexual orientation, or race lies at the "intersection" that makes them who they are. I could not get out of my prison gig fast enough, but there is no escaping the larger prison of racialized, gendered, and identitarian conflicts in which our culture is trapped—and the leaders who, by blindly promoting a facile approach to a couldn't-be-more-complex problem, are refusing to lead.

Band-Aid measures in the form of quotas and cosmetic presences in management, on company boards, or on faculty bodies—rightly criticized, in the case of antiwomen bias, as the "Just add women and stir" approach—are hardly the answer.[73] For my friend Ken's employer, aggressive recruitment efforts and establishing women-friendly policies, like equal pay, paid maternity leave, and flexible hours, would definitely help women attain and remain in positions of power. So would expecting a company to publicly explain any gender gap in hiring and pay. But none of those would go far enough. It has been suggested that, to encourage emerging women leaders, the very concept of leadership must fundamentally change to move away from the ingrained idea of dominance to the idea of exerting influence through other attributes and skills, like conflict resolution abilities.[74] What is needed to get from here to there is a much deeper and more fundamental change at the level of society's unconscious—one that makes us see women and minorities as potential leaders naturally and automatically. Implicit or unconscious bias à la "Think manager, think male" is a formidable obstacle that has to be confronted head-on, repeatedly, creatively, and by society as a whole, not over the course of a "one and done" DEI workshop. Carl Jung, another psychoanalysis great, wrote that "when an inner situation is not made conscious, it happens outside, as fate. That is to say, when an individual . . . does not become conscious of his inner opposite, the world must perforce act out the conflict and be torn into opposing halves."[75] In other words, unless we make the unconscious conscious, it will direct our lives, and we will call it "fate." Until we go through the arduous work of making society's implicit biases explicit, we are "fated" to remain biased and to continue discriminating, and it is hard to see our situation improving. But this is no easy task. If psychoanalysis has taught us anything, it is the power of the unconscious and how accessing and manipulating its content is a committed, open-ended task that can hardly be squeezed into an hour's worth of sensitivity role-play exercises.

Indeed, lessons and tools from psychoanalysis can be helpful in addressing a problem it wasn't developed for. In psychoanalysis, learning how an early unresolved conflict with a parent can "hide" in the unconscious, potentially complicating future relationships and contributing to lifelong trust issues, can explain how unconscious processes exert power on us long after the conflict of origin is forgotten and without us really knowing that it is even happening or how. Implicit bias works similarly and needs to be similarly uncovered. Acknowledging our potential for it is the necessary first step. Learning about stereotypes we internalized during our upbringing and from people who imprinted us early on, including people we may otherwise love and respect but who may harbor racist, sexist, homophobic, or other discriminatory views, is another step. Developing a healthy suspicion of first impressions that automatically elevate one profile and automatically downgrade another is a related task. Along the way, acquiring a level of safety with new realities and new experiences by intentionally and systematically exposing ourselves to them will broaden our "comfort zone" and the scope of what we consider familiar and therefore not threatening. If this feels like a massive and fantastical combination of collective psychoanalysis for society's unconscious and Truth-and-Reconciliation-Commission-style hard work, why not? If you consider the $7.5 billion spent on DEI globally in 2020 without nearly enough to show for it, the cost to our present and future of a narrow and uninspiring pool of leaders, the cost in lost productivity and reduced innovation from workplaces that are not diverse, and the cost of recurring unrest following high-profile racist tragedies, the price tag, practicality, and feasibility of such an undertaking will stop feeling so massive and so fantastical.[76]

"What would happen if women ruled the world?" To really find out, our present leaders would have to model very different ways in leading us to a truly diverse future. I would not bet money on that happening, though. If I were a psychoanalyst, I would wonder, beyond the obvious optics and the desire to cancellation-proof themselves, about other incentives that might be motivating some leaders to promote "solutions" that they know or should know are not making their companies or C-suites meaningfully more diverse and are not helping culture heal. Psychoanalysis trades in ambivalences, resistance to change, dark motives, and secret drives, and begs one to ask the following question: Could our leaders be fundamentally ambivalent about changing the status quo because the status quo has been good to them—thank you very much—and has allowed them to become the leaders that they are? Are they sincerely interested in rocking the system and surrendering their current privilege by opening up the leadership pool in a significant way to more competition? Are they really ready for the floodgates to part? But assuming unsavory intentions on the part of the leadership class would be too Hobbesian on my part, when I'm working hard to be more optimistic.

PART III

THE WAY FORWARD

THE THIRD PART of the book addresses what I call End-Stage Leadership, a terminal stage of leadership bankruptcy that we are now fully ushered into—and how we can correct course. This part will synthesize the issues raised in the first and second parts of the book, showing how the conveyor belt approach of the leadership industrial complex described in Part One, combined with the cultural and technological forces captured in Part Two, have resulted in a system that gives those with narcissistic and sociopathic tendencies a leg up, when, to save leadership culture, it is imperative that we try to weed pathological narcissists and sociopaths out. Therefore, instead of familiarizing ourselves with the leadership potential tests increasingly relied upon in selecting leaders—and with services that, SAT-style, will teach you how to ace those tests—we should familiarize ourselves with scales that quantify narcissistic, sociopathic, and other negative traits that we don't want in our leaders, and think how we can prevent those who have overdosed on them from running our lives.

Part Three also reconsiders the building blocks of good leadership by showing how, in some of the most storied leaderships the world has witnessed, leadership found the leader, not the other way around. When it comes to leadership preparation, one plus one rarely equals two. Leaders should therefore dare to experiment, go on tangents, and free themselves of the straitjacket of overly confident "How to" prescriptions when it comes to acceding to leadership positions and succeeding once there. This means embracing the enormous role that serendipity plays in our lives and not treating it like an enemy to subdue when such an effort is fated to fail.

Another necessity is leading to build again as opposed to just "disrupting." Rather improbably, disruption has become leadership's most vaunted quality, perhaps because breaking down something generates more retweets than building something up. Without denying the need for disruptive solutions to some of our most intractable problems, we have to ask ourselves whether much of the disrupting taking place is simply for disruption's sake and amounts to little more than attention-seeking behavior by attention-loving narcissists that sacrifices long-term strategy and legacy.

Leadership culture may be in its end stage, but going leaderless is a chaotic option we should not want, not least because we would be going against our DNA and acting ahistorically and abiologically. A serious exercise in personal and cultural reflection is therefore necessary to find leaders we can live with and who lead to lift others, not to exercise a God-given right. To find those good leaders, we should decouple self-worth from leadership titles and urge people to follow natural inclinations, drawing as much happiness and doing as much good along the way as possible. If leadership "happens" at the end of this journey, fine; if it doesn't, fine, too.

We should also radically change approaches at the level of parenting, school, higher education, and professional life to blunt the marketing forces imploring us to rise at all costs because leadership is what counts and because it is supposedly within reach. In doing so, we would also be curing society of the dangerous inferiority complex that this psychologically compromising message is giving those who don't become leaders or who aren't interested in leading.

More than anything, we should worry less about leaders and more about followers. After defining what might constitute an "ideal" leader, Part Three ends with an invitation to stop talking about leadership and start talking about the followers without whom no leader can lead. Talk about their well-being, their stability, and the upheaval they must feel when a leadership goes wrong, as so many in this age of end-stage leadership often do. While at it, talk about their economic realities and salaries, too, especially in relation to leaders' pay. A good leadership culture is one that will try to put followers first, and so, I think, is a good leadership book.

8

THE LEADERSHIP CHARACTER
STRESS TEST

Ace It, Don't Fake It

THE "SERENITY PRAYER" popularized by Alcoholics Anonymous and other twelve-step programs is often quoted as: "God,
grant me the serenity to accept the things I cannot change,
courage to change the things I can, and wisdom to know the
difference."[1] Written in the 1930s by the American theologian
Reinhold Niebuhr, it spread through church groups in the 1940s
before appearing in AA publications in the 1950s, where it has
remained, continuing to influence spiritually inclined addiction treatment programs to this day. Its advice could also serve
present-day leadership "addicts" and the leadership programs ca-
tering to them, spiritually inclined or not. There are some facts
about leaders that are hard to change, and that leaders and leadership schools may be better off accepting as more or less fixed,
instead of tricking culture into believing that everyone can,
theoretically speaking, be leadership material. One's magnetism
and emotional IQ, for example, would be difficult to dramatically
augment within any reasonable time frame and should probably
be filed under "Things that I should serenely accept." Posture,
nonverbal cues, and body language, which are responsible for the

majority of how communication occurs, are, on the other hand, less stubborn and more reliably teachable.

Building on a *Forbes* list of body language tools for leaders, one can imagine leadership students learning how to:

- make a practice of noticing the eye color of everyone they meet (shows interest and "transmits energy");
- smile (a sign of approachability);
- shake hands (the quickest way to establish rapport);
- watch their posture (taking up more space makes one act and appear more powerful);
- lean in (communicates engagement);
- avoid finger-pointing (smacks of parental scolding and playground bullying);
- show their arms (hiding them suggests untrustworthiness);
- and "talk with their hands" (communicates enthusiasm, as long as the hands don't go above the shoulders, which we are told can make leaders appear less powerful and less believable).[2]

Similarly, one's online communication patterns, which, as we have seen, can directly influence how a leader is perceived, are another behavior that can be altered with reasonable effort. File these handy tips under "Things I can change" if you are a leadership student, and strive to practice and implement them.

Rather than aim for an overly ambitious and ultimately unachievable character transplant, leaders and their coaches can learn to work around the edges of personality in a sort of leadership "finishing school" that smooths out the messenger as it sharpens the message, making sure, for example, that the "energy" being communicated online or through body language doesn't undermine the intended goal of the communication. There is a lot of leadership wisdom in knowing what lies where on the spectrum of malleability; in sifting the mutable from the immutable; in figuring out the ratio of personal agency to "destiny" in how leaders happen. That wisdom attained, an offering such as "Body Language for Leaders," available for $79 from MindEdge, will start looking more honest and more realistic than a crash course on how someone not known for his caring instinct can become a model of the empathetic leader.[3]

Other changes, likely not taught in leadership school, go deeper than nonverbal cues and TikTok etiquette but would be helpful for leaders and would-be leaders to consider. They amount to conscious decisions people make that, together, can add up to a healthier culture for leaders and followers alike. They include making room for serendipity instead of overused, overtaught "how to" prescriptions; building rather than "disrupting"; and learning about, and expanding, one's reserves of modesty and humility.

Caught up in the determined pursuit, prepping, and politicking, we often overlook a crucial fact: in many leaderships that count, leadership found the leader, not the other way around. There are limits to the planning and the positioning, in other words, and, just like leadership is not a science, the path to it defies precise scientific mapping. In the calculus of professional and personal steps that could secure leadership and leadership success, one plus one sometimes equals infinity and sometimes equals zero, but only rarely equals two.

Nothing in the background of Ukraine's president Volodymyr Zelensky could have predicted that he would become the first worldwide hero of the twenty-first century. The man who would stare down Russia's Vladmir Putin in Ukraine's battered cities, make Putin an international pariah, rally the entire world to Ukraine's cause, infuse NATO with renewed *raison d'être* after it had been declared "brain dead," push Germany to break with its longtime refusal to export weapons to conflict zones, invigorate western Europe toward energy independence from Russia, and leave the Russian military's reputation in tatters, spoke Russian as his first language and hailed from a showbiz career summarized in GQ as being the "voice of Paddington Bear" and the star of "a dozen shitty comedies and one decent one."[4] *Love in the City*, one rather "representative" sampling from his oeuvre, is "about three friends living it up in New York when a curse from a magic fairy

. . . leaves them impotent until they find true love." Also under his belt was having won Ukraine's *Dancing with the Stars*, a show he also produced, which may or may not raise conflict of interest doubts about his true dancing chops.[5] All this makes the B movie and TV career of Ronald Reagan, the fortieth president of the US and a leader idolized by much of the American right, look decidedly high-brow and accomplished.

Surreal does not begin to describe it. The Russian-speaking comedian-dancer-producer then decides, against everything in his bio, to run for president. Everything, that is, except perhaps having *played* one on TV. The show in question, *Servant of the People*, features a high school history teacher who is recorded by a student ranting against the government in a video that goes viral.[6] Then, without asking for it, the teacher is elected president of Ukraine and goes on to heroic leadership. In the real-life version, Zelensky's opponent was Slava Vakarchuk, a popular Ukrainian rocker who had the considerable advantage of never having performed in Russian. Ironically, a big fear among a section of voters during the campaign was whether, should Zelensky prevail, he would be too chummy with Putin.

How do you go from this to sinking the *Moskva*, the jewel in the crown of Russia's navy, named after the capital city itself, whose capacities included the ability to fire 5,000 rounds in one minute as the last of a triple-tiered air defense system meant to make it invincible?[7] You don't. At least not in any linear, conscious, mapped out, overstudied, one-plus-one-equals-two way. As an article in *The Atlantic* put it, history "found" Volodymyr Zelensky.[8] What Volodymyr Zelensky did was rise to the occasion. The rest is history.

So it also arguably went with the greatest hero of the twentieth century. When Churchill replaced Neville Chamberlain as prime minister in 1940, he was a washed-up figure, adrift, out of favor with the British political class, and out of step with the times, his finest hour clearly behind him. He was also nearly bankrupt, with only a bailout from a banker friend in 1938 sparing him from having to sell Chartwell, his beloved home. What would be called his "wilderness years" had gone on a good decade and included the low point when Lady Astor, a British MP and Churchill foe, visited Russia in 1931 and was asked by Joseph Stalin about the man. "Churchill?" she replied. "He's finished."[9] Churchill's "black dog" of recurring depression, discussed earlier, had also probably not helped him stay active, engaged, and relevant in the eyes of his contemporaries.[10]

It might have taken a world war, but the old lion came roaring back. With the benefit of hindsight, Churchill's leadership seems foreordained and inevitable, but nothing about him in those bleak "black dog" or "wilderness" years could have necessarily predicted that he would become the statesman he became. "We tend to view the past as if it could not have been otherwise," writes John Gray for BBC News, "but for Churchill to replace Neville Chamberlain in 1940 was a highly improbable turn of events. Almost no one who counted wanted Churchill as leader."[11] Gray quotes the press baron Lord Beaverbrook, who said the consensus on who to replace Chamberlain with strongly favored Viscount Halifax, then foreign secretary: "Chamberlain wanted Halifax. Labour wanted Halifax. . . . The Lords wanted Halifax. The King wanted Halifax. And Halifax wanted Halifax." Crucially, Gray adds, Churchill himself seems to have wanted Halifax: "Churchill seems to have shared the view that Halifax . . . would be Chamberlain's successor. Churchill took for granted that he would serve under Halifax as minister of defence, and made it clear he felt it was his duty to serve in this way." But history had other plans. It found Churchill, and Churchill rose to the occasion.

The lesson from these examples is not to encourage a passive stance toward one's place in leadership history but to highlight the real limits to how much we can control the larger arc and context of how great leaders happen and how some of the most inspiring leaderships that the world has witnessed have played out when one least expected them to, not as the result of careful prepping and positioning or a well-rehearsed plan by the leader to lead. They were certainly not governed by basic laws of cause and effect or input and output or action and reaction. Rather than a simple "career path" or a "clean" example of how "the shortest distance between two points is a straight line," these leaders took a circuitous route, with twists and turns, ups and downs, and surprises galore. Not to mention long stretches of dead time where nothing seemed to happen. A leadership course more or less promises you the most efficient route possible from where you are at point A to where leadership is at point B. But that would be like turning your career coordinates over to Google Maps or trusting geometry with your professional development, when a professor of leadership should not be playing Archimedes, the third-century BC Greek mathematician credited with first articulating the efficiency and economy of the straight line. To make leadership inspiring again, and to attract the right people to it, we should drop the promises, shortcuts, and "hacks" involved in our approach to it and start making the most of the journey itself. This can happen only if we embrace the serendipity and hairpin turns that may or may not get us there. If *Dancing with the Stars* beckons along the way, by all means go for it. If you're temporarily thrown off course by clinical depression, don't let it be the end of the world. If you don't become a leader, the journey would still have carried valuable meaning. And if you do, you will be the richer for it and can still win a world war and save Western civilization.

IN HIS INFLUENTIAL article "Leading Change," Harvard professor of leadership John Paul Kotter identified eight steps for a leader trying to effect change that must be implemented and—very important—in the right order: create a sense of urgency; form a guiding coalition; outline a vision; communicate said vision; empower others to act on said vision; create short-term wins; consolidate wins; and institutionalize new approaches.[12] Handy tips come with the precise sequence. Here's one for going from vision development (Phase 3) to vision communication (Phase 4): "If you can't communicate the vision to someone in five minutes or less and get a reaction that signifies both understanding and interest, you are not yet done with this phase of the transformation process." Follow these steps in order, and a big payoff seems all but guaranteed: "Your organization flexes with tectonic shifts in competitors, markets, and technologies—leaving rivals far behind." (Never mind that rivals are taking the same popular leadership courses and memorizing the same eight steps.)

Kotter's eight steps sound like an impressive road map for implementing change, but this approach—stepwise, confident, predictable, logical—forgets that leadership, like life, is messy, and that many of the factors that determine whether we get the corner office or succeed once there are out of our control, will not easily yield to a map, and can easily intrude on any grand plan and derail it. Personal qualities and personal history, like temperament, charisma, age, sex, education, class, looks, personal connections, relationship status, and family situation, get in the way. And let's not overlook nepotism; the circumstances of the current occupant of the position you are eyeing; and whether the macroeconomy has registered two consecutive quarters of negative growth, indicating a recession and possible company belt-tightening that might preclude advancement. Even height has established itself as a determining factor for leadership efficacy: according to the "presidential height index," taller presidential candidates have a measurable advantage when it comes to winning, and male Fortune 500 CEOs are ten times more likely than the average American male to be six foot, two inches or taller![13] But most importantly, perhaps, let's not forget the outsize role of pure, cold chance, luck, and serendipity. So very much happens because you are at the right place at the right time, and so very much does not happen because you are in the wrong place at the wrong time. This is reality, and those who call it defeatist have a leadership course to sell you.

Serendipity, while seeming like an enemy of the fixed, step-by-step Kotter-style roadmap, can be an ally. It is worth embracing because it makes the journey worth journeying, even if we don't ultimately make it to the hoped-for destination. When Warren Buffet, chairman and CEO of Berkshire Hathaway and one of the world's most successful investors, showed his calendar to a businessman who had given $650,000 to charity to have lunch with him, the lunch companion was struck by how bare it looked given how busy the man must be. When he asked Buffett about it, the billionaire's poetic response was that he preferred to leave time for serendipity. Having made it, Buffet understood the importance to success of plain old luck, so much so that he "made time" for it.[14] If the lunch companion ended up taking Buffet's advice to heart, the meal would have almost been worth the price tag.

Steve Jobs, too, seems to have been a fan of this "planned serendipity" approach. In his book *Good Strategy/Bad Strategy: The Difference and Why It Matters*, Richard Rumelt of the UCLA Anderson School of Management recounts an opportunity he had to interview Jobs in the summer of 1998:

> I said, "Steve, this turnaround at Apple has been impressive. But everything we know about the personal computer business says that Apple cannot really push beyond a small niche position. The network effects are just too strong to upset the Wintel [Windows-Intel] standard. So what are you trying to do in the longer term? What is the strategy?" He did not attack my argument. He didn't agree with it, either. He just smiled and said, "I am going to wait for the next big thing."[15]

A strategy that consists of "waiting for the next big thing" would seem to reflect someone who is refreshingly liberated from the confines of the strict timeline and the predetermined list of action items, and who is ready to seize the next inspiring opportunity when it strikes. For Jobs, "the next big thing" would mean the iPod in 2001, the iPhone in 2007, and the iPad in 2010.[16] The rest is history.

According to a survey of remote work conducted with over 2,000 workers in the US and the UK by the data analytics firm YouGov, the most missed element of the in-person workplace has been the old watercooler chat—much more so than the more ergonomic workstations, not having to take care of the kids, eating lunch out, or happy hour with colleagues.[17] The move to an all-Zoom workplace has dealt a serious blow to serendipity by doing away with the spontaneous hallway encounter and unpredictable watercooler chat, moving our workday more fully into the straitjacket of the Outlook Calendar grid. Not many people miss the full-time, in-person workplace or want to return to the office if they can help it, but serendipitous contacts and conversations with colleagues are something they actually seem to want back, probably because they know how much they contribute to work creativity, productivity, and satisfaction. Or because they may have had the experience of a "virtual watercooler," as I did during a planned "breakout session" from a long meeting early into the pandemic. Meant as an exercise in spontaneity, this virtual watercooler, with its assigned leader who guided conversation topics such as "Did you partake in the sourdough craze?" and "What is the most bizarre thing your pet has ever done?" was just . . . bizarre. It was also anything but spontaneous. And therein lies a necessary prescription for leadership culture: the need to reintroduce real spontaneity and serendipity in leadership and wrench it back from the tyranny of the handler-coach, the recipe, Google Maps, and the "Eight Steps to (fill in the blanks)" format.

In this regard, leadership, which likes to think of itself as a science, would do well to remember that the history of science is punctuated by unintended discoveries—up to 50 percent by some estimates—that can be attributed almost solely to serendipity.[18] The most famous might be the 1928 discovery of penicillin by Alexander Fleming, a bacteriologist at St. Mary's Hospital in London. Fleming had been growing colonies of the bacterium *Staphylococcus aureus* for an experiment, when he noticed that one of the containers had become contaminated by a mold that had a clear area surrounding it. Instead of sticking to his experiment and discarding the contaminated container, he was intrigued to explore whether, perchance, a substance from the mold had somehow killed the bacterial colony near it. He set out to investigate the putative substance, eventually discovering the life-saving antibiotic now known as penicillin. "I certainly didn't plan to revolutionize all medicine by discovering the world's first antibiotic, or bacteria killer," he famously wrote. "But I guess that was exactly what I did."[19] It's hard to be any humbler—or any more accurate.

Equally unexpected was a 1975 discovery by scientists at the Tate and Lyle food company and King's College London, who were hard at work developing an insecticide by modifying sucrose (the chemical name for table sugar) into a new compound. A graduate student helping on the project was asked to "test" the agent, but he misheard the request as "taste," so he did. (Don't ask.) Instead of poisonous, however, the compound tasted cloyingly sweet, significantly more so than table sugar. The team had just stumbled on an agent that was 1,000 times sweeter than sucrose *and* calorie free. They appropriately dubbed their discovery "Serendipitose," in honor of serendipity, although it would later be named sucralose and is now probably best known under the commercial name Splenda.[20] Similarly serendipitous trails led to the discovery of the microwave oven and even cisplatin, the "gold standard" for cancer chemotherapy drugs.[21] How sweet is that?

Most leadership success stories that are worth telling have more in common with an insecticide-turned-sweetener than with *Inc.* magazine's "Nine Proven Steps to Effective Leadership" or *Fast Company*'s "Twelve Keys to Effective Leadership."[22] The advice that life is about the journey, not the destination, with its hackneyed air of quotes-to-live-by, is not a vacant platitude when it comes to leadership. A lot of good can happen when you leave the beaten path and allow yourself to off-road for a year or two in the "wilderness" and when you open yourself up to serendipitous experiences without a detailed leadership "track." What you will be doing during this interregnum is to build character through novel experiences you would not otherwise have, reflect on things that a monofocus on leadership would prevent you from pondering, and interact with a much broader swath of people than an obsession with leading would allow time for. Then, if "history calls" and you have an opportunity to lead, you will be more in touch with yourself and your followers, and it will be in no small measure because you off-tracked to learn about the world and your place in it. You will be more likely to know if it is not for you and to withdraw honorably if that is what should happen, or to lead with integrity and hard-earned self-confidence. You will be more likely to pass the leadership character stress test when you have to take it. When, early into the Ukraine war, the US government offered to evacuate Zelensky and his entourage from a capital everyone was expecting to fall, his legendary response was, "I need ammo, not a ride."[23] Zelensky passed this most extreme version of the test, probably also because he understood what his resistance would mean to "real" people who could not be airlifted to safety; those who cheered him on *Dancing with the Stars* and enjoyed his bad comedies had never set foot in a leadership school, and probably had no idea such a thing existed.

A good dose of Serendipitose can help in other ways, too. We have seen how the aura of mystery that comes with being a little bit unknown and with leaders protecting their privacy can pay dividends when it comes to allowing followers to project their dreams and best-case-scenario outcomes on them. We have also seen how organically linked mystery and charisma are, and what a valuable asset charisma can be to a leader's ascent and success. "Making time" for serendipity would seem to naturally feed both of these important leadership ingredients.

But leaders are part of the broader culture, and, culture-wide, we have come to view serendipity as something to be suspicious of and protect against. In that, leaders and followers may be more alike than different. Leaders—they're just like us! Perhaps it's the technology-enabled customization, where seemingly every experience from the shows we watch to the music we hear to the ads that are sent our way can be personalized to match our last micro-taste, but we have come to refuse the role that cold chance and uncertainty play in our lives. We know what we like, and we like what we know. Don't subject us to music, content, opinions, or people that are not to our liking or that we disagree with. At best, they are a waste of time. At worst, they might offend our sensibilities. The effect is to make us intolerant of the unknown and anxious when confronted with it. This is reminiscent of some anxiety disorders, in particular obsessive-compulsive disorder, where patients often develop a need to reduce uncertainty to an absolute minimum. In a rather common form of OCD, patients seek 100 percent confirmation that they locked their door, turned the lights off, activated their alarm system, or unplugged their clothes iron before they can safely leave their house, when most of us carry out these daily routines without thinking twice about them. For Claire, a patient in my practice with a disabling form of this doubt, making sure she turned off the stove in her kitchen before leaving for work in the morning involved a painful, hour-long ritual. After checking that her stove was indeed off, she would remove the four electric coils off the top, making a video of the process with her phone "in case I start doubting that I removed them when I get to the office." She would then put the coils in a bucket that she would fill with cold water "in case they might still be hot from last night." After that, she would place the bucket and its contents in her backyard, far from anything remotely flammable. In addition to the medication I prescribed for her OCD diagnosis, Claire's psychotherapy consisted of helping her accept that some level of uncertainty is unavoidable; that, while no one can absolutely, unequivocally guarantee that a burner that perchance had been left on would not cause her kitchen to catch on fire, the risk was so infinitesimally small that she should benefit from trying to learn to accept it and to live with it.

But life today is more about the curated experience that doesn't leave much to chance. Better to protect ourselves from the anxiety of the unknown than run the risk of discovering a new singer we might like or stumble on penicillin. We are not talking about a museum visit here, where "curators" have long played a role, but entire industries that personalize, edit, and refine everything from our Amazon shopping cart suggestions to our music playlist and cannabis strain (Afghan Kush, Hindu Kush, Green Kush, Blueberry Kush, Golden Jamaican, Diesel Haze, and so on).[24] It is, of course, somewhat disingenuous to complain: we all crave tools that save us time and help us zoom in on what we like. But in limiting ourselves to what we already like, we enclose ourselves in a bubble. This narrows our repertoire of what is familiar and comfortable and lowers our threshold for feeling discomfort when something different threatens to burst our bubble. Yet benefits can flow to followers and leaders alike from accepting reasonable uncertainty: it broadens horizons, lowers anxieties, and familiarizes us with other personalities, lifestyles, and experiences. The chance of something majorly bad resulting is probably not as slim as that of Claire's house spontaneously combusting, but it's pretty low.

So, to get back to Kotter's eight-point schema for leaders who want to effect change, go ahead, linger at Point 4 if you like, or take off on a serendipitous tangent from there to learn something new. Return to Point 4 to pick up where you left off eventually. Or never. Despite the near-guarantees suggested in leadership podcasts you may have listened to, leadership success does not necessarily await at Point 8 for many reasons that you can't control, so why not grow and learn and experience as much as you can along the way?

Intriguingly, the popular how-to protocols that would have leaders progress smoothly from Point 1 to Point 2 to Point 3 before achieving a target they set out to achieve don't necessarily mean that much patient, strategic long-term planning is taking place. Larry Fink, CEO of BlackRock, the world's largest investor with more than $10 trillion in managed assets as of January 2022, talks of a plague of "short-termism afflicting corporate behavior."[25] This would seem to undercut much of the multistep planning being taught, and supposedly learned, in leadership school. In a 2016 letter to CEOs of S&P 500 companies and large European corporations, Fink bemoaned leaders' obsession with quarterly returns and whether their companies met analysts' expectations, at the expense of a far-reaching strategy that unfolds over time and that outlives quarters, the fiscal year, and even the CEO's personal tenure. "Today's culture of quarterly earnings hysteria is totally contrary to the long-term approach we need," he wrote. "With clearly communicated and understood long-term plans in place, quarterly earnings reports would be transformed from an instrument of incessant short-termism into a building block of long-term behavior," he added. Detecting that political leaders are drinking from the same well as corporate ones, Fink warned: "In Washington (and other capitals), long-term is often defined as simply the next election cycle, an attitude that is eroding the economic foundations of our country."[26] So, to the extent that leaders are really following "how-to" recipe steps, they seem to be using them to survive analyst-expectation-to-analyst-expectation, quarter-to-quarter, and election-to-election. Instead of a grand plan for "future generations" or longevity across leaders and administrations, the horizon of what has also been dubbed "quarterly capitalism" is depressingly near term.[27] The how-to eight (or other number) steps, then, end up serving short-term objectives rather than a true vision or a goal worth investing time in and being patient about. To return to the recipe metaphor, it's more about learning how to fry an egg than a complex duck confit–type culinary project that would have you forage for goose fat, duck legs, and fresh thyme; marinate the salted, seasoned meat for a couple of days; slow roast at a low temperature submerged in fat; then bury, still submerged, in your basement for weeks while you patiently wait for the shortcut-defying flavors to develop.

THE SHORT-TERMISM AND lack of patience with long-term planning is matched by many of today's leaders' fascination with "disruption," or lack of patience with the status quo. Kotter's steps for effecting change beg the question of what sort of change today's leaders are interested in effecting. For many, change is being sought for change's sake—to mix things up, generate retweets, and say they did something different and left their imprimatur, rather than to fulfill a strategic vision, lift others, give back to society, or even improve the bottom line.

There has always been a chaotic period following the installation of a new leader. On the bright side, the change that happens when a new CEO takes over promises new energy, better company performance, and a fresh direction. On the negative side, employees, including senior ones, know to expect firings, abrupt reshuffles, complicated "reorgs," and shelved projects. "How worried should I be?"; "How do I impress my new boss?"; and "What will happen to me if I get pushed out?" are but some of the questions playing on repeat in the minds and therapist offices of employees whose boss has just been replaced. These employees have reason to be concerned. A study by Kevin Coyne and Edward J. Coyne analyzed data on CEO and other high-level executive turnover from 2002 to 2004 at the top 1,000 US companies, as determined by market cap. In cases where a new CEO came from outside the company, involuntary turnover among senior management averaged a whopping 26 percent—almost four times the rate when the CEO did not change.[28] Much of this can be justified. After all, high-performing companies rarely replace their CEOs with outsiders, and it would make sense for a low-performing or a mid-performing company to undergo significant change by a new leadership trying to reverse its decline. But in the twenty years or so since the study was conducted, the concept of change has, itself, changed, raising new anxieties among those watching a new, impatient CEO swoop in, or even an established one govern. Goodbye, change. Hello, disruption.

Disruptive innovation typically refers to the introduction by a small company of a new product that suddenly convinces us of a need we weren't aware we had. The product becomes a game-changer and makes a lot of money for its inventors in the process. By nature, disruptive companies are subversive, tired of the status quo, and willing to upend everything because they have little to lose. LCD TVs, mobile phones, and streaming services can all be seen as examples; so can more current inventions like app-based ridesharing, 3D printing, and the electric vehicle. They started on the fringes of a rather stable market, then became good enough and affordable enough to try to replace it altogether. Not to mention generative AI, the latest and possibly largest-scale disruption, whose potential to supplant entire professions we are barely beginning to imagine.

Although it was coined to refer to technological innovation, "disruption" has morphed into a catchall designation for the rather heroic rejection of business-as-usual. It even has a leadership style named after it, characterized by "always looking for better solutions and ways to establish new processes."[29] Disruptive leaders will not hesitate to question the basic assumptions of an enterprise running on autopilot or show skepticism toward its most fundamental practices in order to avoid the fate of Blockbuster, Kodak, and the cathode ray tube. They seem hyperaware of a statistic that shows that over half of Fortune 500 companies in 2000 had disappeared two decades later.[30] "Disrupt or be disrupted" seems to be their motto.

If implemented right, disruption can assure a company's survival and the continued stability of its employees' lives and can do the rest of us a lot of good in the form of valuable new products and services. When it becomes a goal onto itself, though, it can start looking psychiatric. There is a "disruption" fixation imbuing leadership culture today that has seen the word shed many of the negative connotations having to do with causing an unwelcome disturbance or interrupting a process in an unproductive way. A 2018 report on CEO outlook by KPMG, a "Big Four" global accounting firm, surveyed 400 US-based CEOs representing all major industries and leading companies with revenues of at least $500 million. Eighty-six percent of those surveyed considered their companies to be active disruptors, and nearly all—98 percent—saw technological disruption as more of an opportunity than a threat.[31] These CEOs' exuberant support for disruption may be attributed to our technological era, and the magic people expect to happen when you apply machine learning tools to Big Data. According to Tim Zanni, Global and US Technology Leader for KPMG, "We are living in one of the most disruptive periods of tech evolution since the Internet first entered the scene decades ago. The Fourth Industrial Revolution is quickly unfolding as the evolution of artificial intelligence, IoT [Internet of Things], and robotics move firmly into the mainstream and upturn media, transportation, health care, security, retail, telco, and many other fields." He describes large-company CEOs as following the lead of tech startups, whose approach to solving problems is "ground-breaking with an acceptance to fail fast and pivot quickly."[32] Their role model might as well be Mark Zuckerberg, whose internal motto in Facebook's early years famously was "Move fast and break things," and who, as a behoodied twenty-something disruptor, now represents an archetype of sorts for today's much more "mature" leaders and seasoned companies.[33] Except it is one thing to drive a nimble startup into the ground and repivot it, and another to try to do it with a Fortune 500 company. The pain grows exponentially with company size, and the nimbleness decreases dramatically. The startups that Fortune 500 CEOs seem to be modeling themselves on may be in the business of disruption, but a full two-thirds of them fail, never delivering a return to investors.[34] One would expect this statistic to keep more disruption-minded leaders up at night.

They might be downplaying expectations, but the CEOs surveyed by KPMG don't necessarily predict that all the disrupting they want to do will necessarily make their companies more money. Commenting on the data, Carl Carande, KPMG's Vice Chair of Advisory, said, "Disruptive innovation has shifted expectations of ROI (return on investment) from linear progression to wildly varying, based on a technology's potential, forcing companies to accept greater volatility in their growth projections."[35] With 98 percent of leaders being enthusiastic fans, there are many more leaders self-identifying as disruptors than there are Uber-style disruptions coming to light or disruption-related fortunes being made. If disruption has become only tenuously linked to successful outcomes and is not even being done in the name of the bottom line, what might explain its popularity? I vote for attention-seeking as being at least partially the answer.

The list of modern-day disruptors would probably include Travis Kalanick, who all but did away with traditional cabs; Elizabeth Holmes, who wanted to do away with needles and run all sorts of laboratory tests on one drop of blood obtained via painless pinprick; and Jack Dorsey, cofounder of X (Twitter) whose mission for it was to be the world's "global consciousness."[36] Travis Kalanick would come to represent douchey behavior to many riders and drivers, and Elizabeth Holmes's only true "success" might be as a popular Halloween costume.[37] As for Dorsey, as if disrupting how we communicate—not to mention democracy— were not enough, he has been busy advocating for cryptocurrency, predicting in 2018 that bitcoin will become the world's single currency within ten years, having disrupted the rest of them out of circulation.[38] (In 2021, ostensibly in honor of how the blockchain would replace banking infrastructure, he changed the name of the digital payments company he cofounded from "Square" to "Block.")[39]

In the political arena, Donald Trump probably fancied himself a disruptive leader. His campaign flaunted every convention—he lacked expected qualifications, bypassed usual channels to communicate with his followers via X (Twitter), ran despite the openly hostile rejection of his party, and won despite every major poll and news outlet consistently predicting otherwise. These disruptions started early in his presidency and continued unabated. Every reality was upended, from the recent and relatively divisive (Obamacare, the Iran nuclear weapons treaty, the Paris climate accord) to forever bipartisan sacred cows (NATO, skepticism toward Russia, friendly relationships with age-old allies). Rather than complete entropy, though, there seemed to be a method to Trump's behavior, a reliable script behind the endless show: take conventional wisdom or what a "standard" leader might do, flip it on its head, rotate it 180 degrees, and you could predict Trump's action with reasonable accuracy. Until, that is, he starts disrupting the disruptions, whiplashing back and forth on the same issues: during his 510-day bid for the White House, Trump was calculated to have taken 141 distinct positions on 23 major causes. Call him predictably unpredictable. Call it business unusual.[40]

One problem with many of today's disruptors is that their disruptions don't seem to stand for much beyond the disruption itself. They do not add up to a clear vision or long-term plan and are not necessarily linked to financial or other awaited rewards. Rather, they seem driven by the attention they get from behaving provocatively, predicting dramatically, and acting unexpectedly. Attention may be why they can be so in-your-face with their disruptions and their intention to break things. The tweets, the hashtags, the antics, the magazine covers (before her fall from grace, Holmes made the covers of *Forbes*, *Fortune*, *Inc.*, and the *New York Times Style Magazine*—all in a black turtleneck that recalled Steve Jobs's) can point to someone who wants to disrupt out of restlessness and for shock value; someone who is less interested in improving lives than in generating clicks; someone for whom likes counters and the number of retweets matter more than performance metrics. Yet they represent another archetype for leaders today: the maximally exposed fast mover who wants to break things now—on stage, in your face—and worry later.

Without putting too much of a damper on the innovations we truly need—think, for example, of global warming and the desperate quest for creative solutions to address it and the desperate necessity to keep artificial intelligence from turning against us—it may be time to inject a little bit of negative charge back into the verb "to disrupt." This can be done with some help from the *Diagnostic and Statistical Manual of Mental Disorders* (DSM), the book that classifies and defines psychiatric diagnoses, where the word makes frequent appearances, none of which are exactly positive. There is, for example, the condition named disruptive mood dysregulation disorder, in which children or adolescents experience ongoing irritability, anger, and frequent, intense temper outbursts. There is also an entire category of conditions named disruptive behavior disorders, which includes diagnoses like oppositional defiant disorder and the more severe conduct disorder. Typically diagnosed in children and adolescents but still diagnosable in adults, these conditions include symptoms such as defiance of authority figures, angry outbursts, lying, stealing, blaming others for the person's own mistakes or misbehavior, and being spiteful or vindictive.[41] Even as no leader wants the label disruptive behavior disorder attached to a son or daughter, leaders have fully embraced "disruptive leadership" as their signature personal style, with a huge proportion of them self-identifying as such and wanting the world to know it. And the world is rewarding them with views, retweets, and magazine covers, because a lot more people will watch a video of somebody breaking something than putting it together. When leaders stop coming with a long-term vision and start adopting positions primarily to go viral, you know we have entered the age of upside-down, inside-out leadership—and that we are deeply in need of disruption.

This, however, would involve leaders shifting from a breaking-in-the-spotlight mentality to a building-in-the-shadows one. Leaders build, that's what they do. They build buildings, monuments, and highways, of course, but also communities, universities, programs, nonprofits, parks, religions, and you name it. That is why the focus on "disruption" as a cornerstone leadership quality is a curious one insofar as it puts the emphasis on shattering rather than patient constructing, on undoing rather than doing, on telling us what you don't like rather than what you want to make happen to replace it. We discussed the overrepresentation of narcissists in the leadership classes, and this fact also complicates the necessary shift from disruptor back to builder. That is because disruptors are guaranteed immediate attention, whereas builders must wait until their edifice is complete and they have something to show for their hard work.

I doubt disruptive leaders' coaching sessions involve a primer in the classics, but it wouldn't be a bad idea. Runaway ego and hubris-as-deadly-sin are themes that permeate much of Greek mythology, with especially colorful punishment—a "special place in hell," to partially requote Madeleine Albright—reserved by the gods for that blinding self-importance that offends both the natural order and the divine. The list of tragic figures is long— Narcissus, of course, for falling in love with his own reflection, as we have seen, and many others—and the moral of the story is almost always the same: some humility, for God's sake! This is as applicable to disruptive present-day Narcissuses as it was at the dawn of Western civilization.

True leadership is also about not allowing leadership to "get to your head." It is about lifting others and turning the focus onto them and away from you. It is about surrounding yourself with quality would-be leaders and potential successors, not a mediocre class that helps assure personal survival by diminishing internal threats and competition. And, crucially, it is about knowing when to stop leading and voluntarily vacating center stage so that someone else may have a chance. Along these lines, recent political history has served several tragic examples of a gerontocracy that is so intent on continuing to lead that it is willing to autodestruct in the name of it. Justice Ruth Bader Ginsburg, despite several bouts of pancreatic cancer and multiple hospitalizations, clung to her Supreme Court seat until her death at eighty-seven, preventing President Obama from nominating a like-minded justice while he was still president and paving the way for a Trump-defined Supreme Court that has been very busy undoing much of what she stood for.[42] Dianne Feinstein, California's late Democratic senator, at ninety and despite loud rumors of dementia and long health-related absences from the Senate, still would not resign her seat or relinquish her position on the all-important Judiciary Committee, complicating her party's ability to advance its nominees and risking that it might fall a vote short on crucial matters such as raising the debt ceiling to avoid default.[43] And Chuck Grassley, Iowa's Republican senator, at eighty-nine, was reelected for an eighth term that ends in 2028, when he would be ninety-five, and, shortly after winning his eighth term, filed paperwork for a 2028 reelection campaign.[44] (He claims impeccable health, is said to be sharp as a Ginsu knife, and apparently celebrates his birthdays by doing an underwater somersault and scuba diving down to the depth of his new age, but still!)[45] And let's not even get into presidential candidates. It's undoubtedly scary for those close to them to communicate, but it's important for these leaders to hear it: it's OK to pass the baton. Your leadership legacy will be enhanced for it, and we the followers will be OK. We promise. Don't make this about us. Instead, the mistake, increasingly, is for leaders who have been at it a long time to think that new blood is overrated, that no other leader can fill their shoes, that they are indispensable. Alas, as

Charles de Gaulle is said to have remarked, the cemeteries are full of indispensable people.[46]

Another narcissistic failure by some leaders today is their de-prioritizing of those they are supposed to be leading in favor of constant "managing up" and prioritizing of those *above*. Defined as successfully influencing the decision-makers one reports to—one's boss, basically—by learning how to speak their language and keep them happy, managing up is crucial to understanding one's role within the organization and to succeeding in it, as well as for raises, bonuses, and advancement within the hierarchy. Investing in managing one's relationship with the boss is typically viewed positively as it implies cultivating a productive working rapport and adapting to, and adopting, the boss's management, leadership, and communication preferences. A study by the consulting firm McKinsey of 1,200 senior executives from seventy-one countries showed that managing up and horizontally (one's peers) increased both business impact and personal career success much more than managing subordinates. For business success, managing up and horizontally was 50 percent more important than managing down (45 percent versus 30 percent). For personal career success, as measured, for example, by promotions and raises, managing up was more than twice as important (47 percent versus 19 percent)—a dramatic, statistically significant endorsement of the art of kissing up.[47]

These rosy associations with managing up belie a negative side that doesn't receive nearly the attention it deserves. It is about the "addiction" of leaders to leading, and its signs include constantly eyeing a further rise in the hierarchy, *no matter how high one gets*. We are not talking here about employees praising their CEO as they gun for a promotion, but, rather, about leaders being disingenuous "yes men" and obsequiously, relentlessly, and unconditionally flattering *their* leaders. We are talking about CEOs brownnosing whomever is above in order to be further promoted to whatever leadership position is above their already lofty current rank. Unless you are "World King" as former UK prime minister Boris Johnson dreamt as a child he would someday become, you will always have a boss to manage up.[48] An academic department chair answers to the dean who answers to the president who answers to the board of trustees. A corporate chief marketing officer answers to the CEO who answers to the board of directors. On every step of this over-simplified ladder, there is opportunity for leaders to manage up, and sometimes it happens at the expense of managing down and side-ways. For a leader who has already made it, though, a fixed upward gaze communicates an insatiable appetite for ever-more leadership; almost an "addiction" where satisfaction can only be guaranteed if the dose of leadership can keep increasing. It's never enough! In this scenario with AA overtones, what matters more than lifting subor-dinates is to score an even bigger leadership dose. Subordinates and peers don't matter as much because their opinion about whether the leader will advance further doesn't matter as much. As such, it's OK to delegate their concerns, ignore their emails, and create all sorts of obstacles, buffers, and fortifications between the leader and them so the leader can focus on what—and who—is "really" important. In practice, this is nothing more than terminal upward mobility by a modern-day Narcissus who is in it exclusively for himself.

THE INTERNET ABOUNDS with tests that purport to measure leadership potential and that are popular with leadership aspirers and those con-sidering hiring them. The "Leadership Potential Indicator" (LPI) is a user-friendly scale that, for ten minutes and $19.95, claims to assess twenty leadership and management competencies covering vision-ing, goals, and the capacity for delivering success. Everyone stands to benefit from the LPI—"leaders, first-time managers, individual con-tributors, administrative staff, health care workers, and students"— and its feedback report comes with development tips.[49] The "Cadillac" of leadership potential scales, however, may be the Korn Ferry Assessment of Leadership Potential, or KFALP, developed and offered by the famed consultancy group.[50] The KFALP is designed to answer the question "Who has the potential to take on higher-level, bigger leadership roles in the future?" The assessment is described as "the choice of employers who want to future-proof their businesses by ensuring that there is not only a current well of effective leaders, but a clear succession of leadership talent."[51] Among other things, it measures leadership drive, experience, competencies, self-awareness, and learning agility, and comes with an elaborate color-coded scoring system and recommendations to map future development.

Unfortunately for many of these assessments, however, the internet also abounds in sites that teach to these tests and help those aspiring to leadership perfect their scores on them, a little bit in the vein of the popular Princeton Review SAT prep course, which promises—the asterisk notwithstanding—a score of "1400+ Guaranteed★" out of a maximum achievable 1600.[52] As such, it is easy to find leadership sample questions, a "KFALP practice test," and mock leadership exams that will make you look like leadership material, regardless of your true capacities and inclinations.[53] JobTestPrep is one such how-to-ace-your-leadership-potential-test service and comes with an impressive 4.8-star rating for its KFALP practice program.[54] "Leadership Assessment tests are often a part of the hiring process for various management positions, such as Directors, Executives, and CEOs," the site explains. "The following guide will cover the types of Leadership Assessment tests, a comprehensive list of different Leadership Assessment tools, sample questions, and Leadership assessment test tips. . . . In addition, you may gain access to a complete preparation plan for leadership tests, with full guidance on what traits you are expected to demonstrate, and how to do it in real-time."[55]

In what can be seen as an invitation to "fake it till you make it," such leadership prep packs teach you how you can pass as an agile, self-aware, emotionally intelligent visionary in your answers, and how you can appear to be in possession of leadership skills that you may or may not possess. This can reduce the requirement for acing the leadership potential exam to a capacity for deceit rather than the other qualities that the test hopes to measure.

So, for our would-be leaders, aspiring politicians, and MBA candidates, a plea: forget the likes of the LPI, the KFALP, and Job-TestPrep, and consider, instead, the previously discussed Narcissistic Personality Inventory (NPI), which measures narcissistic tendencies, and the Levenson Self-Report Psychopathy Scale (LSRP), which measures psychopathic ones.[56] The NPI has been shown to accurately assess for narcissism and consists of forty pairs of statements.[57] For each pair, users are asked to choose between statements such as:

- *Modesty doesn't become me* vs. *I am essentially a modest person.*
- *When people compliment me, I sometimes get embarrassed* vs. *I know that I am good because everybody keeps telling me so.*
- *I am no better or worse than most people* vs. *I think I am a special person.*
- *I can read people like a book* vs. *People are sometimes hard to understand.*
- *I am more capable than other people* vs. *There is a lot I can learn from other people.*
- *I will never be satisfied until I get all that I deserve* vs. *I take my satisfactions as they come.*

NPI scores range from 0 to 40, with higher scores constituting a reason for concern.

The LSRP, on the other hand, was designed to assess psychopathy, which, as we have seen, has also been shown to be overrepresented in leaders and to have a close relationship to white collar crime. It consists of twenty-six statements that users rate based on their level of agreement with the statement (from [1] strongly disagree to [5] strongly agree). Sample statements include:

- *Success is based on survival of the fittest; I am not concerned about the losers.*
- *People who are stupid enough to get ripped off usually deserve it.*
- *Looking out for myself is my top priority.*
- *I have been in a lot of shouting matches with other people.*
- *I tell other people what they want to hear so that they will do what I want them to do.*

A score is generated for "primary psychopathy" (lack of empathy) and, separately, for "secondary psychopathy" (rule-breaking).

There is a real need to weed out extreme narcissists and psychopaths from leadership culture—do we really want leaders who strongly agree with the statement "Looking out for myself is my top priority" or "I am not concerned about the losers"? Here is how this might work in the best of all leadership worlds. A best-case scenario would be when someone contemplating leadership undergoes a journey of self-discovery that identifies unhealthy levels of self-love or disregard for others, then does leadership culture and followers a favor by bowing out of the race. This person might instead be inspired to do everything possible to learn humility and empathy, maybe by twisting Kotter's eight-step model for leading change into a model for leading *self*-change. This is a daunting prospect, to be sure, and comes with a high failure rate; if you are a leader or wannabe leader touched by narcissism, you think you are special and have little to learn and improve upon. With colleagues, Wiley W. Souba, the former Dartmouth medical school dean who has written extensively on leadership in academia, wrote this in an article on leaders and personal change: "The kind of change that causes angst and heartburn is the kind that requires that we fundamentally change ourselves. . . . It is exceedingly difficult, sometimes even terrifying, for highly competent individuals . . . to acknowledge or even realize that they might be incompetent when it comes to learning new ways of thinking and working." "Deep change," the article continues, "must come from within each individual. It requires going deep inside yourself to discover how your mental models were shaped and how you came to be the person you are today. It involves confronting your fears and vulnerabilities, addressing your inauthenticity, and being willing to redesign yourself so your life will work better, personally and professionally."[58] This kind of self-motivated self-change is much harder than most other types, but, if successful, can help address the epidemic of attention seekers, pretenders, and manage-up-ers in the highest posts, and will put the focus squarely back where it belongs—on the followers whom good leaders are supposed to want to manage, inspire, and lift.

Short of self-change, for a healthier leadership culture, it falls to HR departments, executive recruiters, board members, search committees, coaches, therapists, and followers to educate themselves about these tendencies in leaders and to create "obstacles, buffers, and fortifications" between those who possess unhealthy levels of them and leadership positions. As it stands now, though, narcissistic and psychopathic drive is largely ignored by employers and the leadership industry in selecting who gets to rise, and this drive is rewarded by the toxic and cutthroat nature of the leadership culture we have created. Until, that is, an egregious violation is committed by the narcissistic or psychopathic leader we have promoted or elected or been in thrall to—and psychology can no longer be ignored.

Thankfully, a serious self-change leadership student who is intent on transforming for the better can still find inspiring leader role models to emulate. While attending a conference in Omaha, Nebraska, a few years ago, I took a break from scheduled events to sample Gorat's, one of the city's classic steakhouses. Opened in 1944, it looks like it hasn't been touched since, stuck in a time warp of décor, bedecked octogenarians, mushy sides, and beautiful meat. Cutting into my whiskey rib eye, I would have been excused if I had missed the bespectacled white-haired man with the average Midwestern habitus who walked in with a dining companion, despite the collective upward head tilt of nearly everybody in the room. He exchanged brief pleasantries with the hostess, greeted a couple of diners he recognized, then proceeded to take a seat at a semiprivate table he seemed well familiar with. It turned out I was at Warren Buffet's favorite restaurant in his native town and the "Oracle of Omaha" himself was dining there. There was no fanfare, no bodyguards, no limelight desperation, no "gramming" of his plate for the world to salivate—just an unassuming giant of twentieth-century investing enjoying his meal of a protein, a starch, and a veggie. If he "disrupted" our dinner at all, it's not because he had any intention to do so. There was something deeply reassuring about his "meat and potatoes" disposition, which was perfectly matched to the timelessness of the place and perfectly anachronistic if you consider leadership culture today.

Buffet's other tastes are equally simple, as someone researching him will quickly learn. He famously still lives in the same house he purchased in 1958 and has had the same five-minute commute to work for over a half century. He alternates among three McDonald's breakfast options every day and loves his Cherry Coke. Even his tipping is frugal, considering his resources: 25 percent, according to my waitress, who answered the tips question before I could finish asking it, like it had been put to her countless times before. He can invest my money anytime.

They don't make them like that anymore, with "make" being the operative word. There is little emphasis on humility and self-effacement in the conveyor-belt, production-line approach to making leaders, where there is so much "product" being churned out that the only way to stand out and get noticed is to go to extremes, disrupt in the loudest way possible, and saturate our lives by all means necessary. Some coaching and branding practices, with their focus on "owning the message" and disseminating it over as many platforms as possible until a recognizable "brand" sticks, run the risk of selecting for undesirable traits like narcissism, "enriching" leadership culture with them at the expense of more desirable ones. And the glut of leaders churned out by the leadership industry and egged on by a culture obsessed with leadership makes it even more difficult to land at the top of the pyramid, rewarding meaner, fiercer competitors who know how to up the ante and ruthlessly assert themselves. Narcissists and psychopaths have an advantage in such a race because they are undeniably better at these tasks. That they can do it while acing a leadership assessment exam by faking leadership qualities like emotional intelligence and interest in serving others is the cherry (Coke) on the cake.

In summary, and in the spirit of the "Eight Steps" approach to leadership advice popular today, some dos and don'ts for leadership would seem in order. Do change what is changeable but accept that which is likely constant. Don't fake it till you make it, pretending, for example, to possess self-awareness and mindful presence that you may not have or empathy that may not come naturally to you. Learning to the test may help you ace a multiple-choice leadership assessment test just like it helped you ace the SAT, but this is not college admissions, and you risk failing the much more difficult and more "real" leadership character stress test when you are confronted with it.

Also, do manage "down," even if it means delaying the further expansion of your leadership role. You are leader "enough" as it is, so enjoy it and fulfill your current role to the best of your abilities and try to lift others before focusing on what comes next for you, personally. At some point, a leader should stop rising and start leading, and at some point he should exit altogether. As part of this exercise in humility, do accept that life is full of uncertainty; that you are not in total control of your leadership fate; that leadership is far from a shoo-in no matter how good you might be and how hard you prep—and that there is something to be celebrated in the serendipity and the unknowns built into this fact. As such, ease up on the prepping and the leadership "development" and take prescriptions like "Eight steps to," "Nine tips for," and "Ten skills that" with eleven large grains of salt, opting, instead, for experiences that can expand your horizon and help you better understand yourself and your place in the world.

Finally, do dethrone disruption as a value unto itself in favor of the patient building up of something people can remember you by. A trending Google story will get you briefly noticed, and a quarterly fiscal triumph will help you survive the next board meeting, but legacy is what you should be shooting for, and its shelf life is orders of magnitude longer than a winning TikTok video or a hashtag that takes the Twitterverse by storm. Follow these dos, avoid these don'ts, and your personal reward might well be a newfound serenity that rubs off on your followers and on leadership culture at large.

9

THE CURE
(IF YOU CAN AFFORD IT)

An Ode to Followers

TO A LARGE degree, great leaders are born, or happen, with the help of innate temperament, character, talent, opportunity, timing, and circumstance, in ways that we do not fully understand and can certainly not completely control. So many ingredients have to come together and so many stars have to align that the default should be to assume that most people will not have what it takes to become that rare successful and happy leader. This reality should not depress us, given how many other paths there are to success and happiness. Instead, it should spur us to invest in followers and the need to allow their nonleadership talent to emerge in its own peculiar way. While this talent may not guide them to a leadership position, there is a good chance it will guide them somewhere more in sync with who they are, and they will be the better for it. It should also spur us to support them, first and foremost by changing the cultural narrative playing out at home, at school, and at work that is giving them an inferiority complex and making them question their very self-worth. Leaders have sucked up too much oxygen; it is time to put followers front and center. A healthy leadership culture starts with appreciating followers.

Just how rare is a good leader who has what it takes to rise and lead? Bringing together what we have discussed so far to stitch together a composite of that "ideal" leader might give us a hint. In outlining the profile of such a person, the wish list would have to start with strength of character and the ability to model resilience in times of fear, uncertainty, and pain. But along with strength and resilience comes a long list of "soft" prerequisites. There is, of course, the leader's IQ. But there is also the ability to empathize, self-regulate, and take one's and others' psychological temperature—a quality that has been labeled emotional quotient or EQ, and that has been estimated to account for as much as 90 percent of what distinguishes leaders from peers with otherwise similar technical skills and IQ.[1]

There is also the genuine desire to lift others, which can only be present if the leader has a deficit of narcissism and psychopathy, and a surplus of humility. A humility surplus, however, does not mean poor self-confidence. A healthy supply of that is an absolute requirement for the crucial leader quality of being able to go against accepted dogma or any course of action that doesn't align with personal values. If this means a fight for one's principles, so be it. Leaders, as our comparison of the Barack Obama and George W. Bush presidencies showed, shouldn't be trigger-happy—but they shouldn't be gun-shy, either.

Personality-wise, while we do not want our leaders to have narcissistic or antisocial personality disorder, we still want them to have *a* personality; one that is their unique and recognizable signature. This requires dropping all talk of "branding" if it implies Brand Bland and a milquetoast, blunted, personality-less leadership, in favor of leaders who stand for something and are not just parroting the least controversial positions du jour. It also requires dropping, in favor of a personality that is real, the artifice that seems to go into some of the more toxic brands, from Elizabeth Holmes's black turtlenecks and reportedly artificial baritone to SBF's disheveled wunderkind who is so dedicated to making everybody else rich that he doesn't have time to comb his hair.[2] We don't want Brand Bland, but we don't want Brand Fake, either.

Then there is the ability to inspire others to work toward a common goal. Here, a leader "dreams big" and visualizes imaginative solutions to problems for which no template exists, then moves followers to pursue that same dream. Translating this "vision thing" into a shared goal is aided by superior communication and social skills, which have also been loosely grouped under the EQ umbrella, and an auspicious charisma quotient, which is an ingredient so important that it deserves an acronym of its own. How about CQ?

All this communicating, glad-handing, and social extraversion, however, should not lead to overexposure and overfamiliarity, since, as we have seen, an inner core of unknowability is necessary, allowing followers to project desires and aspirations onto the leadership. Therefore, the extroverted leader should stay simultaneously removed, distant, and a touch, dare I say, out of touch.

Leaders should also incorporate just the right dose of manager. In the classic leader versus manager Manichaean approach to leading, leaders lead by vision, strategy, and influence whereas managers organize, implement, and sweat the details. Yet a leader who is too anxiety-free about details can easily become unanchored. So, rather than a rigid dichotomy where leader and manager are mutually exclusive and never the twain shall meet, leaders should have a "just right" amount of manager in them. Not too much, lest their leadership get bogged down in the weeds, and not too little, lest they appear too given to whims of fantasy.

The profile of the ideal leader, then, is very much a yin-and-yang jumble of contradictions, where soft balances strong, combat-ready offsets battle-weary, social flirts with asocial, managerial concretizes leaderly, and brand is in a dialectic with personality. It is rife with paradox and difficult to engineer or piece together if it didn't come more or less "ready-made" with the leader.

As if this composite were not rare enough, there is, beyond the difficult-to-engineer profile, luck, which, itself, can be a rarity. Yes, leaders should be lucky. It is said that when inquiring about an officer he was considering for a promotion to division general, Napoleon said: "I know he's a good general, but is he lucky?"[3] One of the greatest military commanders of all time had a "lucky star" that guided him on battlefields. Besides loving his wife, Josephine, for fulfilling his destiny (his wedding gift to her was a gold medallion inscribed "To Destiny"), he loved her because he believed she brought him good luck.[4] His campaigns may have been taught in military academies for a couple of centuries, but deep down, it is possible he agreed with those who attributed some of his achievements to sheer luck.[5] Luck, Napoleon might concur, defies the ability of a leader or coach to attract, predict, or channel it, yet it can be what decides when a meaningful opportunity comes knocking and whether it's recognized for what it is when it does. No amount of leadership training or even committed psychotherapy can help us there, since this mercurial determinant of success has, if you choose to believe in it, more in common with astrology and horoscope than anything objective, controllable, or scientific that you can pick up in leadership school.

Finally, ideal leadership requires a favorable context in which to play out, both at the "local" level of the leader's organization or institution, and at the level of culture at large. The latter, as we have seen, conspires against stable and successful leadership, making one's rise more challenging than perhaps it has ever been. If this sounds like a difficult formula, that is because it is. This reality highlights the—there's no other word—narcissism of an industry that, in the face of such a forbidding landscape, still thinks it can reliably produce good leaders with this unique mix of personality, disposition, good fortune, and conducive context.

It also highlights how easy it is to be duped when people uncritically follow a leader, only because one or two ingredients on the long list of necessary qualities seem to be present. A seemingly brilliant vision—*Lab tests from a pinprick! Crypto for the masses!*—might be a necessary ingredient for leadership and makes for a tantalizing startup idea, but it is hardly sufficient. There was absolutely no reason why, solely by virtue of an idea that sounded good, Elizabeth Holmes and SBF should have been assumed to be biotech or finance leaders worth worshipping, emulating, and featuring in fawning article after fawning article and on magazine cover after magazine cover. One leadership ingredient suffices, and the rest can be learned or sacrificed, seemed to be the message. Sure, Elizabeth Holmes and SBF could have been visionary leaders in a Steve Jobs uniform or with a nerd's phenotype, but they could have just as likely been scam artists, which is what their subsequent trajectories would suggest they had been all along. They were far from having earned the leadership mantle, so why were so many so premature in elevating them and partaking in their leadership cult? That so many—including George Shultz, Henry Kissinger, and James Mattis in the case of Holmes, and Larry David, Tom Brady, Steph Curry, and Shaquille O'Neal in the case of SBF— were enthralled and in awe speaks to how even the most powerful and celebrity-jaded of followers can contribute to the failed leadership culture by following unproven, unworthy "leaders."[6] Holmes's and SBF's visions proved far from workable, but even if they had worked, this would not in and of itself have constituted good leadership—exhibit A: Travis Kalanick and cab-hailing apps. The moral of the story is that no leader should be prematurely anointed based solely on a tantalizing vision or other single leadership ingredient. Leaders should earn their leadership, and nothing but the long list of proven qualities should satisfy us, since no training may satisfactorily make up for the missing ones.

A heartwarming example of "earning one's leadership" may forever belong to President Jimmy Carter, described by his biographer Kai Bird as "probably the most intelligent, hard-working and decent man to have occupied the Oval Office in the 20th century." His widely dismissed one-term presidency came with real accomplishments: the Camp David peace accords between Egypt and Israel; the SALT II arms control treaty; normalization of relations with China; deregulating the airline industry in a way that made travel affordable to middle-class Americans; deregulating natural gas in a way that prepared for today's energy independence; tripling the size of protected wilderness areas; and being among the first presidents to warn about climate change. Still, these accomplishments have been overshadowed by failure, notably his handling of the 444-day hostage crisis that followed the seizing of the US embassy in Tehran and his refusal to order military retaliation. What came after his 1980 reelection defeat, however, can be seen as four decades of Carter earning his leadership. Writing in the *New York Times* in 2023, Bird says: "If I once believed that Mr. Carter was the only president to use the White House as a steppingstone to greater things, I see now that the past 43 years have really been an extension of what he thought of as his unfinished presidency." As such, his Carter Center has helped reduce Guinea worm disease by 99.99 percent, making it likely to be the first disease since smallpox to be eradicated. His devotion to democratic ideals saw him monitor 114 elections in 39 countries. And his work building decent and affordable housing with Habitat for Humanity has inspired millions around the globe and earned him the moniker "one of the world's most distinguished humanitarians."[7] How is that for title and for earned leadership? (And how is that for elevating "building" over "disrupting?")

Assuming they do not go to jail, fallen or prematurely anointed leaders whom we had no business elevating have a lot of support they can count on and many second chances and second lives. From the hallowed halls of MBA programs and leadership institutes, from the desks of professors of leadership, whenever a leader who had all sorts of access to leadership training and coaching opportunities falls from grace, there is no throwing down of the towel or acknowledgment that we do not know the first thing about how to predictably produce good leaders or prevent bad ones from emerging. Rather than see the many costly and soul-sapping leadership crises as proof that our current approach to leadership is counterproductive and that many of the industry's services may be of limited value in a post-leadership age; rather than viewing the situation as an opportunity for humility about what can and cannot be accomplished when it comes to leadership development, the industry sees "antileaders" as convenient cautionary vignettes that can be integrated into more leadership training activities. There is, instead, a sort of doubling down as more business school courses, company trainings, after-hours seminars, and articles from professors of leadership are devoted to teaching how to rehabilitate failed leaders and how *not* to lead. More leadership training simply *must* be the answer is the industry's perhaps unsurprising reaction.

You will perhaps not be surprised to learn, then, that the modern leadership industry is not limited to training you to become a leader. It also nurses you when you succumb to the position; a position that perhaps you weren't meant for and shouldn't have been coaxed into in the first place. As leaders who were not natural fits for leadership start feeling lonely at the top; as they are squeezed to conform to a tight leadership mold or are subjected to endless haranguing for defying it; as they get tired of faking it and the façade starts to crack, some will break under the stress.

And so, in 2017, Johnson & Johnson announced an intervention for the executive on the verge: a $100,000 antiburnout program offered in partnership with the famed Mayo Clinic and executed by a team of experts that includes, besides the ubiquitous coach, a dietitian and a physiologist.[8] No sticker shock necessary: $100,000 a head is a small price to pay when you consider the loss in a company's valuation when its CEO abruptly quits, including due to burnout, according to a study by the consulting firm PwC Strategy+Business. (Not to mention direct payments to the CEO in the form of "golden parachute"–type severance guarantees and gilded retirement benefits.) All in all, the PwC Strategy+Business study estimates that "large companies that underwent forced successions in recent years would have generated, on average, an estimated US$112 billion more in market value in the year before and the year after their turnover if their CEO succession had been the result of planning."[9]

A company has every incentive, then, to make sure its executives don't crash and burn, and J&J's program would, as *Bloomberg* put it, "surround (a company's) leadership class with specialists like the medical crew around an astronaut after splashdown." Having tested it on seven of their own executives, J&J decided to roll it out for the benefit of other Fortune 100 companies. "What's unique here is we're sending clear messages to this individual that we support you," Peter Fasolo, executive vice president and chief human resources officer at J&J told *Bloomberg*. "We get to the root causes. . . . It's more than stress management."[10]

Among other components, "getting to the root cause" involves an abdominal ultrasound at the Mayo Clinic, the executives writing down their life story for their life coach as a kind of "narrative therapy," and, if needed, the life coach interviewing family members and friends to identify the executives' "fault lines." In parallel, the dietician and physiologist develop a diet and exercise regimen and make a home visit, complete with a "cupboard analysis," presumably to make sure the CEO is eating healthily and enough.[11]

Acronyms, crucial as we have seen to teaching today's leaders handy tips on how to rise, also play a role in educating them in digestible ways on obstacles to watch out for that might bring down their leadership. As such, VUCA—volatility, uncertainty, complexity, and ambiguity—has gained ground as an explicator for why executives may fracture along their fault lines and require something like J&J's intervention.[12] Talking to *Bloomberg*, Seymour Adler of the consulting firm Aon said, "Our research shows that leaders in organizations operate in a VUCA environment. It takes its toll."[13] Leaders, it turns out, may not be as resilient as we had assumed, but there's nothing that a bespoke $100,000 program cannot fix. Lucy Kellaway of the *Financial Times* commented on it this way: "We are hoodwinking companies into thinking resilience can be bought. So long as the program is 'holistic' and 'personalised,' a CEO can be turned from a frail human into a superhero."[14]

However, as we fret about the physiology of the burned-out CEO, it is urgent we also ask ourselves who is worrying about the VUCA being created in followers' lives; about the volatility, uncertainty, complexity, and ambiguity that necessarily roll downhill whenever a leader is indisposed; about the aftershocks followers have to absorb when a trembler shakes the C-suite. Are *followers* eating healthily and enough? Who's analyzing *their* cupboards? Who's offering *them* abdominal ultrasounds? Who's taking *their* psychological temperatures?

The masses of misled followers whose lives are upended whenever a leader fails somehow fall through the cracks. Followers—destabilized, disillusioned, or deceived by a leadership gone off the rails—are often ignored. Don't expect much research into their mental health, fate, or next career move from an industry that is now focused on rehabilitating the leader or turning the failed leadership into a case study. Several patients who were relatively junior in their companies but still bore the brunt of turmoil occurring several rungs above their heads come to mind: Camilla, who could no longer afford her medicine when her job was eliminated by a disruptive CEO, causing her to relapse and causing us to desperately try to find a more affordable alternate. George, whose long-dormant symptoms returned in full force after his successful division was closed simply because it was closely associated with the outgoing CEO when the incoming one was desperate to leave his own imprimatur. Susan, who worked in housekeeping for years but whose services were no longer needed when the CEO took the company fully remote, causing her to become unemployed, and depressed, for the first time in her life. Or Jarrod, a sixty-two-year-old divorced man, who, after working for a tech company for twenty-five years, woke up one morning to a work email account that wouldn't open, a magnetic ID badge that wouldn't let him into his office building, and an online calendar from which all appointments had mysteriously disappeared. Without forewarning, Jarrod had been laid off as part of a massive cost-cutting workforce reduction by a CEO who had failed to meet his quarterly earnings forecasts, with only an email message to an old personal account announcing the decision. Jarrod's identity had become so attached to his longtime job that he never recovered from this loss. Combined with other risk factors, it would lead to his suicide nearly to the day a year later.

It is often the fallen leader who receives much of the focus and help when a leadership fails and when all the training and coaching prove insufficient, but it is the followers who are almost always the bigger victims—and deserve most of the attention and support. According to data published in *Forbes*, CEOs in 2021 made 324 times more than their median workers.[15] This represents a worsening of a trend long underway: From 1978 to 2020, CEO compensation rose 1,322.2 percent, adjusted for inflation, compared to 18 percent for employees. The COVID-19 pandemic accelerated the gap, contributing to a compensation increase of 14.1 percent from 2019 to 2020 for the 200 highest-paid public company CEOs, compared to an increase of only 1.9 percent for workers. And lest you should think that charities meant to provide a public benefit are above this, there is an entire class of nonprofit millionaire CEOs presiding over a sometimes largely volunteer workforce of followers.[16]

In leadership culture, too much attention is being spent on the metabolism, caloric intake, and stress level of generally very well compensated leaders and CEOs, and not enough on the well-being of their followers. Yet the first step toward a better leadership culture is a healthy, committed, and inspired followership. But to the extent that the leadership industry focuses on followers, it is often to try to turn them into leaders and send the message that the path to success and happiness must necessarily go through the C-suite—not to improve their current lives. A good place to begin helping followers is by not giving them an inferiority complex if they fail to become leaders.

It all starts with education, yet our educational system has turned into a billboard of sorts for the leadership industry in that it has fully embraced leadership development as a crucial cornerstone of educational institutions' missions and vision statements. We are not just talking about business schools, where the goal *should* be to try to teach students how to lead companies, and where slogans like "We unite the best minds in business education to shape the next generation of leaders" from the Association to Advance Collegiate Schools of Business, a global community of business schools, do make sense.[17] We are talking about everyone in all types of educational settings wanting to teach that next generation of leaders, rather than the next generation of responsible, engaged, and educated citizens. At West Catholic High School in Grand Rapids, Michigan, for example, "students develop the leadership skills, critical thinking, experience and values necessary to lead in today's world."[18] De Anza, an otherwise unassuming local community college in my neck of the woods, wants to teach its students to become "leaders in their communities, the nation and the world."[19] As for universities, LeaderU is a program from the coaching company FranklinCovey that tries to remind every stakeholder in higher education of the centrality of the leadership topic to university life and students' curriculum: "We help your institution develop exceptional leaders, engage staff and faculty, build a high-trust culture, and empower students." They deploy their trademarked "Principle-Centered Leadership" in higher education settings to "teach leaders at all levels how to stop managing and start leading."[20] Even high-seas students are not spared the leadership spiel, as suggested by the US Naval War College's guiding mission, which seems to prioritize "(informing) today's decision makers" and "(educating) tomorrow's leaders" over sailors' combat preparedness and how to pass a literal sink-or-swim challenge.[21]

This misguided leadership message is being inculcated into ever-younger minds and has seamlessly invaded even daycare settings, where it is now common to find centers with names like Tiny Leaders Children's Center, Little Leaders Institute, Lil' Leaders Childcare, Tomorrow's Leaders Childcare, and Future Leaders Christian Learning Center.[22] Not to mention Future S.T.E.A.M Leaders Academic Child Care, which prepares children aged zero to twelve for a lifetime of leadership in Science, Technology, Engineering, Arts, and Mathematics. (They do deserve credit for incorporating "Arts" and expanding their leadership focus beyond traditional STEM fields!)[23] Our leadership fixation knows no minimum age or prerequisites and spares no one, as handy leadership tips in the mode of 7 *Habits of Highly Effective People* are seemingly dispensed earlier and earlier, literally with breast milk.

Rather than worry about producing STEAM leaders, how about our educational institutions worry about improving student performance on STEAM subjects, where dramatic declines have been documented, especially during the COVID-19 pandemic?

Before they become leaders in science, tech, and the arts, they need to master English and simple algebra, which is not happening if you believe the National Assessment of Educational Progress, often called "The Nation's Report Card."[24] The program tracks students' academic achievement at the national, state, and district levels, and its fall 2022 results showed significant declines in math and reading proficiency between 2019 and 2022 in an overwhelming majority of states. Nationally, the average math score for fourth graders fell five points compared to 2019, while the score for eighth graders dropped eight points. In reading, average scores for both grades fell three points. In addition, the percentage of students performing below the "basic" level, defined as the lowest level of academic achievement, grew—to 25 percent of fourth graders and 38 percent of eighth graders in math. The dismal report card led Education Secretary Miguel Cardona to sound an alarm: "I want to be very clear: The results of today's nation's report card are appalling and unacceptable."[25]

These results should constitute much more immediate concerns than the business of leveraging the educational system to produce child leaders or funnel countless students to leadership courses. Other "bigger fish to fry" that might also deserve to be prioritized include improving teacher pay to attract the best to the profession, understanding the legacy of online education, and figuring out what to do about the epidemic of school shootings. On that topic, there is no reason why mission statements should not focus more on how schools will strive to make the kids' learning environment a safe and conducive one, rather than how they will turn themselves into a platform for precocious executives.

Universities, in particular, should resist perpetuating the leadership cult by signing on to services like LeaderU or making "leadership qualities" "the" aspect to showcase in a personal statement. A quick review of university websites suggests that they are fully partaking in, and magnifying, this fixation with leadership. Who needs a cello virtuoso when you can admit the president of ten clubs? And from an applicant's perspective, why hone your musicianship when you can focus on other extracurricular pursuits that carry more bang for the buck with the admissions committee? The financial reference here is apt because leadership is increasingly understood in economic and political terms. "To lead" used to bring up "to lead by example," as in setting and following a certain high standard, the equivalent of walking one's talk. Today, to lead suggests an ability to attract attention, subdue opponents, and maximize returns by skewing even more that 324 to 1 salary ratio. Power and profiteering seem to permeate the definition as exemplary behavior, humaneness, and morality take a back seat. Writing for the *New York Times'* "On Campus" column, Susan Cain, the author of *Quiet: The Power of Introverts in a World That Can't Stop Talking*, says, "Many students I've spoken with read 'leadership skills' as a code for authority and dominance and define leaders as those who 'can order other people around.' And according to one prominent Ivy League professor, those students aren't wrong; leadership, as defined by the admissions process, too often 'seems to be restricted to political or business power.'"[26] For universities to obsess about leaders to the exclusion of students who don't want to, or cannot, lead is bad enough, but for them to contribute to reducing leadership to dominance or a dollar value is actively doing leadership culture and all of us a disservice.

Universities, of all places, should know better when it comes to the societal benefits of supporting passionate but inhibited, even awkward, young students; those with a solid moral compass but who may not fulfill a leader's profile and don't want to fake it; those who may never become huge donors and may never have dorms, auditoriums, or gymnasiums named after them, and for whom money is a means not an end. Instead, universities seem to be feeding the cult of the alpha leader that began in daycare, making those who don't qualify feel left out and like failures. Any good university worthy of its designation as an academic center for higher education will address its services to the entire spectrum of its student body—would-be leaders or not—and will not make followers or those uncomfortable leading feel excluded and unwelcome, like they are set to fail. Diversity, equity, and inclusion starts there, too.

And then there is the irony of the rise of the leadership studies major, minor, or track as liberal arts departments are being decimated.[27] The soft skills of leadership that are a nonnegotiable contributor to a leader's success are also the bread and butter of a traditional liberal arts education. Liberal arts degrees teach students creative thinking, analytical reasoning, communication skills, and how to make a persuasive argument. They teach that much of life happens in a gray zone, not in the certainty and comparative simplicity of the "black and white" universes of engineering and computer science. This can make graduates with liberal arts degrees more comfortable navigating the world's ambiguity with strong critical thinking skills and intellectual humility, arguably making them better leaders. Indeed, a reasonable answer to the age-old question "What are you going to do with that liberal arts degree?" might be "Why, I'm going to become CEO!"

But these competencies that play so well in leadership are not the ones that universities are prioritizing as STEM majors increasingly dominate campus identity, rankings, and offerings, and as political science, sociology, English, and history undergo a disappearing act of sorts. Fewer than one in ten college graduates obtained a humanities degree in 2020, a 25 percent decline just since 2012.[28] The old English major, which used to account for a third of all humanities degrees, saw a third less graduates in 2020 compared with 2009. History is in freefall, too, down 35 percent over the same period. Students, who may be lining up to take leadership courses, are not learning from Shakespeare about conflict and resolution, order and disorder, hubris and modesty, and appearance and reality. They are not learning about Churchill.

There is little benefit in taking Churchill out of history and teaching him in leadership studies. Students and future leaders are less served trying to fit him into a particular leadership style—was it "transformational," "situational," "visionary," "commanding," "charismatic," "disruptive," or "tipping point"?—than understanding the complex path to his rise, what could have happened had he not been in the right place at the right time, and how formidable personal demons can be so outweighed by inner strength that a man can still utter words like: "We shall go on to the end, we shall fight in France, we shall fight on the seas and oceans, we shall fight with growing confidence and growing strength in the air, we shall defend our Island, whatever the cost may be, we shall fight on the beaches, we shall fight on the landing grounds, we shall fight in the fields and in the streets, we shall fight in the hills; we shall never surrender."[29]

Absent the nuanced and textured backdrop of a history curriculum, context can be lost, complexity sacrificed, legacy diminished, and leadership oversimplified. An educational system that is truly keen on training the "next generation of leaders" would bring back the liberal arts major and make sure that history and English don't go the way of the classics. There is little for leadership culture to gain from forcing professors of history into early retirement as we recruit professors of leadership and offer them tenure. There is little for leadership culture to gain from shutting down English language departments, then acknowledging that leaders can't write and, therefore, need a speech writer along with the executive coach. Before rushing to open leadership studies departments and announcing leadership courses and tracks, the educational system should try to rehabilitate the image of the liberal arts major and advertise its incredible relevance to our world today. And, at a time of high student debt and high demand for STEM skills, the educational system should work to maximize the return on investment for that brave soul who still dares pursue a bachelor's in anthropology.

A related, parallel process in universities is their increased insistence on leadership training for a big percentage of their faculty and staff. While this can often be easily justified as part of the "development" opportunities any employer should offer and any employee looks for in a job, it can have the same effects it has on that passionate but inhibited freshman—namely to make staff and faculty members who are not "natural" leaders and who want to excel at what they do without the pressures of leadership feel like their contributions are less valued and that they are somehow less themselves. How about, in lieu of paying for "leadership development" classes that mostly benefit the further development of the leadership industry, universities offer employees other opportunities, such as funding attendance at professional conferences and supporting participation in mindfulness classes where employees can learn to de-stress and avoid professional burnout? Perhaps better yet, why not give them pay raises so we can start to make a small dent in the 324 to 1 leader-to-follower salary ratio? (This is also largely true of the corporate world, where employee "development" is increasingly confused with leadership workshops.)

It all starts with education. Or does it? If there is a Bright Little Leaders Daycare, Inc., in Chicago, a "Leader in Me" curriculum adopted by over 5,000 schools in all fifty states and over fifty countries, leadership minors and majors at many colleges and universities, and professors of leadership, it is also because parents and students of all ages are signing up.[30] In that sense, it all starts at home. Fed up, understandably, with leaders at their workplaces, in politics, and in culture at large; moved by a genuine desire for better leaders and a better life for their children; inspired by a cultural message that leadership can be taught and nonleaders don't count as much, parents are nurturing the leadership kernel in their children and eating up educational offerings and other activities that claim to unearth and grow it. This, however, may be happening at the expense of other talents and abilities that are also worth nurturing but that are going underappreciated or ignored.

Martha is a forty-eight-year-old married woman in a senior leadership position who made an appointment to see me to better understand a perfectionistic tendency that had been diagnosed as OCD in college when she was very anxious about preserving her 4.0 GPA. Still very focused on maximizing her performance over two decades later, she wanted to explore what may, and may not, be OCD in her professional drive. In particular, she wondered whether her "OCD" may have actually helped her reach the upper echelons of her corporation, and, if so, is it really a "disorder"? Martha explained how her bosses could always trust that no i's would be left undotted or t's uncrossed in any project she oversaw, so they diverted high-stakes jobs to her and rewarded her handsomely for her perfect execution, including with successive promotions. "Why is that so bad?" she wondered.

It may have been partially driven by anxiety, but her "obsessiveness" was undoubtedly part of Martha's success, and she had no regrets about it: "You want your CPA or your doctor to be a little OCD, don't you?" she joked. "Otherwise, you know things will fall through the cracks." Martha was making a good argument. Up to a certain point, OCD tendencies can be adaptive and are at the basis of the "evolutionary theory" of the illness, which posits that, if OCD exists in the population at all, it is because, in our ancient history, avoiding catching a virus, checking for lurking danger, and hoarding food for lean times were self-protective behaviors that conferred an advantage on the individual and species. Of course, when these behaviors become totally disinhibited, a serious and sometimes debilitating condition results, but "a little OCD," as she put it, where the degree doesn't rise to the level of a full-blown pathology that is negatively impacting one's functioning, may not be so bad.

Where Martha's perfectionism did seem to add up to a problem, however, was in how it transposed itself onto her sixteen-year-old son, Jordan, latching on to the teenager's life with the goal of guaranteeing his success the only way she could define success. In a sort of "OCD by proxy," Martha's anxiety focused on what she viewed as Jordan's lackadaisical approach to his grades, future, and career. Yet Jordan was far from most people's definition of a failure. A B-average student, he had close friends and a girlfriend, loved football and multiplayer video games, and did not smoke, drink, or do drugs. Middling grades were hardly acceptable in Martha's family of overachievers, however, and a girlfriend at sixteen was a major distraction. As for video games, nothing good has ever come out of them. Martha had "diagnosed" in her son what she called "Ambition Deficit Disorder"—"My version of ADD!" she said—that could complicate admission into a good college and appropriate "launching," leading to a B-average life and, God forbid, no chance at a senior-level job such as the one she and her husband occupied.

To "rescue" Jordan's CV, Martha enlisted her husband to convince him to take on new activities that her executive coach and the college admission counselor said could kickstart his "executive function" and make him a more competitive candidate for college. Those included volunteering to tutor middle school kids, serving on the school's homecoming parade committee, and helping run an after-school antivaping awareness event. Her plan came with a meticulous schedule grid to help her son with time management, complete with arrows, graphs, and color-coded tasks and subtasks.

Jordan had nothing against tutoring, or a good parade, and was certainly no fan of e-cigarettes, but none of these initiatives resonated. When it came to enjoyable extracurricular activities, he really just wanted to play video games! Still, he agreed, and applied himself to follow the yearlong executive function "curriculum." The results were decidedly mixed: although Jordan could now boast of "leadership experience" having tutored some students, done a decent job on the homecoming committee, and spent many a night designing antivaping banners that were well received, his grades suffered, decreasing from a B to B- average. Martha's detailed grid did not make an allowance for video games, Jordan's main passion, so gaming time had to come from somewhere else, and it came from Algebra II, American Literature, and US History.

Anxious to perfect her son's college application by incorporating what colleges are looking for, Martha inadvertently caused Jordan's grades to suffer, which may or may not have hurt his college admission chances, since some colleges seem to be giving more weight to leadership experience than grades. What seemed certain is that, in her narrow focus on giving him executive experience, Martha missed a true if unusual talent in her son. Jordan, you see, was not your run-of-the-mill teenage gamer. Without Martha really noticing it, he had competed in several online tournaments of his favorite game and performed well enough to earn some monetary rewards and get the attention of South Korea, the e-sports capital of the world. The kid whose mom diagnosed him with ADD for "Ambition Deficit Disorder" may not have looked like your prototypical leader but had international gaming sponsors reaching out to recruit him for his superlative scores commanding his favorite video game character! In his very unique niche, he showed plenty of ambition.

Martha wanted her son's college application personal statement to be perfect, and it took some work to convince her to use the limited space they had to highlight the e-sports experience that Jordan naturally excelled at over the e-cigarette leadership initiative that she forced him into. She ultimately agreed, and thanks to following a genuine passion that made him stand out for all the right reasons, Jordan would get into a very good university.

Jordan may not have had the leadership instincts of his mother, but he was far from devoid of unique, superior talents that deserve to be supported and that can bring him happiness and success. Parents should look for, and promote, all the talent they see in their kids, not just an executive seedling that may or may not be there, and they should avoid tying their children's self-esteem to whether they develop leadership experience or become leaders, unless they want to contribute to a therapy fund in parallel with the 529 college savings plan. There is nothing automatically perfect about leading and nothing automatically imperfect about following other passions or simply being a follower. The leadership obsession driving parents, students, the educational system, and the entirety of culture is meant, on the surface of it, to stoke ambition, but it comes with considerable side effects. For one, it immunizes people, very early on, against the fundamental truth that not everyone can be a leader, and opens them up, very early on, to the misleading message that all that counts is rising to a leadership position. For, as leadership has been glorified, the concept of "follower" has taken on negative connotations and now can be seen as shorthand for someone who is easy to control or who is not an independent thinker. In a sense, it's a zero-sum game. The more we idolize leading, the more we look down our noses on followers. All this ensures "business" for the leadership industry for generations to come. Not to mention for therapists treating people's inferiority complexes: years later, the former kindergarten and college students will still carry this notion in them, which can make them easier prey to the leadership training I described in Part One of the book, and to feeling inadequate or like a lesser human being if they fail. It can also encourage the unhealthy traits required when one is desperately trying to rise and needs to somehow eclipse the crowded competition. Those that are better at manipulation and at pushing others out of the way will be emboldened. Rather than stoking followers' ambitions, then, the ultimate effect may be to make people more psychologically vulnerable and to encourage unflattering personality traits in some of them.

Being weaned on this idea of leadership can also put off potentially good leaders as an environment is created where the better leader is not necessarily the one with a leg up. To avoid this destiny, the message to all, starting as early as possible, should be that it's OK to be a leader, but it's also OK not to be one. You are a worthwhile contributor to society either way, and there are many roads to happiness, success, self-respect, and respect by others that don't go through a leadership station. Leaders have no monopoly on those. Being a leader does not—should not—automatically imply someone who has it made, and being a follower does not—should not—automatically imply someone who would rather be leading. Followers should have nothing to explain if they are "just" followers, and leaders should be constantly "earning" their leadership title. Followers should listen to their natural inclinations: try your hand at a leadership role if it seems to complete you and to complement who you are, otherwise eschew it with no regret and no looking back. Know thyself and don't lead if it means transforming into someone you don't recognize, for you might rue the day and want to reverse course. Leadership trappings, though, can be a trap, and it is sometimes harder to change course and go from leader to follower than it is to go from follower to leader. So, give up the follower role and walk into the leadership one with awareness, conviction, and eyes wide open, for you may not be able to walk back even if you really wanted to.

When I started working with Nick, a thirty-nine-year-old engineer and immigrant from India who had a new wife and young son, he was struggling at his job as CEO of an AI startup. After completing his PhD at a California university, Nick spent ten years as an engineer then chief engineer at a data analytics firm, an eternity to spend with one company in his fast-moving field. "I was what you might call a techno-nerd," he explained. "I started out at the company coding on multiple screens all day, then advanced to supervising people who were coding on multiple screens all day." Nick's big break came when, through a high school friend he knew from India, he discovered that he could outsource much of the work they were doing to Bangalore and figured out the logistics for doing it. The huge savings that came with this move and the original thinking he displayed around it got Nick noticed as somebody who might have leadership instincts, so opportunities started coming. He batted them away, initially. Nick was enjoying the familiarity and flexibility of his new-old job. It let him focus on his newborn and on a remodeling project that he and his wife had started and that was dragging on. He was also well paid, so there was no huge financial incentive. At some point, though, Nick started feeling like something was wrong with him for not wanting to rise further. "Should I not be seeking new challenges?" he wondered. "Am I letting my CV go stale? Did I have no aspirations? Why am I the only member of the original engineering team still with the company?" These questions churned, unanswered, in his brain, until an AI startup came knocking on his door with a CEO position offer, to which Nick answered, "Why not?"

AI researchers had become such a hot commodity—with some commanding salaries as high as a million dollars barely a couple of years postgraduation—that the only way for AI startups to make it seemed to be to outsource their coding. Given Nick's experience doing this, he became a hot target for all sorts of aggressive recruitment. "It was an offer I couldn't refuse," he said, hinting at the incentives package. And so began a CEO journey that lasted three years. As was his mandate, Nick successfully outsourced most of his company's engineering needs, to the delight of the company board and large company investors. Meanwhile, the relatively contained house remodel turned into a sprawling total home upgrade and an extension—vertically and into the backyard—to accommodate the grander entertaining of investors, recruits, and other executives that he felt he had to do as CEO. He also purchased a nearby cottage for when his parents visited and made an offer on a small vacation home in the wine country. Besides real estate, new, expensive habits quickly anchored themselves in the family as a function of the new company they were keeping. He took up golfing, for example, and the family started taking skiing trips. He had a wine cellar installed in his basement and began collecting wine. He got his son wait-listed at the most exclusive local school. There was much to discover, and like, about this new lifestyle, and, for a while, this "CEO thing" didn't seem bad at all. "What took me so long?" he wondered.

Then things took an unpredictable turn. An American political war broke out that the immigrant engineer was swept up in, totally unawares. We are talking about the newly hot-button issue of offshoring high tech. Was Nick responsible for the loss of local jobs in his community? Was his company in violation of intellectual property laws? Was he compromising the US lead on AI by sharing tech "secrets"? Was he endangering national security? The fact that he was Indian-born and that the company was sending jobs to India made it even more uncomfortable as some of the accusations questioned his very allegiance.

"You'd think I singlehandedly killed off manufacturing in the Rust Belt by outsourcing the grand old industries of the Midwest!" he said of the blowback he felt. Talk about VUCA! And no speech writer could translate his state of mind, no company executive coach could help him figure out a way out of this pickle, and no therapist could help calm his anxiety down.

When asked at the height of his career why he did not engage in politics, Michael Jordan responded: "Republicans buy sneakers, too."[31] For a long time, corporate leaders could similarly keep their politics to themselves and chart a company course that was essentially apolitical. Today, with a more politically vocal workforce, and with an online audience eager to scrutinize companies' political leanings, corporate silence on politics becomes a political choice in and of itself—and a losing one. Add to the CEO's must-have skills, then, the ability to navigate turbulent, no-win political currents, taking stances that appeal to some stakeholders, and that, by definition, alienate others. For Nick, this was more than he had bargained for. The engineer who wore his politics close to his chest was comfortable talking machine learning, not the consequences on congressional balance of the forces of globalization. Knowing that this storm would not be subsiding anytime soon, Nick wished he could walk back on his career decision to accept an executive post. Could he return to "just" being a coder making "only" an engineer's salary? Maybe work as an AI consultant? In his low moments, imagining any of these scenarios brought some measure of peace, but, in a way, his life had moved past him and there could be no redo. His parents had gotten used to staying in their own place when they visited. There were Alpine vacations already on the calendar and Grand Crus he had developed a taste for. His wife had become increasingly reliant on assistants. His son had just gotten accepted at the fancy private school he was wait-listed at. Rather than things he and his family were genuinely enjoying, though, these luxuries felt more like a status prison.

But before anything else, there was the notion that a "demotion" from leader to anything resembling a follower would cause people to lose respect for him and maybe cause him to lose respect for himself. For if we are making followers feel like failures when they don't rise, leaders feel it even more when they fall. As he put it, "I didn't set out to be rich. I didn't care to leave a big impact. I wasn't desperate to make the world a better place. I felt bypassed by events and by the time I tried to get my simpler life back, it was too late." This perhaps "natural follower" now felt like he had no option but to always be a leader. Despite therapy aimed to help him realign with his values, Nick would eventually resign his post for another politically dicey executive position; one that, given his personality, seemed to come with red flags all over it. The simpler pleasures of his life as "techno-nerd" seemed permanently out of reach, and, sooner or later, he seemed destined to a $100,000 antiburnout intervention and an abdominal scan.

In some ways, that would be an easier way out. You may be able to teach leaders some yoga positions at a wellness retreat or image them and check lab results at a J&J program, but you cannot reliably teach them how to become political animals. Similarly, the top-ten qualities that, according to *Forbes*, make a great leader defy teaching. No, you cannot teach "discernment," "integrity," "vision," "strong charisma," "altruism," "ambition," and "formidability," and you can barely teach "effective communication," "eloquence," and "teamwork." The push to sell leadership as something whose qualities can be purchased and learned, the desire by followers to buy it and buy into it, the obstinacy of leaders never to relinquish it—all defy logic. This is especially true in an age where many of the ingredients for successful leadership are missing. What we are left with is a large class of burned-out leaders being propped up by coaches, speech writers, a leadership industry, and an offshoot wellness industry—and an even larger class of frustrated would-be leaders who feel they were robbed of their "right" to lead.

And their cure—the culture's cure—is something beyond what J&J can offer. It is a total and urgent rethinking of leadership. We live in an era of end-stage leadership, that is, the terminal stage of leadership—its last gasps. "Zero leadership," used, rather positively, to describe the laissez-faire leadership style defined by Kurt Lewin in the 1930s, might serve as another good, if negative, descriptor for our current state, not so much for the hands-off approach of many of our leaders as for their bankruptcy. The "businessification" of leadership, combined with the moment's unique cultural and technological forces, have helped usher in an era of inside-out, upside-down, disrupt-for-the-sake-of-disrupting leadership, where the dominant arrival and survival skill required of leaders seems to be out-of-bounds narcissism. We need to question the conveyor belt system manufacturing leaders today and suggest a different way forward. Current leadership culture is untenable, but giving up on leaders to go leaderless is an invitation for chaos. We humans need real leaders to guide us. This need for leaders, as old as our DNA, is not going away, even when all around us points to crises in leadership. A rigorous exercise of cultural reflection and some serious soul-searching are therefore required if we do not want this end-stage to be prolonged indefinitely. Too much is at stake for us to allow this, for us not to all display some collective leadership behavior and take courageous steps to lift society and rescue civilization. Besides the steps discussed in the previous chapter, the whole cultural narrative must change to be in sync with an inescapable reality: the world also needs followers. There is a moral imperative to end the hypocrisy and start respecting people who can be good at something other than a leadership position, and it plays out on several critical front lines, including parenting, education, and professional life. Rather than an unproven detox or spending billions on HR-required leadership training and executive coaching, we need to start celebrating human productivity in all its forms and at all its levels, starting with the followers, without whom no successful leader has ever been possible. Support them, invest in them, and respect them for their intrinsic value, not their "leadership potential." Parents should support all the talent they find in their kids, not just their executive capabilities. Schools should go back to obsessing about building students' character and forming responsible citizens, not the "next generation of leaders." College admissions committees should stop poring over applicants' statements for evidence of leadership behavior and go back to figuring out who is the most likely to learn, discover, and grow over the course of a college education.

Above all, we need to urgently bring back psychology. Before it was a business, before it was a science, leadership was about psychology. Yet as a culture we have deluded ourselves into believing that leadership is a discipline that can be broken into digestible lessons, then transmitted and replicated. The person's unique personality and psychological profile are perplexingly minimized in assessing fitness to lead, the drive to rise, how leaders rise, and how they lead once they have risen. Yet it is impossible to understand leaders and leadership other than through the lens of psychology.

And said psychology is difficult to fashion. The same applies to personality, which is sticky, not malleable, and can viciously resist attempts at manipulating it into something it is not. There is a futility to trying to instill a wish list of leadership traits into a gullible or coerced audience. The natural end result of this type of "forced" leadership is end-stage leadership, where an over-abundance of fakers—people who pretend to have the necessary building blocks when what they really have is an ability to deceive, clothed in abundant charm and undeniable smarts—rule in leadership roles. To that end, the data suggesting that the rate of psychopathy among leaders may be higher than in the general population should give us pause.[32]

Instead of the kind of leadership training I've described in this book—the kind that assumes that individuals of all personalities can essentially be diamond-in-the-rough leaders waiting for the right training course—let's encourage people to take advantage of the kind of reflection and soul-searching that helps them understand what they are truly good at, what they really like to do, what they are willing to sacrifice to become leaders, and how they want to be remembered. This is what counseling was invented for, and this is why a therapist is almost always a better destination than an executive coach or a management rehab camp for someone contemplating leadership or struggling under its weight.

It is so basic as not to require stating, but it does: not everyone can be a leader. So be happy with who you are and what you are able to accomplish given your psychology, temperament, interests, strengths, limitations, and the unique circumstances of your life and the time you were born in. Not being a leader does not doom you, and being one does not save you. Whether you are a leader or not, don't tie your life's meaning to leading. Life is too complicated, layered, and interesting to limit yourself that way. Plenty of other arenas for success and failure exist that are worthier of our anxiety, doggedness, and obsessing. Do what you are naturally inclined to do, extracting as much happiness doing it as you can and producing as much good along the way as you are capable of. Hard as it may be, ignore the deafening cultural message imploring you to rise at all costs, as well as the accompanying marketing message trying to sell you a rosy path to leadership. And, all other things being equal, if you are ever faced with a choice between a Rainbow Children Day Care and a Future S.T.E.A.M Leaders Academic Child Care for your little one, go for Rainbow Children Day Care. Not feeding the cult of leadership has become a necessity, and it starts with little decisions like that.

And for those who—through psychology, skills, or a little lucky star—do make it to the top: stay true to yourselves. Don't be forced into a mold that doesn't suit you or blindly adopt formulas that are sold as guarantors of success. The oversimplification implied in the latter should offend your intelligence, and the repression that comes with the former might cause you to explode. Lead with personality—yours. Be a leader because you have what it takes and happened to fall into propitious circumstances that allowed your leadership talent to blossom, not because you compromised basic values, reinvented yourself chameleon-style to meet the moment's checklist, took a gazillion courses, always felt "destined" to lead, or won the Narcissism Olympics. On that last point, lead to help others, not to ensconce yourself.

Good leaders today must swim against daunting cultural currents. The headwinds are strong. The followers are restive. The hierarchies are unstable. For good reason, we should be suspicious of the motives, recipes, limitations, and very possibility of leadership today. But if true leaders manage to emerge, they will be all the more celebrated, for what they will have had to face will have been unique in history. And this might be the silver lining: somebody lucky enough to possess the right mix of trait and opportunity, who makes it to the top with intact values and a well-meaning drive, and who leads to serve rather than fulfill a God-given right, is sure to be remembered among the greats.

ACKNOWLEDGMENTS

I WISH TO thank Rachel Sussman for first seeing the "there" there in this project; Howard Yoon for his patient and expert support as I processed ambivalence and opportunity cost; and John Mahaney for a master class in erudite and cultivated editing. I am also grateful for my patients; they teach me something new every day.

NOTES

PROLOGUE

1.   Mike Prokopeak, "Follow the Leader(ship) Spending," Chief Learning Officer, March 21, 2018, https://www.chieflearningofficer.com/2018/03/21/follow-the -leadership-spending; "The Leadership Training Market," Training Industry, November 20, 2020, https://trainingindustry.com/wiki/leadership/the-leadership-training -market.

2.   Katanga Johnson, "Sam Bankman-Fried's Bahamas Jail Is Nothing Like His $30 Million Penthouse," *Fortune*, December 21, 2022, https://fortune.com/2022/12 /21/sam-bankman-fried-bahamas-jail-ftx-extradition.

3.   Stephanie Saul, "At N.Y.U., Students Were Failing Organic Chemistry. Who Was to Blame?," *New York Times*, October 3, 2022, https://www.nytimes .com/2022/10/03/us/nyu-organic-chemistry-petition.html; Danielle Ofri, "Why Are Nonprofit Hospitals So Highly Profitable?," *New York Times*, February 20, 2020, https:// www.nytimes.com/2020/02/20/opinion/nonprofit-hospitals.html.

4.   Stephanie Saul, "Stanford President Will Resign After Report Found Flaws in His Research," *New York Times*, July 19, 2023, https://www.nytimes.com/2023/07/19 /us/stanford-president-resigns-tessier-lavigne.html.

CHAPTER 1: HOW AN INDUSTRIAL COMPLEX FUELS AN INFERIORITY COMPLEX

1.   Alyssa Pereira, "California Tesla Driver Appears to Be Asleep at the Wheel as Car Goes 75 MPH on Freeway," *San Francisco Chronicle*, March 7, 2019, https://www .sfchronicle.com/technology/article/tesla-autopilot-sleeping-driver-video-illegal -13670993.php.

2.   KPIX5, "Dead-End SF Street Plagued with Confused Waymo Cars Trying to Turn Around 'Every 5 Minutes,'" CBS News, October 14, 2021, https://www .cbsnews.com/sanfrancisco/news/dead-end-sf-street-plagued-with-confused-way mo-cars-trying-to-turn-around-every-5-minutes.

3.   Jason Dearen, "Buses for Google, Facebook Employees Cause Traffic Problems in San Francisco," CTV News, January 7, 2014, https://www.ctvnews.ca/world

/buses-for-google-facebook-employees-cause-traffic-problems-in-san-francisco-1
.1628252.

4. Rachel Sandler, "San Francisco Threatens to Punish the Controversial Scooter Startups for Their Riders' Bad Behavior," *Business Insider*, April 16, 2018, https://www.businessinsider.com/san-francisco-cease-desist-bird-lime-spin-electric -scooter-startups-2018-4.

5. Megan Rose Dickey, "Former Uber Software Engineer Alleges Sexism from Female Manager," https://techcrunch.com/2017/03/03/former-uber-software -engineer-alleges-sexism-from-female-manager; Keala Denea, "Sexism at Uber from Female Management," *Medium*, March 3, 2017, https://medium.com/@kealadenea /sexism-at-uber-from-female-management-uberstory-238874075bbb#.hwx1ihj9y.

6. Megan Rose Dickey et al., "Uber's SVP Amit Singhal Leaves Company Because He Didn't Disclose a Sexual Harassment Allegation at Google," *TechCrunch*, February 27, 2017, https://techcrunch.com/2017/02/27/ubers-svp-amit-singhal-leaves -company-because-he-didnt-disclose-a-sexual-harassment-allegation.

7. Mike Isaac, "How Uber Deceives the Authorities Worldwide," *New York Times*, March 3, 2017, https://www.nytimes.com/2017/03/03/technology/uber-greyball -program-evade-authorities.html.

8. "Uber CEO Caught on Video Berating Company Driver," *Wall Street Journal*, March 1, 2017, https://www.wsj.com/video/uber-ceo-caught-on-video-berating -company-driver/E909CB38-2594-4308-A637-2661CBE58038.html.

9. Travis Kalanick, "A Profound Apology," *Uber*, March 1, 2017, https://www .uber.com/newsroom/a-profound-apology.

10. Pierre Gurdjian et al., "Why Leadership Development Programs Fail," McKinsey & Company, January 1, 2014, https://www.mckinsey.com/featured-insights /leadership/why-leadership-development-programs-fail.

11. Harvard Business School, "Comprehensive Leadership Programs," Executive Education, https://www.exed.hbs.edu/comprehensive-leadership-programs.

12. Harvard Business School, "Admission Requirements," Executive Education, https://www.exed.hbs.edu/admissions/requirements.

13. Harvard Business School, "Admission Requirements."

14. "Harvard Requirements for Admission," Prep Scholar, https://www.prepscholar .com/sat/s/colleges/Harvard-admission-requirements.

15. Alexandra A. Chaidez and Samuel W. Zwickel, "Meet the Class of 2022," *Harvard Crimson*, https://features.thecrimson.com/2018/freshman-survey/makeup-narrative.

16. Harvard Business School, "Comprehensive Leadership Programs."

17. Harvard Business School, "Program for Leadership Development: Accelerating the Careers of High-Potential Leaders," Executive Education, https://www.exed .hbs.edu/leadership-development; Harvard Business School, "Program for Leadership Development Module 5: Earning HBS Alumni Status," https://www.exed.hbs.edu /leadership-development-module-5.

18. The Wharton School, University of Pennsylvania, "History of Wharton," https://www.wharton.upenn.edu/history; "University of Pennsylvania (Wharton)," *US News and World Report*, https://www.usnews.com/best-graduate-schools/top-business -schools/university-of-pennsylvania-01194.

19. The Wharton School, University of Pennsylvania, "Global C-Suite Program," https://executiveeducation.wharton.upenn.edu/online-learning/self-paced-online -programs/global-cxo-program.

20. "The Ten Most Popular Leadership Courses of 2022," Find Courses, December 8, 2022, https://www.findcourses.com/prof-dev/top-10/top-10-leadership -courses-18399.

21. "Ten Most Popular Leadership Courses of 2022," Find Courses; "Great Leaders Are Great Speakers," Speak by Design University, https://www.speakbydesign .com/speak-by-design-university.

22. "Ten Most Popular Leadership Courses of 2022," Find Courses.

23. Northwestern Kellogg, "The Strategy of Leadership," https://www.kellogg .northwestern.edu/executive-education/take-action/request-brochure-form/thank -you.aspx.

24. PBS NewsHour, "Inside Garrison Keillor's Fabled World of 'A Prairie Home Companion,'" July 26, 2014, https://www.pbs.org/newshour/show/40-years -counting-inside-garrison-keillors-fabled-world-prairie-home-companion.

25. Sara Bobolz, "Yep, Martin Shkreli's 5,000 Percent Drug Price Hike Is Still in Effect," *Huffington Post*, March 9, 2018, https://www.huffpost.com/entry /martin-shkreli-aids-drug-price-the-same_n_5aa3117fe4b07047bec694cb; Adam Klasfeld, "'Pharma Bro' Martin Shkreli Gets a Slap on the Wrist for Using Contraband Phone to Discuss Pharma Business Behind Bars," Law and Crime, June 1, 2021, https:// lawandcrime.com/high-profile/pharma-bro-martin-shkreli-gets-a-slap-on-the -wrist-for-using-contraband-phone-to-discuss-pharma-business-behind-bars.

26. Michael Kaplan, "The Shocking and Rude Ways WeWork's ex-CEO Adam Neumann Treated Staff," *New York Post*, July 17, 2021, https://nypost.com/2021/07/17 /the-shocking-ways-weworks-ex-ceo-adam-neumann-treated-staff.

27. Martha Ross, "Elizabeth Holmes' Voice: 'The Dropout' Devotes an Entire Episode to Her 'Odd' Baritone," *Mercury News*, February 9, 2022, https://www .mercurynews.com/2022/02/09/elizabeth-holmes-voice-the-dropout-devotes-an -entire-episode-to-her-odd-baritone.

28. Scottie Andrew, "The US Has 4% of the World's Population but 25% of Its Coronavirus Cases," CNN, June 30, 2020, https://www.cnn.com/2020/06/30/health /us-coronavirus-toll-in-numbers-june-trnd/index.html.

29. "Lil' Leaders Childcare," Yelp, https://www.yelp.com/biz/lil-leaders-childcare -san-mateo; "Emily Luchetti: Chief Pastry Officer," Waterbar, https://www.waterbarsf .com/emily-luchetti.

30. "Leadership Express Series," Blue Point Leadership, https://store.blr.com /complete-les-series-participant-pack.

31. Luke Gilfillan, "41 Leadership Tips for Teenagers," 2021, https://www.amazon .com/41-Leadership-Tips-Teenagers-Ultimate/dp/B08RZ7FHVF#:~:text=In%20 %2241%20Leadership%20Tips%20for,from%20every%20corner%20of%20humanity.

32. Ben Jacobs, "Did George Santos Lie About Everything?," *Vox*, February 24, 2023, https://www.Vox.com/policy-and-politics/23520848/george-santos-fake-resume; Grace Ashford and Michael Gold, "Santos Charged," *New York Times*, May 10, 2023, https://www.nytimes.com/live/2023/05/10/nyregion/george-santos-charges-news; Lazaro Gamio, Josh Williams, Ashley Wu, and Molly Cook Escobar, "How Every Member Voted on the Expulsion of George Santos from Congress," *New York Times,* December 1, 2023, https://www.nytimes.com/interactive/2023/12/01/us/politics/santos -expulsion-vote-tracker.html.

33. The Wharton School, University of Pennsylvania, "Chief Receptionist Officer? Title Inflation Hits the C-Suite," *Knowledge at Wharton* (podcast), May 30, 2007,

https://knowledge.wharton.upenn.edu/article/chief-receptionist-officer-title-inflation-hits-the-c-suite.

34. The Wharton School, "Chief Receptionist Officer?"

35. Sita Slavov, "How to Fix College Grade Inflation," *US News and World Report*, December 26, 2013, https://www.usnews.com/opinion/blogs/economic-intelligence/2013/12/26/why-college-grade-inflation-is-a-real-problem-and-how-to-fix-it.

36. Stewart Rojstaczer and Christopher Healy, "Where A Is Ordinary: The Evolution of American College and University Grading, 1940–2009," Teachers' College Record (2012), https://www.tcrecord.org/content.asp?contentid=16473.

37. "Why Have College Completion Rates Increased? An Analysis of Rising Grades," NBER Working Paper Series, https://www.nber.org/system/files/working_papers/w28710/w28710.pdf.

38. Derek Newton, "Grade Inflation Is Real," *Forbes*, September 28, 2021, https://www.forbes.com/sites/dereknewton/2021/09/28/grade-inflation-is-real/?sh=6ab2747ae46a.

39. Matthew Q. Clarida and Nicholas P. Fandos, "Substantiating Fears of Grade Inflation, Dean Says Median Grade at Harvard College Is A–, Most Common Grade Is A," *Harvard Crimson*, December 3, 2013, https://www.thecrimson.com/article/2013/12/3/grade-inflation-mode-a.

40. WBUR, "Harvard Professor Gives Two Sets of Marks to Combat Grade Inflation," *Here and Now* (radio), December 4, 2013, https://www.wbur.org/hereandnow/2013/12/04/harvard-grade-inflation.

41. Vicky Ge Huang et al., "FTX Tapped into Customer Accounts to Fund Risky Bets, Setting Up Its Downfall," *Wall Street Journal*, November 11, 2022, https://www.wsj.com/amp/articles/ftx-tapped-into-customer-accounts-to-fund-risky-bets-setting-up-its-downfall-11668093732; David Yaffe-Bellany et al., "Prosecutors Say FTX Was Engaged in a 'Massive, Yearslong Fraud,'" *New York Times*, December 13, 2022, https://www.nytimes.com/2022/12/13/business/ftx-sam-bankman-fried-fraud-charges.html.

42. Gideon Lewis-Kraus, "Sam Bankman-Fried, Effective Altruism, and the Question of Complicity," *New Yorker*, December 1, 2022, https://www.newyorker.com/news/annals-of-inquiry/sam-bankman-fried-effective-altruism-and-the-question-of-complicity.

43. Tony Romm, "Congress Took Millions from FTX. Now Lawmakers Face a Crypto Reckoning," *Washington Post*, November 17, 2022, https://www.washingtonpost.com/us-policy/2022/11/17/congress-crypto-ftx-regulations-law.

44. Stefania Palma et al., "Sam Bankman-Fried's Fall Cuts Off Big Source of Funds for US Democrats," *Financial Times*, November 13, 2022, https://www.ft.com/content/428c7800-c72d-4c59-9940-4376fea6e263.

45. Ben Schreckinger, "Bitcoin Crashes the Midterms," *Politico*, January 16, 2022, https://www.politico.com/news/2022/01/16/bitcoin-crashes-the-midterms-527126.

46. Romm, "Congress Took Millions from FTX."

47. Renae Merle, "A Guide to the Financial Crisis—10 Years Later," *Washington Post*, September 10, 2018, https://www.washingtonpost.com/business/economy/a-guide-to-the-financial-crisis--10-years-later/2018/09/10/114b76ba-af10-11e8-a20b-5f4f84429666_story.html.

48. Daniel Roberts, "5 Lessons from the Stunning Implosion of SBF and FTX," Yahoo! Finance, https://finance.yahoo.com/news/5-lessons-stunning-implosion-sbf-212433718.html.

CHAPTER 2: BRING ME YOUR TOXIC LEADERS AND FAST-TRACKERS

1. Colin Baker, "Are Leaders Born or Made?," *Leaders*, September 7, 2022, https://leaders.com/articles/leadership/are-leaders-born-or-made.

2. "Vince Lombardi's Story," Official Website of Vince Lombardi, 2023, https://www.vincelombardi.com/about.html.

3. Jeffrey E. Auerbach, "The Increasing Demand for Executive Coaching," Chief Learning Officer, June 1, 2022, https://www.executivecoachcollege.com/research-and-publications/increasing-demand-for-executive-coaching.php.

4. Mikaela Kiner, "Why Every HR Leader Needs a Coach," *Forbes*, August 1, 2019, https://www.forbes.com/sites/forbeshumanresourcescouncil/2019/08/01/why-every-hr-leader-needs-a-coach/?sh=2612d6ea6887.

5. "Higher Education," FranklinCovey, https://www.franklincovey.com/solutions/education/higher-education.

6. "All Things Coaching," International Coaching Federation, 2023, https://coachingfederation.org/about. See "What Is Coaching?" on this site.

7. Elias Aboujaoude, "Where Life Coaching Ends and Therapy Begins: Toward a Less Confusing Treatment Landscape," *Perspectives in Psychological Sciences* 15, no. 4 (July 2020): 973–977, https://doi.org/10.1177/1745691620904962.

8. Darren Perucci, "6 Methods to Improve Management Coaching—HR Experts Weigh In," BambooHR, September 21, 2018, https://www.bamboohr.com/blog/improve-management-coaching-hr-experts-weigh-in.

9. Alexandra Levit, "Retention Coaching," Association for Talent Development, September 4, 2012, https://www.td.org/insights/retention-coaching.

10. Arthur Schnitzler, *La Ronde*, trans. Eric Bentley (New York: Samuel French, 2014).

11. "ACC vs. PCC vs. MCC: Understanding ICF Accreditation Levels," Institute for Coaching Studies, https://coachingstudies.org/resources/articles/icf-accreditation-levels.

12. Robert Taibbi, "There Are 5 Types of Relationships. Which One Is Yours?," *Psychology Today*, May 4, 2019, https://www.psychologytoday.com/za/blog/fixing-families/201905/there-are-5-types-relationships-which-one-is-yours.

13. Elias Aboujaoude, "Life Coaching Is Unregulated and Growing Rapidly. Should It Be Reined In?," *Psyche*, September 2, 2020, https://psyche.co/ideas/life-coaching-is-unregulated-and-growing-rapidly-should-it-be-reined-in.

14. "Person-Centered Therapy," *Psychology Today*, July 1, 2022, https://www.psychologytoday.com/us/therapy-types/person-centered-therapy.

15. Nathan Thoma et al., "Contemporary Cognitive Behavior Therapy: A Review of Theory, History, and Evidence," *Psychodynamic Psychiatry* 43, no. 3 (September 2015): 423–461, https://doi.org/10.1521/pdps.2015.43.3.423.

16. Shi Min Lim et al., "Chatbot-Delivered Psychotherapy for Adults with Depressive and Anxiety Symptoms: A Systematic Review and Meta-Regression," *Behavior Therapy* 53, no. 2 (March 2022): 334–347, https://doi.org/10.1016/j.beth.2021.09.007.

17. Suzy Green et al., "Cognitive-Behavioral, Solution-Focused Life Coaching: Enhancing Goal Striving, Well-Being, and Hope," *Journal of Positive Psychology* 1, no. 3 (February 2007): 142–149, https://doi.org/10.1080/17439760600619849; Gordon B. Spence et al., "The Integration of Mindfulness Training and Health Coaching: An Exploratory Study," *Coaching: An International Journal of Theory, Research and Practice* 1, no. 2 (November 2008): 145–163, https://doi.org/10.1080/17521880802328178.

18. Gardiner Morse, "Executive Psychopaths," *Harvard Business Review*, October 2004, https://hbr.org/2004/10/executive-psychopaths.

19. Jack McCullough, "The Psychopathic CEO," *Forbes*, December 9, 2019, https://www.forbes.com/sites/jackmccullough/2019/12/09/the-psychopathic -ceo/?sh=d2f7175791e3.

20. Karen Landay et al., "Shall We Serve the Dark Lords? A Meta-Analytic Review of Psychopathy and Leadership," *Journal of Applied Psychology* 104, no. 1 (2019): 183–196, https://doi.org/10.1037/apl0000357.

21. Clive R. Boddy et al., "The Influence of Corporate Psychopaths on Corporate Social Responsibility and Organizational Commitment to Employees," *Journal of Business Ethics* 97, no. 1 (November 2010): 1–19.

22. "2023 Edelman Trust Barometer," Edelman, January 15, 2023, https://www .edelman.com/news-awards/2023-edelman-trust-barometer#:~:text=January%20 15%2C%202023%20%E2%80%94%20NEW%20YORK,30%20points%20ahead%20 on%20ethics.

23. Alex L. Rubenstein et al., "Surveying the Forest: A Meta-Analysis, Moderator Investigation, and Future-Oriented Discussion of the Antecedents of Voluntary Employee Turnover," *Personnel Psychology* 71, no. 1 (February 2017), https://doi .org/10.1111/peps.12226.

24. Joachim Klement, "Employees Quit Bosses, Not Jobs," Klement on Investing, November 3, 2022, https://klementoninvesting.substack.com/p/employees-quit -bosses-not-jobs.

25. Hervey M. Cleckley, *Mask of Sanity: An Attempt to Clarify Some Issues About the So-Called Psychopathic Personality*, 5th ed. (Augusta, GA: Emily S. Cleckley, 1988), 338–339.

26. Cleckley, *Mask of Sanity*, 173–174.

27. American Psychiatric Association, *Diagnostic and Statistical Manual of Mental Disorders*, 5th ed. (Washington, DC: American Psychiatric Publishing, 2013).

28. Bo Bach and Michael B. First, "Application of the ICD-11 Classification of Personality Disorders," *BMC Psychiatry* 18 (October 2018): 351, https://doi.org/10.1186 /s12888-018-1908-3.

29. Mirel Zaman, "Why Will Men Do Literally Anything to Avoid Going to Therapy?," Refinery29, May 21, 2021, https://www.refinery29.com/en-us /2021/05/10442178/why-do-men-avoid-therapy-memes.

30. Hettie O'Brien, "Grin and Bear It: On the Rise and Rise of Neo-Stoicism," *The Baffler*, October 28, 2020, https://thebaffler.com/latest/grin-and-bear-it-obrien.

31. David Whitford, "The Strange Existence of Ram Charan," CNN Money, April 30, 2007, https://money.cnn.com/magazines/fortune/fortune_archive/2007/04 /30/8405482/index.htm.

32. Whitford, "Strange Existence."

33. Jeanne Meister, "Do You Have a Distraction Prevention Coach? Your HR Department Is About to Be Transformed," Brink News, October 24, 2021, https://www .brinknews.com/do-you-have-a-distraction-prevention-coach-your-hr-department -is-about-to-be-transformed.

CHAPTER 3: NATURE OR NURTURE

1. Leadership Express Series, Blue Point Leadership, https://bluepointleadership .com/leadership/express-series (site discontinued).

2. "List of 365 Fear Not Bible Verses," Believers Portal, March 6, 2018, https://believersportal.com/list-365-fear-not-bible-verses.

3. "How Much Do Instagram Ads Cost?," Thrive Agency, https://thriveagency.com/news/how-much-do-instagram-ads-cost.

4. Robert F. Bruner, "Repetition Is the First Principle of All Learning," University of Virginia Darden School Foundation, August 17, 2001, https://papers.ssrn.com/sol3/cf_dev/AbsByAuth.cfm?per_id=66030.

5. Larry Dressler, "Leaders, Use the OARRs Model to Start Your Next Meeting," LinkedIn, January 9, 2020, https://www.linkedin.com/pulse/leaders-use-oarrs-model-start-your-next-meeting-larry-dressler.

6. "Meet Our Team: Larry Dressler," 3rd Conversation, August 23, 2021, https://www.3rdconversation.org/post/meet-our-team-larry-dressler.

7. Rajiv Talreja, "Why Is It Important to Know the 4W 1H 1Y of Your Business?," LinkedIn, December 26, 2018, https://www.linkedin.com/pulse/why-important-know-4w-1h-1y-your-business-rajiv-talreja.

8. "Rajiv Talreja," *Entrepreneur India*, https://www.entrepreneur.com/en-in/author/rajeev-talreja.

9. "Our Mission," CORO Northern California, https://coronorcal.org/purpose/#history; Courtney Young-Law, "Leading Through Ambiguity," CORO Northern California, June 22, 2020, https://coronorcal.org/2020/06/22/leading-and-ambiguity.

10. Nnenna Ozobia, "Cultivate a More Balanced Perspective: Coro's FIAO Tool," CORO Northern California, April 8, 2020, https://coronorcal.org/2020/04/08/fiao.

11. "Credible Leaders Walk the Talk: An Updated Leadership Framework from MIT's Deborah Ancona," MIT Sloan School, April 20, 2019, https://exec.mit.edu/s/blog-post/credible-leaders-walk-the-talk-an-updated-leadership-framework-from-mit-s-debora-MC5CD6A6UEORAV5GYB6C5Y5FFZNY.

12. Leading Effectively Staff, "The Core Leadership Skills You Need in Every Role," Center for Creative Leadership, November 24, 2022, https://www.ccl.org/articles/leading-effectively-articles/fundamental-4-core-leadership-skills-for-every-career-stage.

13. "Developing Yourself as a Leader," Harvard Business School, https://www.exed.hbs.edu/Documents/developing-yourself-leader-virtual-brochure.pdf.

14. Young-Law, "Leading Through Ambiguity."

15. Louise Altman, "The 3 R's of Leadership—Reflection, Relationships and Resiliency," Intentional Communication Consultants, https://intentionalcommunication.com/the-3-rs-of-leadership-reflection-relationships-resiliency; Paul LaRue, "Rules, Relationship, and Respect—Balance the 3 R's of Leadership," Connection Culture Group, June 12, 2017, https://www.connectionculture.com/post/rules-relationship-respect-balance-3-rs-leadership; Ronald E. Riggio, "The Three 'R's' of Leadership," *Psychology Today*, October 29, 2017, https://www.psychologytoday.com/us/blog/cutting-edge-leadership/201710/the-three-rs-of-leadership; John Maxwell, "The 3 R's of Decision-Making," *John C. Maxwell* (blog), August 17, 2010, https://www.johnmaxwell.com/blog/the-3-rs-of-decision-making; Doug Dickerson, "The 3 R's of Service-Based Leadership," Leaders Beacon, 2012, https://www.leadersbeacon.com/the-3-rs-of-service-based-leadership.

16. Michael Gusenbauer, "Google Scholar to Overshadow Them All? Comparing the Sizes of 12 Academic Search Engines and Bibliographic Databases," *Scientometrics* 118 (January 2019): 177–214, https://doi.org/10.1007/s11192-018-2958-5.

17. "Learn. Engage. Accelerate. Disrupt: Transforming Business Leaders into Change Makers," Stanford Graduate School of Medicine, https://image.gsbcommu nications.stanford.edu/lib/fe5515707c630c75741c/m/2/b2af8172-cb80-4988-b0df -a67efc2263d2.pdf.

18. George Bradt, "The Fundamental Difference Between Leading and Managing: Influence Versus Direction," *Forbes*, November 24, 2015, https://www.forbes .com/sites/georgebradt/2015/11/24/the-fundamental-difference-between-leading -and-managing-influence-versus-direction; "Our Top 10 Clients Have Used Us Over 180 Times," PrimeGenesis, https://www.primegenesis.com/clients.

19. C. L. Langford, "George Bush's Struggle with the 'Vision Thing,'" in *The Rhetorical Presidency of George H. W. Bush*, ed. Martin J. Medhurst (College Station, TX: Texas A&M University Press, 2006), 19–36.

20. Pierre Gurdjian et al., "Why Leadership Development Programs Fail," McKinsey & Company, January 1, 2014, https://www.mckinsey.com/featured-insights /leadership/why-leadership-development-programs-fail.

21. Kristi Hedges, "If You Think Leadership Development Is a Waste of Time You May Be Right," *Forbes*, September 23, 2014, https://www.forbes.com/sites/work -in-progress/2014/09/23/if-you-think-leadership-development-is-a-waste-of-time -you-may-be-right/?sh=5189803c5bf4.

22. Miriam Solomon, "On 'Cookbook Medicine,' Cookbooks, and Gender," *OUPblog* (Oxford University Press blog), July 24, 2015, https://blog.oup.com/2015/07 /history-cookbook-medicine.

23. Daniel Patterson, "Do Recipes Make You a Better Cook?," *Food & Wine*, March 31, 2015, https://www.foodandwine.com/news/do-recipes-make-you-a-better- cook.

24. Sam Sifton, *The New York Times Cooking No-Recipe Recipes* (Berkeley, CA: Ten Speed Press, 2021).

25. Daniel Goleman, "What Makes a Leader?," *Harvard Business Review*, January 2004, https://hbr.org/2004/01/what-makes-a-leader.

26. Daniel Goleman and Richard E. Boyatzis, "Social Intelligence and the Biology of Leadership," *Harvard Business Review*, September 2008, https://hbr.org/2008/09 /social-intelligence-and-the-biology-of-leadership.

27. Rodrigo Perez Ortega, "'Breakthrough' Finding Shows How Modern Humans Grow More Brain Cells Than Neanderthals, *Science*, September 8, 2022, https://www .science.org/content/article/breakthrough-finding-shows-how-modern-humans -grow-more-brain-cells-neanderthals.

28. Temma Ehrenfeld, "Reflections on Mirror Neurons," *Psychological Science*, February 27, 2011, https://www.psychologicalscience.org/observer/reflections-on-mirror -neurons.

29. Goleman and Boyatzis, "Social Intelligence and the Biology of Leadership."

30. "How Is Southwest Different from Other Airlines?," Investopedia, September 10, 2021, https://www.investopedia.com/articles/investing/061015/how-south west-different-other-airlines.asp.

31. Kevin Freiberg and Jackie Freiberg, "20 Reasons Why Herb Kelleher Was One of the Most Beloved Leaders of Our Time," *Forbes*, January 4, 2019, https://www .forbes.com/sites/kevinandjackiefreiberg/2019/01/04/20-reasons-why-herb-kelleher -was-one-of-the-most-beloved-leaders-of-our-time/?sh=4aaf28f1b311.

32. Carmine Gallo, "Southwest Airlines Founder Herb Kelleher Was the Brand's Storyteller-In-Chief," *Forbes*, January 4, 2019, https://www.forbes.com/sites/carmine

gallo/2019/01/04/southwest-airlines-founder-herb-kelleher-was-the-brands-story
teller-in-chief/?sh=6f6aa481620b.

33. Zachary Crockett, "How Southwest Airlines Settled a Legal Dispute with
Arm Wrestling," Priceonomics, November 3, 2014, https://priceonomics.com/how
-southwest-airlines-settled-a-legal-dispute.

34. Justin H. Williams et al., "Imitation, Mirror Neurons and Autism," *Neuroscience and Biobehavioral Reviews* 25, no. 4 (June 2001): 287–295, https://doi.org/10.1016
/S0149-7634(01)00014-8.

35. Tomas Chamorro-Premuzic, "What Science Tells Us About Leadership Potential," *Harvard Business Review*, September 21, 2016, https://hbr.org/2016/09/what
-science-tells-us-about-leadership-potential.

36. Chamorro-Premuzic, "What Science Tells Us."

37. Chamorro-Premuzic, "What Science Tells Us."

38. Chamorro-Premuzic, "What Science Tells Us."

39. Karen Scholz, "Wolf Pack Leadership: Insights for Effectively Leading a
Team," Leadership Depot, https://leadershipdepot.com/wolf-pack-leadership-insights
-for-effectively-leading-a-team.

40. Connor Meyer et al., "Parasitic Infection Increases Risk-Taking in a Social,
Intermediate Host Carnivore," *Communications Biology* 5 (November 2022): 1180,
https://doi.org/10.1038/s42003-022-04122-0.

41. Emma Marris, "Parasite Gives Wolves What It Takes to Be Pack Leaders," *Nature*, November 24, 2022, https://www.nature.com/articles/d41586-022-03836-9.

42. "Navigating Workplace Conflict," Northwestern Kellogg, https://www.iedp
.com/programs/kel-navigating-workplace-conflict-dec-2019.

43. "High-Performance Negotiation Skills," Northwestern Kellogg, https://
www.kellogg.northwestern.edu/executive-education/individual-programs
/executive-programs/neg.aspx.

44. Drew Dudley, "Everyday Leadership," https://embed.ted.com/talks/drew
_dudley_everyday_leadership.

CHAPTER 4: INTROVERT OR SOCIAL ANIMAL

1. Peter Lattman, "The Origins of Justice Stewart's 'I Know It When I See It,'"
Wall Street Journal, September 27, 2007, https://www.wsj.com/articles/BL-LB-4558.

2. Wilford Robert Francis Browning, "A Dictionary of the Bible," Oxford Reference, 2010, https://www.oxfordreference.com/display/10.1093/acref/9780199543984
.001.0001/acref-9780199543984-e-373;jsessionid=89DCD563AB314000AFC386C382
AEDDB7?rskey=elxCS5&result=341.

3. Max Weber, *The Theory of Social and Economic Organization* (New York: Free
Press, 1924/1947), 328.

4. Linda Woodhead on "Charisma," *In Our Time* (radio), March 17, 2022, https://
www.bbc.co.uk/programmes/m0015b6r.

5. Joseph Roach, *It* (Ann Arbor, MI: University of Michigan Press, 2007).

6. Veracifier, "Democratic Presidential Debate," YouTube, January 5, 2008,
https://www.youtube.com/watch?v=K3DeCLPwxXI.

7. Laurence Rees, "His Dark Charisma," BBC News, November 12, 2012,
https://www.bbc.com/news/magazine-20237437; Steven J. Zipperstein, "Enlight-
enment All Around," *New York Times*, November 24, 2002, https://www.nytimes
.com/2002/11/24/books/enlightenment-all-around.html.

8. John Mattone, "Is Charisma a Learned Leadership Skill?," John Mattone Global (blog), January 25, 2018, https://johnmattone.com/blog/is-charisma-a-learned-leadership-skill.

9. Valerie Gauthier, "Charismatic Leadership," HEC Paris, https://www.coursera.org/lecture/leading-sense/1-2-charismatic-leadership-6VEu6.

10. Leading People and Teams Specialization, "Inspiring and Motivating Individuals," Coursera, https://www.coursera.org/learn/motivate-people-teams#syllabus.

11. Corey Robin, "The Professor and the Politician," *New Yorker,* November 12, 2020, https://www.newyorker.com/books/under-review/max-weber-the-professor-and-the-politician.

12. Kendra Cherry, "What Are the Big 5 Personality Traits?," Verywell Mind, October 19, 2022, https://www.verywellmind.com/the-big-five-personality-dimensions-2795422.

13. Carl Lindberg, "Kurt Lewin Leadership Styles," Leadership Ahoy, November 28, 2022, https://www.leadershipahoy.com/kurt-lewin-leadership-styles.

14. Carl Lindberg, "Criticism of the Lewin Leadership Styles: Why They Are Bad, and Why You Should Avoid Them," Leadership Ahoy, August 20, 2022, https://www.leadershipahoy.com/criticism-of-the-lewin-leadership-styles-why-they-are-bad-and-why-you-should-avoid-them.

15. Kendra Cherry, "How to Lead: 6 Leadership Styles and Frameworks," Verywell Mind, November 14, 2022, https://www.verywellmind.com/leadership-styles-2795312; Mind Tools Content Team, "Leadership Styles," Mind Tools, https://www.mindtools.com/a7m23wp/leadership-styles; Sander G. Tideman et al., "Sustainable Leadership: Towards a Workable Definition," *Journal of Corporate Citizenship* 49 (2013), https://www.researchgate.net/publication/263604448_Sustainable_Leadership_Towards_a_Workable_Definition; Charlene Li, "Four Simple Steps to Develop Your Disruptive Leadership Skills," LinkedIn, May 19, 2022, https://www.linkedin.com/pulse/four-simple-steps-develop-your-disruptive-leadership-skills-li; W. Chan Kim and Renee Mauborgne, "Tipping Point Leadership," *Harvard Business Review,* April 2003, https://hbr.org/2003/04/tipping-point-leadership.

16. Rosy Callejas, "The 3 Types of Leadership Styles in Business—Which One Is Right for You?," *360 Blog,* November 4, 2021, https://www.salesforce.com/blog/3-common-leadership-styles.

17. Kristen Barker, "Working Styles (Leadership Compass)," Study Collaboration, https://studycollaboration.com/practice/working-styles-leadership-compass; "Strengthening Solidarity, The Leadership Compass Activity," Study Collaboration, https://media.studycollaboration.com/pdfs/8-Leadership_Compass.pdf.

18. Deborah Ancona, "MasterClass: Leadership Coaching and the 4 Capabilities," Institute of Coaching, McLean, Affiliate of Harvard Medical School, https://instituteofcoaching.org/resources/masterclass-leadership-coaching-and-4-capabilities.

19. Grant W. Edmonds et al., "Personality Stability from Childhood to Midlife: Relating Teachers' Assessments in Elementary School to Observer- and Self-Ratings 40 Years Later," *Journal of Research in Personality* 47, no. 5 (October 1, 2013): 505–513, https://www.sciencedirect.com/science/article/abs/pii/S0092656613000792?via%3Dihub.

20. Stephen Soldz and George E. Vaillant, "The Big Five Personality Traits and the Life Course: A 45-Year Longitudinal Study," *Journal of Research in Personality* 33, no. 2 (June 1999): 208–232, https://doi.org/10.1006/jrpe.1999.2243.

21.   Ruth Deller, "63 Up: Long-Running Documentary Series Shows How Reality TV Should Be Done," The Conversation, June 6, 2019, https://theconversation.com/63-up-long-running-documentary-series-shows-how-reality-tv-should-be-done-118304.

22.   William Wordsworth, "My Heart Leaps Up," Poets, https://poets.org/poem/my-heart-leaps.

23.   Robert R. McCrae and Paul T. Costa Jr., *Emerging Lives, Enduring Dispositions: Personality in Adulthood* (Glenview, IL: Scott Foresman, 1984), 61.

24.   Paul T. Costa Jr. and Robert R. McCrae, "Personality Stability and Its Implications for Clinical Psychology," *Clinical Psychology Review* 6, no. 5 (1986): 407–423.

25.   "The Leader Within," Blue Point Leadership, https://bluepointleadership.com/workshop/the-leader-within.

26.   *Your Brain at Work*, (podcast), NeuroLeadership Institute, https://neuroleadership.com/your-brain-at-work/psychological-safety.

27.   Jennifer Senior, "Sorry, Your Time Is Not Up," *New York Magazine*, August 20, 2001, https://nymag.com/nymetro/health/features/5091.

28.   Sigmund Freud, *The Standard Edition of the Complete Psychological Works of Sigmund Freud*, trans. James Strachey, vol. 12 (London: Hogarth Press, 1913), 130.

29.   "Leadership Express Series," Blue Point Leadership, https://bluepointleadership.com/leadership/express-series (site discontinued); "Complete Leadership Express Series Participant Pack," blr store, https://store.blr.com/complete-les-series-participant-pack.

30.   Joe Carroll, "Bush Fails to Convince on Question of Cocaine Use," *Irish Times*, August 21, 1999, https://www.irishtimes.com/news/bush-fails-to-convince-on-question-of-cocaine-use-1.218905.

31.   David Smith, "George Bush Sr. Book Denies Jeb Was Family's First Pick for President," *The Guardian*, November 10, 2015, https://www.theguardian.com/us-news/2015/nov/10/george-bush-sr-book-denies-jeb-was-familys-first-pick-for-president.

32.   Reed Johnson, "Revenge: A Family Affair," *Los Angeles Times*, December 11, 2002, https://www.latimes.com/archives/la-xpm-2002-dec-11-et-johnson11-story.html.

33.   Caitlin Fitzsimmons, "Watch George Bush's Finest Gaffes," *The Guardian*, January 19, 2019, https://www.theguardian.com/media/pda/2009/jan/19/george-bush-gaffes.

34.   Jacob Weisberg, *George W. Bushisms: The Slate Book of the Accidental Wit and Wisdom of Our 43rd President* (New York: Fireside Books, 2001).

35.   John Kreiser, "Bush: 'The Decider-in-Chief,'" CBS News, April 20, 2006, https://www.cbsnews.com/news/bush-the-decider-in-chief.

36.   George W. Bush, *Decision Points* (New York: Crown Publishers, 2010).

37.   David Rothkopf, "Obama's 'Don't Do Stupid Shit' Foreign Policy," *Foreign Policy*, June 4, 2014, https://foreignpolicy.com/articles/2014/06/04/obama_dont_do_stupid_shit_foreign_policy_bowe_bergdahl; The White House Office of the Press Secretary, "Remarks by the President to the White House Press Corps," Obama White House Archives, August 20, 2012, https://obamawhitehouse.archives.gov/the-press-office/2012/08/20/remarks-president-white-house-press-corps (site discontinued).

38.   Press Release, "Thousands Suffering Neurotoxic Symptoms Treated in Hospitals Supported by MSF," Médecins Sans Frontières, August 24, 2013, https://www.msf.org/syria-thousands-suffering-neurotoxic-symptoms-treated-hospitals-supported-msf.

39. Jeffrey Goldberg, "Hillary Clinton: 'Failure' to Help Syrian Rebels Led to the Rise of ISIS," *The Atlantic*, August 10, 2014, https://www.theatlantic.com/international/archive/2014/08/hillary-clinton-failure-to-help-syrian-rebels-led-to-the-rise-of-isis/375832.

40. Goldberg, "Hillary Clinton."

41. Doyle McManus, "Leading from Behind in Syria," *Los Angeles Times*, February 22, 2014, https://www.latimes.com/opinion/op-ed/la-oe-0223-mcmanus-syria-obama-options-20140223-column.html; Ryan Lizza, "Leading from Behind," *New Yorker*, April 26, 2011, https://www.newyorker.com/news/news-desk/leading-from-behind.

42. Frank Dobbin and Alexandra Kalev, "Why Doesn't Diversity Training Work? The Challenge for Industry and Academia," *Anthropology Now* 10, no. 2 (September 2018): 48–55, https://doi.org/10.1080/19428200.2018.1493182; Frank Dobbin and Alexandra Kalev, "Why Diversity Programs Fail," *Harvard Business Review*, July 2016, https://hbr.org/2016/07/why-diversity-programs-fail.

43. Dobbin and Kalev, "Why Doesn't Diversity Training Work?"

44. Joshua Wolf Shenk, "Lincoln's Great Depression," *The Atlantic*, October 2005, https://www.theatlantic.com/magazine/archive/2005/10/lincolns-great-depression/304247.

45. "Newly Discovered Poem Likely Lincoln's," *Talk of the Nation*, National Public Radio, June 9, 2004, https://www.npr.org/2004/06/09/1951239/newly-discovered-poem-likely-lincolns.

46. Susan Paddock, "Depression Helped Fuel President's Greatness," *Gettysburg Times*, January 31, 2022, https://www.gettysburgtimes.com/life_entertainment/columns/article_4cc3d272-5927-5e7b-9976-1685dc4a8361.html.

47. Shenk, "Lincoln's Great Depression."

48. Nassir Ghaemi, "Winston Churchill and His 'Black Dog' of Greatness," The Conversation, January 23, 2015, https://theconversation.com/winston-churchill-and-his-black-dog-of-greatness-36570.

49. Wilfred Attenborough, *Diagnosing Churchill: Bipolar or "Prey to Nerves"?* (Jefferson, NC: McFarland and Company, 2019), 111.

50. Nina Martyris, "Hitler Couldn't Defeat Churchill, but Champagne Nearly Did," National Public Radio, April 1, 2016, https://www.npr.org/sections/thesalt/2016/04/01/472459579/hitler-couldnt-defeat-churchill-but-champagne-nearly-did; Ian Johnston, "At least David Cameron Kept His Kit On," *Independent*, February 2, 2014, https://www.independent.co.uk/news/uk/politics/at-least-david-cameron-kept-his-kit-on-unlike-winston-churchill-the-surprising-history-of-the-prime-minister-as-host-9101651.html; Jason Diamond, "Winston Churchill, Man of Style," *Paris Review*, April 16, 2012, https://www.theparisreview.org/blog/2012/04/16/winston-churchill-man-of-style; "The Books of Sir Winston Churchill," International Churchill Society, October 17, 2008, https://winstonchurchill.org/resources/reference/the-books-of-sir-winston-churchill; Richard M. Langworth, "Old Kerfuffles Die Hard: The Churchill Papers Flap Is Back," January 21, 2021, https://richardlangworth.com/churchill-papers; Julia Gillard, "The Stigma Around Mental Health Nearly Cost Australia Its Greatest Leader," *The Guardian*, June 28, 2017, https://www.theguardian.com/commentisfree/2017/jun/29/julia-gillard-the-stigma-around-mental-health-nearly-cost-australia-its-greatest-leader; Max Kutner, "London Mayor Boris Johnson on Winston Churchill's Cheekiest Quotes," *Smithsonian Magazine*,

December 17, 2014, https://www.smithsonianmag.com/history/london-mayor-boris
-johnson-winston-churchill-legacy-180953538.

51. Ghaemi, "Winston Churchill and His 'Black Dog.'"

52. Ghaemi, "Winston Churchill and His 'Black Dog.'"

53. Ghaemi, "Winston Churchill and His 'Black Dog.'"

54. Oliver James, "Alastair Campbell on Whether Extraordinary Achievement Has a Dark Side," *Financial Times*, March 8, 2017, https://www.ft.com/content/99cc5f60 -f9bb-11e6-bd4e-68d53499ed71.

55. "Quotes," Brittanica, https://www.britannica.com/quotes/Marcel-Proust.

56. Rafael Euba, "Happy Days—Psychiatry in History," *British Journal of Psychiatry* 214, no. 6 (2019): 328, https://www.cambridge.org/core/journals/the-british -journal-of-psychiatry/article/happy-days-psychiatry-in-history/DFE0D1D 9758A8C54BB2E993EA1FF4194.

57. Chris Haroun, "Want Success? Learn from Apple's Simplicity and Intel's Paranoia," *Inc.*, April 6, 2016, https://www.inc.com/chris-haroun/want-success-learn -from-apples-simplicity-and-intels-paranoia.html; Jay Yarow, "Paranoid Steve Jobs Makes WSJ Editor Erase a Tweet Sent from the iPad," *Business Insider*, February 8, 2010, https://www.businessinsider.com/steve-jobs-makes-the-wall-street-journal -2010-2.

58. Steve Jobs, "Review," Amazon, https://www.amazon.com/Only-Paranoid -Survive-Exploit-Challenge-ebook/dp/B0036S4B2G/ref=cm_cr_arp_d_product _top?ie=UTF8.

59. Andy Dunn, "I Built Bonobos into a Major Brand—While Secretly Harboring a Mental Illness That Nearly Cost Me Everything," *Business Insider*, May 8, 2022, https://www.businessinsider.com/bonobos-founder-andy-dunn-bipolar-mental -health-burn-rate-2022-5.

60. Simon Kyaga, "Creativity and Psychopathology," Karolinska Institute Open Archive Home, March 21, 2014, https://openarchive.ki.se/xmlui/handle/10616/41931.

61. John Patty, "In Praise of Mavericks," *Vox*, August 28, 2018, https://www.Vox .com/mischiefs-of-faction/2018/8/28/17788108/john-mccain-maverick.

CHAPTER 5: OUT OF THE WILD AND INTO THE SOCIAL MEDIA SWAMP

1. Alexis de Tocqueville, *Democracy in America and Two Essays on America* (London: Penguin, 2003), 300.

2. Nir Boms, "Slavery and Freedom on the Internet," *Jerusalem Post*, August 21, 2007, https://www.jpost.com/opinion/op-ed-contributors/slavery-and-freedom -on-the-internet.

3. *Medical School Year Two Questionnaire, 2017 All Schools Summary Report*, Association of American Medical Colleges, 2018, https://aamc.org/system/files/reports/1 /y2q2017report.pdf.

4. Petroc Taylor, "Volume of Data/Information Created, Captured, Copied, and Consumed Worldwide from 2010 to 2020, with Forecasts from 2021 to 2025," Statista, September 8, 2022, https://www.statista.com/statistics/871513/worldwide -data-created.

5. Kim Parker and Amanda Lenhart, "The Digital Revolution and Higher Education Overview of Findings," Pew Research Center, August 28, 2011, https://www .pewresearch.org/internet/2011/08/28/main-report-17.

6. Jonathan Bailey, "How Bad Was the Pandemic for Academic Integrity?," Plagiarism Today, April 22, 2021, https://www.plagiarismtoday.com/2021/04/22/how-bad-was-the-pandemic-for-academic-integrity.

7. Susan D'Agostino, "ChatGPT Advice Academics Can Use Now," Inside Higher Ed, January 12, 2023, https://www.insidehighered.com/news/2023/01/12/academic-experts-offer-advice-chatgpt.

8. Elias Aboujaoude et al., "From MOOCs to MOOIs: Attrition as Law in Online Learning and Online Therapy," Educause, August 3, 2020, https://er.educause.edu/articles/2020/8/from-moocs-to-moois-attrition-as-law-in-online-learning-and-online-therapy.

9. Steven Leckhart and Tom Cheshire, "University Just Got Flipped: How Online Video Is Opening Up Knowledge to the World," *Wired*, April 16, 2012, https://www.wired.co.uk/article/university-just-got-flipped.

10. Steven Leckhart, "The Stanford Education Experiment Could Change Higher Learning Forever," *Wired*, March 20, 2012, https://www.wired.com/2012/03/ff-aiclass.

11. Laura Pappano, "The Year of the MOOC," *New York Times*, November 2, 2012, https://www.nytimes.com/2012/11/04/education/edlife/massive-open-online-courses-are-multiplying-at-a-rapid-pace.html.

12. Eric Westervelt, "The Online Education Revolution Drifts Off Course," NPR News, December 31, 2013, https://www.wbur.org/npr/258420151/the-online-education-revolution-drifts-off-course.

13. Tamar Lewin, "After Setbacks, Online Courses Are Rethought," *New York Times*, December 10, 2013, https://www.nytimes.com/2013/12/11/us/after-setbacks-online-courses-are-rethought.html.

14. Ryan DeRousseau, "California's Multimillion-Dollar Online Education Flop Is Another Blow for MOOCs," Herchinger Report, April 14, 2015, https://hechingerreport.org/californias-multi-million-dollar-online-education-flop-is-another-blow-for-moocs.

15. Aboujaoude et al., "From MOOCs to MOOIs"; Laura Perna et al., "The Life Cycle of a Million MOOC Users," The University of Pennsylvania Graduate School of Education, December 5, 2013, https://www.gse.upenn.edu/pdf/ahead/perna_ruby_boruch_moocs_dec2013.pdf.

16. John Warner, "MOOCs Are 'Dead.' What's Next?," Inside Higher Ed, October 11, 2017, https://www.insidehighered.com/blogs/just-visiting/moocs-are-dead-whats-next-uh-oh.

17. "Kids' Cell Phone Use Survey 2019," Sell Cell, 2019, https://www.sellcell.com/blog/kids-cell-phone-use-survey-2019.

18. Teresa Correa, "Bottom-Up Technology Transmission Within Families: Exploring How Youths Influence Their Parents' Digital Media Use with Dyadic Data," *Journal of Communication* 64, no. 1 (December 2, 2013): 103–124, https://doi.org/10.1111/jcom.12067.

19. "Teens, Smartphones, and Texting," Pew Research Center, March 19, 2012, https://www.pewresearch.org/internet/2012/03/19/teens-smartphones-texting.

20. Emily C. Stasko and Pamela Geller, "Reframing Sexting as a Positive Relationship Behavior," American Psychological Association Press Releases, 2015, https://www.apa.org/news/press/releases/2015/08/reframing-sexting.pdf.

21. "2020 Essential Facts About the Video Game Industry," Entertainment Software Association, 2020, https://www.theesa.com/resource/2020-essential-facts.

22. Zoe Ruderman, "Damn It, My Mom Is on Facebook," *Cosmopolitan*, October 11, 2010, https://www.cosmopolitan.com/entertainment/celebs/news/a8876/snl-digital-short-mom-on-facebook.

23. "Finding and Evaluating Online Resources," National Center for Complementary and Integrative Health, US Department of Health and Human Services, 2017, https://www.nccih.nih.gov/health/finding-and-evaluating-online-resources.

24. Daniel Powell and Andrew Stebbins, "How Medical Providers Can Remove and Respond to Negative Medical Reviews," Minc Law, August 26, 2021, https://www.minclaw.com/how-doctors-can-respond-to-negative-online-reviews.

25. Powell and Stebbins, "How Medical Providers Can Remove and Respond."

26. Charles Ornstein, "Doctors Fire Back at Bad Yelp Reviews—and Reveal Patients' Information Online," *Washington Post*, May 27, 2016, https://www.washingtonpost.com/news/to-your-health/wp/2016/05/27/docs-fire-back-at-bad-yelp-reviews-and-reveal-patients-information-online.

27. Carl Malamud, *Exploring the Internet: A Technical Travelogue* (Englewood Cliffs, NJ: PTR Prentice Hall, 1992), 284.

28. Matthew Karsten, "How to Become a Digital Nomad (Work Online from Anywhere!)," Expert Vagabond, January 2, 2023, https://expertvagabond.com/digital-nomad-tips.

29. "Insurance for Nomads," Safety Wing, 2023, https://safetywing.com; "Explore Your Boundaries," World Nomads, 2023, https://www.world nomads.com/usa.

30. "From Your Mailbox to Your Inbox," Earth Class Mail, 2023, https://www.earthclassmail.com.

31. J. D. Shadel, "Like Summer Camp for Grownups," *Washington Post*, February 22, 2021, https://www.washingtonpost.com/travel/2021/02/22/digital-nomad-visas-covid; Eliot Brown and Maureen Farrell, "Behind the Fallout from We-Work's Troubled IPO," *Fortune*, July 20, 2021, https://fortune.com/longform/book-excerpt-cult-of-we-work.

32. Shadel, "Like Summer Camp for Grownups."

33. Joseph Fuller and William Kerr, "The Great Resignation Didn't Start with the Pandemic," *Harvard Business Review*, March 23, 2022, https://hbr.org/2022/03/the-great-resignation-didnt-start-with-the-pandemic.

34. Kim Parker and Juliana Menasce Horowitz, "Majority of Workers Who Quit a Job in 2021 Cite Low Pay, No Opportunities for Advancement, Feeling Disrespected," Pew Research Center, March 9, 2022, https://www.pewresearch.org/fact-tank/2022/03/09/majority-of-workers-who-quit-a-job-in-2021-cite-low-pay-no-opportunities-for-advancement-feeling-disrespected.

35. Jeanne Meister, "The Great Resignation Becomes the Great ReShuffle: What Employers Can Do to Retain Workers," *Forbes*, April 19, 2022, https://www.forbes.com/sites/jeannemeister/2022/04/19/the-great-re-shuffle-of-talent-what-can-employers-do-to-retain-workers/?sh=547837394cf3.

36. Brian Rashid, "The Rise of the Freelancer Economy," *Forbes*, January 26, 2016, https://www.forbes.com/sites/brianrashid/2016/01/26/the-rise-of-the-freelancer-economy/?sh=14b94e483bdf.

37. Michelle Fox, "The Great Resignation Has Changed the Workplace for Good," CNBC, May 10, 2022, https://www.cnbc.com/2022/05/10/-the-great-resignation-has-changed-the-workplace-for-good-.html.

38. Emma Goldberg, "A Full Return to the Office? Does 'Never' Work for You?," *New York Times*, June 9, 2022, https://www.nytimes.com/2022/06/09/business/return -to-work-office-plans.html.

39. Yasmeen Serhan, "How the Rest of the World Is Doing," *The Atlantic*, June 29, 2022, https://www.theatlantic.com/international/archive/2022/06/remote-in-person -work-rto-policies/661407.

40. Goldberg, "A Full Return to the Office?"

41. Huileng Tan, "Airbnb Said More Than 800,000 People Flocked to Its Ca-reers Page After It Announced That Employees Could Live and Work Anywhere," *Business Insider*, May 5, 2022, https://www.businessinsider.com/airbnbs-careers-page -viewed-800k-times-work-from-anywhere-benefit-2022-5.

42. Christopher Hirst, "Cheese: The Big Ingredient," *The Independent*, July 31, 2004, https://www.independent.co.uk/life-style/food-and-drink/features/cheese-the -big-ingredient-556040.html.

43. "This Is How Much the French Are Obsessed with Cheese," *The Local*, Au-gust 10, 2016, https://www.thelocal.fr/20160810/this-is-how-much-the-french-are -obsessed-with-cheese.

44. Cheyenne Babaco, "The Outdated Methodology of Pack Theory and Its In-fluence on Modern Dog Training," *American Journal of Canine Science*, October 27, 2018, http://ajcs.org.uk/uncategorized/the-outdated-methodology-of-pack-theory-and -its-influence-on-modern-dog-training (site discontinued); Virginia Morell, "How Wolf Became Dog," *Scientific American*, July 1, 2015, https://www.scientificamerican .com/article/how-wolf-became-dog.

45. Kate Wong, "Tiny Genetic Differences Between Humans and Other Pri-mates Pervade the Genome," *Scientific American*, September 1, 2014, https://www .scientificamerican.com/article/tiny-genetic-differences-between-humans-and-other -primates-pervade-the-genome.

46. Erna Walraven, "What Wild Animals Can Teach You About Leadership," *Financial Review*, September 4, 2019, https://www.afr.com/work-and-careers/leaders /what-wild-animals-can-teach-you-about-leadership-20190902-p52n64.

47. Mayo Clinic Staff, "Paleo Diet: What Is It and Why Is It So Popular?," Mayo Clinic, October 20, 2022, https://www.mayoclinic.org/healthy-lifestyle/nutrition-and -healthy-eating/in-depth/paleo-diet/art-20111182.

48. Elias Aboujaoude, *Virtually You: The Dangerous Powers of the e-Personality* (New York: W. W. Norton, 2011), 212–213.

49. Elissa Liu, "Most Fortune 500 CEOs Are on Social Media in 2020," Influen-tial Executive, August 24, 2020, https://influentialexecutive.com/how-many-fortune -500-ceos-social-media-2020.

50. Aboujaoude, *Virtually You*, 280.

51. Michael Cavna, "'Nobody Knows You're a Dog': As Iconic Internet Cartoon Turns 20, Creator Peter Steiner Knows the Joke Rings As Relevant As Ever," *Wash-ington Post*, July 31, 2013, https://www.washingtonpost.com/blogs/comic-riffs/post /nobody-knows-youre-a-dog-as-iconic-internet-cartoon-turns-20-creator-peter -steiner-knows-the-joke-rings-as-relevant-as-ever/2013/07/31/73372600-f98d-11e2 -8e84-c56731a202fb_blog.html.

52. Katharine Q. Seelye and Jess Bidgood, "Guilty Verdict for Young Woman Who Urged Friend to Kill Himself," *New York Times*, June 16, 2017, https://www .nytimes.com/2017/06/16/us/suicide-texting-trial-michelle-carter-conrad-roy.html; "I Love You Now Die," HBO, 2019, https://www.imdb.com/title/tt9614090/.

53. Paul LeBlanc, "The Text Messages That Led Up to Teen's Suicide," CNN, June 16, 2017, https://www.cnn.com/2017/06/08/us/text-message-suicide-michelle-carter-conrad-roy/index.html.

54. Sigmund Freud, *New Introductory Lectures on Psychoanalysis: The Standard Edition*, trans. James Strachey (New York: W. W. Norton, 1965), 91.

55. Ibram X. Kendi, "The Day Shithole Entered the Presidential Lexicon," *The Atlantic*, January 13, 2019, https://www.theatlantic.com/politics/archive/2019/01/shithole-countries/580054; Ron Hart, "Corporate America's Bi-Coastal Liberal Elites' Risky Lurch Left," *Chattanooga Times Free Press*, December 8, 2022, https://www.timesfreepress.com/news/2022/dec/08/opinion-go-woke-go-broke; Amy Chozick, "Hillary Clinton Calls Many Trump Backers 'Deplorables,' and G.O.P. Pounces," *New York Times*, September 11, 2016, https://www.nytimes.com/2016/09/11/us/politics/hillary-clinton-basket-of-deplorables.html; Anthony Zurcher, "Cancel Culture: Have Any Two Words Become More Weaponised?," BBC News, February 18, 2021, https://www.bbc.com/news/world-us-canada-55959135.

56. Edith Hamilton, *Mythology* (Boston: Little, Brown, 1942), 88.

57. Clay Dillow, "Yahoo's New Ad Blitz: It's All About 'Y!ou,'" *Fast Company*, September 22, 2009, https://www.fastcompany.com/1369876/yahoos-new-ad-blitz-its-all-about-you.

58. Kevin Down, "Adam Neumann Gives $5.9M Trademark Payment Back to WeWork," Yahoo! Finance, September 3, 2019, https://finance.yahoo.com/news/adam-neumann-gives-5-9m-050000715.html.

59. American Psychiatric Association, *Diagnostic and Statistical Manual of Mental Disorders*, 5th ed. (Arlington, VA: American Psychiatric Association, 2013) 669–670.

60. Paola Rovelli and Camilla Curnis, "The Perks of Narcissism: When Behaving Like a Star Speeds Up Career Advancement to the CEO Position," *Leadership Quarterly* 32, no. 3 (June 2021): https://doi.org/10.1016/j.leaqua.2020.101489.

61. Elias Aboujaoude, "Problematic Internet Use: An Overview," *World Psychiatry* 9, no. 2 (2010): 85–90, https://doi.org/10.1002/j.2051-5545.2010.tb00278.x.

62. Ian Rowlands et al., "The Google Generation: The Information Behaviour of the Researcher of the Future," *Aslib Proceedings* 60, no. 4 (July 6, 2008): 290–310, https://doi.org/10.1108/00012530810887953.

63. Farhad Manjoo, "You Won't Finish This Article," *Slate*, June 6, 2013, https://slate.com/technology/2013/06/how-people-read-online-why-you-wont-finish-this-article.html.

64. Yasmeen Sarhan, "François Hollande's Legacy," *The Atlantic*, December 2, 2016, https://www.theatlantic.com/news/archive/2016/12/francois-hollande-reelection/509387; Emmanuel Carrère, "Orbiting Jupiter: My Week with Emmanuel Macron," *The Guardian*, October 20, 2017, https://www.theguardian.com/news/2017/oct/20/emmanuel-macron-orbiting-jupiter-emmanuel-carrere.

65. Saim Saeed, "Emmanuel Macron's 'Jupiterian' Meeting at Versailles," *Politico*, July 3, 2017, https://www.politico.eu/article/emmanuel-macrons-jupiterian-meeting-at-versailles.

66. James McAuley, "President Macron Spent $30,000 on Makeup Services in Just Three Months," *Washington Post*, August 25, 2017, https://www.washingtonpost.com/news/worldviews/wp/2017/08/25/french-president-macron-has-spent-30000-on-makeup-services-in-just-3-months; Pierre Briançon, "Macron's 'Jupiter' Model Unlikely to Stand Test of Time," *Politico*, June 16, 2017, https://www.politico.eu/article/emmanuel-macron-jupiter-model-unlikely-to-stand-test-of-time-leadership-parliamentary-majority.

67.   Carrère, "Orbiting Jupiter."

68.   "Madoff Scheme 'Too Good to Be True,'" National Public Radio, August 17, 2009, https://www.npr.org/2009/08/17/111959024/madoff-scheme-too-good-to-be-true.

69.   Erin Arvedlund, *Too Good to Be True: The Rise and Fall of Bernie Madoff* (New York: Portfolio, 2009).

70.   Stephanie Yang and Grace Kay, "Bernie Madoff Died in Prison After Carrying Out the Largest Ponzi Scheme in History," *Business Insider*, April 14, 2021, https://africa.businessinsider.com/finance/bernie-madoff-died-in-prison-after-carrying-out-the-largest-ponzi-scheme-in-history/8m8djvm.

71.   Nicholas Reimann, "Bernie Madoff Dies in Federal Prison at 82," *Forbes*, April 14, 2021, https://www.forbes.com/sites/nicholasreimann/2021/04/14/bernie-madoff-dies-in-federal-prison-at-82/?sh=30f9d4d63fad.

72.   Ron Carucci and David Lancefield, "Every Leader Has Flaws. Don't Let Yours Derail Your Strategy," *Harvard Business Review*, September 29, 2021, https://hbr.org/2021/09/every-leader-has-flaws-dont-let-yours-derail-your-strategy.

73.   William Saletan, "The Computer Made Me Do It," *New York Times*, February 11, 2011, https://www.nytimes.com/2011/02/13/books/review/Saletan-t.html.

74.   Nadine M. Post, "1,070-Foot Salesforce Tower Elevates Seismic Design," Engineering News Record, September 14, 2017, https://www.enr.com/articles/42725-070-foot-salesforce-tower-elevates-seismic-design; Laura Bliss and Sarah Holder, "What Happens When a City's Largest Employer Goes 'Work from Anywhere,'" *Bloomberg*, February 12, 2021, https://www.bloomberg.com/news/articles/2021-02-12/what-will-remote-work-do-to-salesforce-tower.

CHAPTER 6: MAGICAL THINKING

1.   Polly Sprenger, "Sun on Privacy: 'Get Over It,'" *Wired*, January 26, 1999, https://www.wired.com/1999/01/sun-on-privacy-get-over-it.

2.   Elias Aboujaoude, "Facial Recognition: The Other Reason We May Need a Face Mask," *The Hill*, May 16, 2020, https://thehill.com/opinion/cybersecurity/498113-facial-recognition-the-other-reason-we-may-need-a-face-mask.

3.   Andrew Rosenberg, "The Fist of the Sender: How Much Does Typing Reveal About Us?," Columbia Entrepreneurship, July 22, 2015, https://entrepreneurship.columbia.edu/2015/07/22/columbia-startup-lab-programming-the-fist-of-the-sender-how-much-does-typing-reveal-about-us.

4.   Lynn Yarris, "George Smoot Wins Nobel Prize in Physics," Lawrence Berkeley National Laboratory, 2006, https://www2.lbl.gov/Publications/Nobel.

5.   "Nobel Literature Prize 2021: Abdulrazak Gurnah on the Moment He Found Out He Won," BBC News, October 7, 2021, https://www.bbc.com/news/av/entertainment-arts-58838532.

6.   "Nobel-Winning Economist Angus Deaton Worried Prize Phone Call Was Prank," *Economic Times*, October 13, 2015, https://economictimes.indiatimes.com/news/international/world-news/nobel-winning-economist-angus-deaton-worried-prize-phone-call-was-prank/articleshow/49329924.cms.

7.   Steven Erlanger and Sheryl Gay Stolberg, "Surprise Nobel for Obama Stirs Praise and Doubts," *New York Times*, October 9, 2009, https://www.nytimes.com/2009/10/10/world/10nobel.html.

8.   "The Nobel Prize 1906," Nobel Prize, https://www.nobelprize.org/prizes/peace/1906/roosevelt/biographical; "The Nobel Prize 1919," Nobel Prize, https://

www.nobelprize.org/prizes/peace/1919/wilson/facts; "The Nobel Prize 1990," Nobel Prize, https://www.nobelprize.org/prizes/peace/1990/gorbachev/facts; "The Nobel Prize 1993," Nobel Prize, https://www.nobelprize.org/prizes/peace/1993/summary.

9. Mark Memmott, "Obama Got Peace Prize 'For What He Has Done,' Nobel Committee Chairman Says," National Public Radio, October 13, 2009, https://www.npr.org/sections/thetwo-way/2009/10/nobel_obama_peace_prize_commit.html.

10. Robert Creamer, "Obama's Nobel Prize Is Really a Tribute to American Voters," *Huffington Post*, March 18, 2010, https://www.huffpost.com/entry/obamas-nobel-prize-is-rea_b_316375.

11. Memmott, "Obama Got Peace Prize."

12. Jonathan Freedland, "US Elections: Obama Wows Berlin Crowd with Historic Speech," *The Guardian*, July 24, 2008, https://www.theguardian.com/global/2008/jul/24/barackobama.uselections2008; Todd Holzman, "Obama Seeks 'New Beginning' With Muslim World," National Public Radio, June 4, 2009, https://www.npr.org/2009/06/04/104891406/obama-seeks-new-beginning-with-muslim-world.

13. Adam Hodges, "'Yes, We Can' and the Power of Political Slogans," *Anthropology News,* October 21, 2019, https://www.anthropology-news.org/articles/yes-we-can-and-the-power-of-political-slogans.

14. Harry Cheadle, "Judging Obama's Progressive, Flawed, Conflicting Legacy," *Vice*, January 19, 2017, https://www.vice.com/en/article/gvvpz9/judging-obamas-progressive-flawed-conflicting-legacy.

15. Libby Nelson, "Is Hillary Clinton Really the Most Qualified Candidate Ever?," *Vox*, August 1, 2016, https://www.Vox.com/2016/8/1/12316646/hillary-clinton-qualified.

16. Anthony Zurcher, "What Happened: The Long List of Who Hillary Clinton Blames," BBC News, September 13, 2017, https://www.bbc.com/news/world-us-canada-41244474.

17. Megan Garber, "Hillary Clinton Traveled 956,733 Miles During Her Time as Secretary of State," *The Atlantic*, January 29, 2013, https://www.theatlantic.com/politics/archive/2013/01/hillary-clinton-traveled-956-733-miles-during-her-time-as-secretary-of-state/272656.

18. Tessa Berenson, "A Brief History of Public Fascination with Hillary Clinton's Hair," *Time*, November 12, 2015, https://time.com/4110060/history-hillary-clinton-hair.

19. Darren Samuelsohn, "Hillary Clinton's Fear of Leaks," *Politico*, January 23, 2015, https://www.politico.com/story/2015/01/hillary-clinton-2016-elections-114476.

20. Casey Hicks, "Timeline of Hillary Clinton's Email Scandal," CNN, November 7, 2016, https://www.cnn.com/2016/10/28/politics/hillary-clinton-email-timeline; Ken Kamisar and Martin Matishak, "Timeline: Hillary's Benghazi Emails," *The Hill*, May 28, 2015, https://thehill.com/policy/defense/243218-timeline-hillarys-benghazi-emails; Jonathan Allen, "Clinton Should Come Clean on Her Relationships with Donors," Roll Call, August 12, 2016, https://rollcall.com/2016/08/12/clinton-should-come-clean-on-her-relationships-with-donors.

21. Hicks, "Timeline."

22. Adam Goldman and Alan Rappeport, "Emails in Anthony Weiner Inquiry Jolt Hillary Clinton's Campaign," *New York Times*, October 29, 2016, https://www.nytimes.com/2016/10/29/us/politics/fbi-hillary-clinton-email.html.

23. Eric Bradner, "Hillary Clinton on Emails: 'It is a Drip-Drip-Drip,'" CNN, September 27, 2015, https://www.cnn.com/2015/09/27/politics/hillary-clinton-emails-meet-the-press/index.html.

24. Susan Cornwell and Lawrence Hurley, "Senior Democrat Says Trump Court Pick Avoided Questions 'Like the Plague,'" Reuters, February 7, 2017, https://www.reuters.com/article/usa-court-gorsuch-schumer/senior-democrat-says-trump-court-pick-avoided-questions-like-the-plague-idINKBN15M2D5.

25. Elena Kagan, "Review: Confirmation Messes, Old and New," *University of Chicago Law Review* 62, no. 2 (Spring 1995): 919–942, https://doi.org/10.2307/1600153.

26. Catherine Cheney and Josh Gerstein, "Sessions Questions Kagan's 'Honesty,'" *Politico*, June 30, 2010, https://www.politico.com/story/2010/06/sessions-questions-kagans-honesty-039157.

27. Peter Cappelli, "Your Approach to Hiring Is All Wrong," *Harvard Business Review*, May–June 2019, https://hbr.org/2019/05/your-approach-to-hiring-is-all-wrong.

28. The Editors, "JFK's Womanizing: Why Americans Just Don't Care," *The Atlantic*, July 11, 2012, https://www.theatlantic.com/politics/archive/2012/07/jfks-womanizing-why-americans-just-dont-care/258771; ML Cavanaugh, "Wear Pink Underwear Like Churchill, and Nine Other Principles of Defense Entrepreneurship," Modern War Institute, August 8, 2017, https://mwi.usma.edu/wear-pink-underwear-like-churchill-nine-principles-defense-entrepreneurship.

29. David Smith, "Over 70 Years Queen Elizabeth Met 13 US Presidents (and Graciously Overlooked Several Faux Pas)," *The Guardian*, September 11, 2022, https://www.theguardian.com/uk-news/2022/sep/11/queen-elizabeth-us-presidents-met-biden-trump.

30. Jane Ridley, "The Secrets Behind 94-Year-Old Queen Elizabeth's Longevity," *New York Post*, December 7, 2020, https://nypost.com/2020/12/07/secrets-behind-94-year-old-queen-elizabeths-longevity.

31. Corey Atad, "Kim Kardashian Says She Is Done 'Oversharing' on Social Media," ET Canada, October 9, 2019, https://etcanada.com/news/520527/kim-kardashian-says-she-is-done-oversharing-on-social-media.

32. "Mission," SpaceX, https://www.spacex.com/mission.

33. Walter Isaacson, "The Real Leadership Lessons of Steve Jobs," *Harvard Business Review*, April 2012, https://hbr.org/2012/04/the-real-leadership-lessons-of-steve-jobs.

34. Joe Nocera, "Apples' Culture of Secrecy," *New York Times*, July 26, 2008, https://www.nytimes.com/2008/07/26/business/26nocera.html.

35. Kate Dailey, "The Cult of Steve Jobs," BBC News, October 7, 2011, https://www.bbc.com/news/magazine-15194365.

36. Maia J. Young et al., "Managerial Mystique: Magical Thinking in Judgments of Managers' Vision, Charisma, and Magnetism," *Journal of Management* (March 26, 2001), https://ssrn.com/abstract=1791984.

37. Dailey, "Cult of Steve Jobs."

38. "Zuckerberg Watches Jobs Defend User Privacy," 2010, YouTube video, https://www.youtube.com/watch?v=3NT7CFLdq-c.

39. Ben Lovejoy, "Steve Jobs Nailed the Tech Privacy Issue Back in 2010," 9to5Mac, October 24, 2018, https://9to5mac.com/2018/10/24/tech-privacy.

40. Nikhil Vemu, "'What is Privacy?'—As Explained by Steve Jobs in 2010," Medium, May 6, 2022, https://medium.com/macoclock/what-is-privacy-as-explained-by-steve-jobs-in-2010-9c110ef9f2cd.

41. Brooke Auxier et al., "Americans and Privacy: Concerned, Confused and Feeling Lack of Control Over Their Personal Information," Pew Research Center, November 15, 2019, https://www.pewresearch.org/internet/2019/11/15/americans-and -privacy-concerned-confused-and-feeling-lack-of-control-over-their-personal -information.

42. Monica Anderson, "Many Smartphone Owners Don't Take Steps to Secure Their Devices," Pew Research Center, March 15, 2017, https://www.pewresearch .org/fact-tank/2017/03/15/many-smartphone-owners-dont-take-steps-to-secure -their-devices.

43. Deepa Seetharaman, "Facebook to Streamline Privacy Settings," *Wall Street Journal*, March 28, 2018, https://www.wsj.com/articles/facebook-to-streamline-privacy -settings-1522234802.

44. Antti Oulasvirta et al., "Long-Term Effects of Ubiquitous Surveillance in the Home" (Proceedings of the 2012 ACM Conference on Ubiquitous Computing, Pittsburgh, Pennsylvania, September 2012), 41–50, https://doi.org/10.1145/2370216 .2370224.

45. Elias Aboujaoude, "Protecting Privacy to Protect Mental Health: The New Ethical Imperative," *Journal of Medical Ethics* 45, no. 9 (2019): 604–607, http://dx.doi.org /10.1136/medethics-2018-105313.

46. Darhl M. Pedersen, "Psychological Functions of Privacy," *Journal of Environmental Psychology* 17, no. 2 (June 1997): 147–156, https://doi.org/10.1006/jevp.1997 .0049.

47. Aboujaoude, "Facial Recognition."

48. Aboujaoude, "Protecting Privacy."

49. "Fourth Amendment," Legal Information Institute of Cornell Law School, https://www.law.cornell.edu/wex/fourth_amendment.

50. "Universal Declaration of Human Rights," United Nations General Assembly, 1948, https://www.digitalhistory.uh.edu/disp_textbook.cfm?smtID=3&psid=4062.

51. "EU Charter of Fundamental Rights," European Union Agency for Fundamental Rights, 2009, https://fra.europa.eu/en/eu-charter/article/7-respect-private-and -family-life.

CHAPTER 7: LEADERS AND THE UNCONSCIOUS

1. Virginia Chamlee, "A Timeline of CNN Host Don Lemon's Controversies," *People*, February 22, 2023, https://people.com/politics/don-lemon-controversy-time line; Oliver Darcy, "Don Lemon to Return to CNN, Will Undergo Formal Training Following Sexist Comments, Network Boss Says," CNN, February 21, 2023, https://www.cnn.com/2023/02/20/media/don-lemon-cnn-this-morning/index .html; Madeleine Marr, "After His 'Prime' Comment, CNN Host Don Lemon Seen Soaking Up the Sun in Miami Beach," *Miami Herald*, February 21, 2023, https://www .miamiherald.com/miami-com/miami-com-news/article272559686.html; Loree Seitz and Joseph Kapsch, "'CNN This Morning' Is the Network's Lowest-Rated Morning Show in a Decade," The Wrap, February 10, 2023, https://www.thewrap .com/cnn-this-morning-ratings-morning-show-iterations.

2. Allie Griffin, "Don Lemon's Fiery Exchange with GOP Candidate Vivek Ramaswamy Left CNN Leaders 'Exasperated,'" *New York Post*, April 24, 2023, https: //nypost.com/2023/04/24/don-lemons-fiery-exchange-with-gop-candidate-left-cnn -leaders-exasperated; Michael M. Grynbaum, John Koblin, and Benjamin Mullin,

"Don Lemon Ousted from CNN in Move That Left Him 'Stunned,'" *New York Times*, April 24, 2023, https://www.nytimes.com/2023/04/24/business/media/don-lemon -cnn.html.

3. Samantha Grindell, "People Are Loving an Adorable Video of Kamala Harris Telling Her 4-Year-Old Niece She Could Be President Someday," Insider, November 5, 2020, https://www.insider.com/kamala-harris-niece-told-her-shell-be -president-one-day-2020-11.

4. Jennifer E. Smith et al., "Obstacles and Opportunities for Female Leadership in Mammalian Societies: A Comparative Perspective," *Leadership Quarterly* 31, no. 2 (2020): 101267, https://doi.org/10.1016/j.leaqua.2018.09.005.

5. Mark J. Perry, "Women Earned the Majority of Doctoral Degrees in 2020 for the 12th Straight Year and Outnumber Men in Grad School 148 to 100," American Enterprise Institute, October 24, 2021, https://www.aei.org/carpe-diem/women -earned-the-majority-of-doctoral-degrees-in-2020-for-the-12th-straight-year-and -outnumber-men-in-grad-school-148-to-100; Brendan Murphy, "Women in Medical Schools: Dig into Latest Record-Breaking Numbers," American Medical Association, September 29, 2021, https://www.ama-assn.org/education/medical-school-diversity /women-medical-schools-dig-latest-record-breaking-numbers.

6. "Women CEOs in America 2021 Report," Women Business Collaborative, 2022, https://www.wbcollaborative.org/wp-content/uploads/2021/10/Women-CEOS -in-America_2021_1013-2.pdf.

7. "Women CEOs Speak," Korn Ferry Institute, 2017, https://www.kornferry .com/content/dam/kornferry/docs/pdfs/kf-rockefeller-women-ceos-speak.pdf.

8. Jeff Green, "Ouster of Gap CEO Syngal Follows Trend of Women Being Fired Faster," *Bloomberg*, July 13, 2022, https://www.bloomberg.com/news/articles /2022-07-13/ouster-of-gap-ceo-syngal-follows-trend-of-women-being-fired-faster #xj4y7vzkg.

9. Vishal K. Gupta et al., "Research: Activist Investors Are More Likely to Target Female CEOs," *Harvard Business Review*, January 22, 2018, https://hbr.org/2018/01 /research-activist-investors-are-more-likely-to-target-female-ceos.

10. Andrew Ross Sorkin, "Do Activist Investors Target Female CEOs?," *New York Times*, February 9, 2015, https://archive.nytimes.com/dealbook.nytimes.com/2015 /02/09/the-women-of-the-s-p-500-and-investor-activism.

11. "Facts and Figures: Women's Leadership and Political Participation," United Nations, 2022, https://www.unwomen.org/en/what-we-do/leadership-and-political -participation/facts-and-figures.

12. Virginia E. Schein et al., "Think Manager—Think Male: A Global Phenomenon?," *Journal of Organizational Behavior* 17, no. 1 (January 1996): 33–41, https://www .jstor.org/stable/2488533.

13. Elizabeth Judge, "Women on Board: Help or Hindrance," *The Times*, November 11, 2003, https://www.thetimes.co.uk/article/women-on-board-help-or-hindrance -2c6fnqf6fng.

14. Michelle K. Ryan and S. Alexander Haslam, "The Glass Cliff: Evidence That Women Are Over-Represented in Precarious Leadership Positions," *British Journal of Management* 16, no. 2 (February 2005): 81–90, https://doi.org/10.1111/j.1467-8551.2005 .00433.x.

15. Michelle K. Ryan et al., "Politics and the Glass Cliff: Evidence that Women are Preferentially Selected to Contest Hard-to-Win Seats," *Psychology of Women Quarterly* 34, no. 1 (March 1, 2010): 56–64, https://doi.org/10.1111/j.1471-6402.2009.01541.x.

16. Michelle K. Ryan et al., "Getting on Top of the Glass Cliff: Reviewing a Decade of Evidence, Explanations, and Impact," *Leadership Quarterly* 27, no. 3 (June 2016): 446–455, https://doi.org/10.1016/j.leaqua.2015.10.008.

17. Alison Cook and Christy Glass, "Glass Cliffs and Organizational Saviors: Barriers to Minority Leadership in Work Organizations?," *Social Problems* 60, no. 2 (May 2013): 168–187, https://doi.org/10.1525/sp.2013.60.2.168.

18. "Examples of the Glass Cliff," Context, Identity and Choice, University of Exeter, https://psychology.exeter.ac.uk/cic/about/theglasscliff.

19. "Chart-Topping 'Pops': Statistics of the Internet Bubble," PBS, https://www.pbs.org/wgbh/pages/frontline/shows/dotcon/thinking/stats.html.

20. Robert Hof, "Yahoo Fires CEO Carol Bartz—Here's Why," *Forbes*, September 6, 2007, https://www.forbes.com/sites/roberthof/2011/09/06/report-yahoo-cans-ceo-carol-bartz-heres-what-went-wrong/?sh=1bccff512e07.

21. Brad Plumer, "The GM Recall Scandal of 2014," *Vox*, May 11, 2015, https://www.vox.com/2014/10/3/18073458/gm-car-recall; Brad Plumer, "GM Just Recalled Another 8.4 Million Cars—Bringing This Year's Total Up to 28 Million," *Vox*, June 30, 2014, https://www.Vox.com/2014/6/30/5858128/gm-just-recalled-another-7-6-million-cars.

22. Daniel Kurtzleben, "What Happened to Jill Abramson Shows Everything That Sucks About Being a Woman Leader," *Vox*, May 14, 2014, https://www.vox.com/2014/5/14/5717926/the-jill-abramson-story-highlights-everything-thats-bad-about-being-a.

23. Miguel Helft, "The Last Days of Marissa Mayer?," *Forbes*, November 19, 2015, https://www.forbes.com/sites/miguelhelft/2015/11/19/the-last-days-of-marissa-mayer/?sh=5b0387da141f; Mike Myatt, "Marissa Mayer: A Case Study in Poor Leadership?," *Forbes*, November 20, 2015, https://www.forbes.com/sites/mikemyatt/2015/11/20/marissa-mayer-case-study-in-poor-leadership/?sh=74a4e2bb3b46.

24. Sam Knight, "Theresa May's Impossible Choice," *New Yorker*, July 23, 2018, https://www.newyorker.com/magazine/2018/07/30/theresa-mays-impossible-choice.

25. "Timeline of Events in Britain's Exit from the European Union," Associated Press, September 24, 2020, https://apnews.com/article/europe-general-elections-elections-referendums-david-cameron-f673af169925d30e524169ef92c4f386.

26. Annabelle Dickson, "What Has Michael Gove Ever Done for Us?," *Politico*, October 4, 2021, https://www.politico.eu/article/michael-gove-boris-johnson-levelling-up-housing-brexit-uk; Paul Armstrong, "Nigel Farage: Arch-Eurosceptic and Brexit 'Puppet Master,'" CNN, July 15, 2016, https://www.cnn.com/2016/06/24/europe/eu-referendum-nigel-farage; Irene Finel-Honigman, "Boris Johnson's Brexit Showdown," *Columbia News*, July 26, 2019, https://news.columbia.edu/news/boris-johnson-brexit.

27. Knight, "Theresa May's Impossible Choice."

28. Knight, "Theresa May's Impossible Choice."

29. Thomas Wright, "How Trump Undermined Theresa May," Brookings, June 1, 2019, https://www.brookings.edu/blog/order-from-chaos/2019/06/01/how-trump-undermined-theresa-may.

30. "Read Theresa May's Full Statement," CNN, May 24, 2019, https://www.cnn.com/europe/live-news/theresa-may-resignation-announcement-0524-gbr-intl/h_44ca20af878fa06b6389120312cf1cf0.

31. "Theresa May's Full Statement."

32. Amy Chozick and Jonathan Martin, "Clinton '16 Would Give Gender More of a Role Than Clinton '08 Did," *New York Times*, February 25, 2015, https://www.nytimes.com/2015/02/25/us/politics/to-break-highest-glass-ceiling-clinton-gives-nod-to-gender.html.

33. Vanessa Friedman, "Why Hillary Wore White," *New York Times*, June 29, 2016, https://www.nytimes.com/2016/07/30/fashion/hillary-clinton-democratic-national-convention.html.

34. Libby Nelson, "Hillary Clinton Concedes, Telling 'Little Girls . . . You Are Valuable and Powerful,'" *Vox*, November 9, 2016, https://www.vox.com/2016/11/9/13574496/hillary-clinton-concession-speech.

35. Stefan Stern, "Like Many Women Before Her, Theresa May Was Set Up to Fail," *The Guardian*, May 25, 2019, https://www.theguardian.com/commentisfree/2019/may/25/women-theresa-may-set-up-to-fail.

36. Allison Cook and Christy Glass, "Above the Glass Ceiling: When Are Women and Racial/Ethnic Minorities Promoted to CEO?," *Strategic Management Journal* 35, no. 7, July 2014: 1080–1089, https://doi.org/10.1002/smj.2161.

37. "Boris Johnson: The Backstory to the PM's Dramatic Resignation," BBC News, July 7, 2022, https://www.bbc.com/news/uk-62062510.

38. "At Yahoo, Scott Thompson Takes Helm As CEO," CNET, January 4, 2012, https://www.cnet.com/tech/services-and-software/at-yahoo-scott-thompson-takes-helm-as-ceo-roundup; Martin LaMonica, "Fiorina Steps Down at HP," CNET, February 9, 2005, https://www.cnet.com/tech/tech-industry/fiorina-steps-down-at-hp; Krishnadev Calamur, "*New York Times* Replaces Jill Abramson as Executive Editor," NPR, May 14, 2014, https://www.npr.org/sections/thetwo-way/2014/05/14/312516951/new-york-times-replaces-jill-abramson-as-executive-editor; J. Jennings Moss, "Yahoo Details Leadership Change, Mayer to Be Replaced by Former IAC Executive," *Silicon Valley Business Journal*, March 13, 2017, https://www.bizjournals.com/sanjose/news/2017/03/13/yahoo-details-leadership-change-mayer-to-be.html.

39. Tate Delloye, "How Has Adam Neumann WeWorked His Way Back to the Top of a Billion Dollar Real Estate Business?," *Daily Mail*, August 16, 2022, https://www.dailymail.co.uk/news/article-11113895/How-did-Adam-Neumann-secure-350M-investment-44BN-WeWork-failure.html.

40. Samar Marwan, "Here's What to Know About Flow: Adam Neumann's Newly Flush-with-Cash Real Estate Startup," *Fast Company*, August 15, 2022, https://www.fastcompany.com/90779384/heres-what-to-know-about-flow-adam-neumanns-newly-flush-with-cash-real-estate-startup.

41. Delloye, "How Has Adam Neumann WeWorked His Way Back?"; Marwan, "Here's What to Know About Flow."

42. Dave Lee and Tim Bradshaw, "Microsoft Invests in Travis Kalanick's CloudKitchens Start-Up," *Financial Times*, September 6, 2022, https://www.ft.com/content/5a768a67-1d0c-4c8a-9f14-de5ba06432ee.

43. Sam Coates, "Being a Mother Gives Me Edge on May—Leadsom," *The Times*, July 9, 2016, https://www.thetimes.co.uk/article/being-a-mother-gives-me-edge-on-may-leadsom-0t7bbm29x.

44. Georgina Stubbs, "Theresa May Reveals Heartbreaking Struggle to Have Children Which 'Affected' Both Her and Husband," *Mirror*, July 3, 2016, https://www.mirror.co.uk/news/uk-news/theresa-reveals-heartbreaking-struggle-children-8337595.

45. Schein et al., "Think Manager—Think Male."

46. Graham Staines et al., "The Queen Bee Syndrome," *Psychology Today* 7, no. 8 (1974): 55–60.

47. Klea Faniko et al., "The Queen Bee Phenomenon in Academia 15 Years After: Does It Still Exist, and If So, Why?," *British Journal of Social Psychology* 60, no. 2 (July 2020): 383–399, https://doi.org/10.1111/bjso.12408.

48. Mechelle Voepel, "Albright Empowers All-Decade Team at Luncheon," ESPN, July 12, 2006, https://www.espn.com/wnba/columns/story?columnist=voepel _mechelle&id=2517642.

49. Faniko et al., " Queen Bee Phenomenon in Academia."

50. Staines et al., "Queen Bee Syndrome"; Olga Khazan, "Why Do Women Bully Each Other at Work?," *The Atlantic*, August 3, 2017, https://www.theatlantic.com /magazine/archive/2017/09/the-queen-bee-in-the-corner-office/534213.

51. Faniko et al., "Queen Bee Phenomenon in Academia."

52. Belle Derks et al., "Extending the Queen Bee Effect: How Hindustani Workers Cope with Disadvantage by Distancing the Self from the Group," *Journal of Social Issues* 71, no. 3 (September 2015): 476–496, https://doi.org/10.1111/josi.12124; Faniko et al., "Queen Bee Phenomenon in Academia."

53. "Implicit Bias," Stanford Encyclopedia of Philosophy, February 26, 2015, https://plato.stanford.edu/entries/implicit-bias.

54. Elizabeth J. McClean et al., "The Social Consequences of Voice: An Examination of Voice Type and Gender on Status and Subsequent Leader Emergence," *Academy of Management Journal* 61, no. 5 (2018): 1869–1891.

55. Kieran Snyder, "The Abrasiveness Trap: High-Achieving Men and Women Are Described Differently in Reviews," *Fortune*, August 26, 2014, https://fortune .com/2014/08/26/performance-review-gender-bias.

56. Phillip Atiba Goff et al., "The Essence of Innocence: Consequences of Dehumanizing Black Children," *Journal of Personality and Social Psychology* 106, no. 4 (2014): 526–545, https://doi.org/10.1037/a0035663.

57. Marianne Bertrand, "This Problem Has a Name: Discrimination," *Chicago Booth Review*, May 21, 2016, https://www.chicagobooth.edu/review/problem-has-name -discrimination.

58. Sandra Shullman, "We Are Living in a Racism Pandemic," American Psychological Association, May 29, 2020, https://www.apa.org/news/press/releases/2020/05 /racism-pandemic.

59. Anna Johansson, "Why Workplace Diversity Diminishes Groupthink and How Millennials Are Helping," *Forbes*, July 20, 2017, https://www.forbes.com /sites/annajohansson/2017/07/20/how-workplace-diversity-diminishes-groupthink -and-how-millennials-are-helping/?sh=345a9e4f4b74.

60. Rocío Lorenzo et al., "How Diverse Leadership Teams Boost Innovation," Boston Consulting Group, January 23, 2018, https://www.bcg.com/publications/2018 /how-diverse-leadership-teams-boost-innovation.

61. Theresa Walker, "LA Riots 25 Years Later: Rodney King's 'Can We All Get Along' Still Matters," *Orange County Register*, April 30, 2017, https://www.ocregister .com/2017/04/30/la-riots-25-years-later-rodney-kings-can-we-all-get-along-still -matters.

62. Zulekha Nathoo, "Why Ineffective Diversity Training Won't Go Away," BBC, June 16, 2021, https://www.bbc.com/worklife/article/20210614-why-ineffective -diversity-training-wont-go-away.

63. Nathoo, "Why Ineffective Diversity Training Won't Go Away."

64. Frank Dobbin and Alexandra Kalev, "Frank Dobbin and Alexandra Kalev Explain Why Diversity Training Does Not Work," *The Economist*, May 21, 2021, https://www.economist.com/by-invitation/2021/05/21/frank-dobbin-and-alexandra -kalev-explain-why-diversity-training-does-not-work.

65. Nathoo, "Why Ineffective Diversity Training Won't Go Away."

66. Frank Dobbin and Alexandra Kalev, "Why Doesn't Diversity Training Work? The Challenge for Industry and Academia," *Anthropology Now* 10, no. 2 (September 2018): 48–55, https://doi.org/10.1080/19428200.2018.1493182.

67. Tessa L. Dover et al., "Diversity Policies Rarely Make Companies Fairer, and They Feel Threatening to White Men," *Harvard Business Review*, January 4, 2016, https://hbr.org/2016/01/diversity-policies-dont-help-women-or-minorities-and -they-make-white-men-feel-threatened.

68. Sarah Cordivano, "How Much Does Diversity, Equity and Inclusion Really Cost?," *Medium*, April 7, 2021, https://medium.com/sarah-cordivano/how-much-does -diversity-equity-and-inclusion-really-cost-f3dae9e410f8.

69. Sara Rynes and Rosen Benson, "A Field Survey of Factors Affecting the Adoption and Perceived Success of Diversity Training," *Personnel Psychology* 48 (1995): 247–270.

70. Sangeeta Gupta, "Three Characteristics of Effective DEI Leadership," *Forbes*, August 19, 2021, https://www.forbes.com/sites/forbescoachescouncil/2021/08/19/three -characteristics-of-effective-dei-leadership/?sh=49f0704c10dc.

71. Ashitha Nagesh, "US Election 2020: Why Trump Gained Support Among Minorities," BBC News, November 22, 2020, https://www.bbc.com/news/world -us-canada-54972389.

72. Iris Kuo, "The 'Whitening' of Asian Americans," *The Atlantic*, August 31, 2018, https://www.theatlantic.com/education/archive/2018/08/the-whitening-of-asian -americans/563336; Janice Omadeke, "Why the Model Minority Myth Is So Harm-ful," *Harvard Business Review*, June 15, 2021, https://hbr.org/2021/06/why-the -model-minority-myth-is-so-harmful; Kearie Daniel, "Why BIPOC Is an Inad-equate Acronym," Chatelaine, November 12, 2020, https://www.chatelaine.com /opinion/what-is-bipoc; Ernest Owens, "White People, Please Stop Declaring Your-self Allies," *Philly Mag*, June 15, 2020, https://www.phillymag.com/news/2020/06/15 /white-people-ally-culture; James Doubek, "Linguist John McWhorter Says 'White Fragility' Is Condescending Toward Black People," NPR, July 20, 2020, https: //www.npr.org/2020/07/20/892943728/professor-criticizes-book-white-fragili ty-as-dehumanizing-to-black-people; Katelyn Burns, "The Rise of Anti-Trans 'Rad-ical' Feminists Explained," *Vox*, September 5, 2019, https://www.vox.com/identities /2019/9/5/20840101/terfs-radical-feminists-gender-critical; Nicholas Kristof, "Inclu-sive or Alienating? The Language Wars Go On," *New York Times*, February 1, 2023, https://www.nytimes.com/2023/02/01/opinion/inclusive-language-vocabulary .html; Evan Odegard Pereira, "For Most Latinos, Latinx Does Not Mark the Spot," *New York Times*, June 15, 2021, https://www.nytimes.com/2021/06/15/learning /for-most-latinos-latinx-does-not-mark-the-spot.html.

73. Katelyn Jones, "'Just Add Women and Stir'—A Perfect Recipe for Dashed Hopes and Disappointment," *The Hill*, January 24, 2019, https://thehill.com/blogs /congress-blog/lawmaker-news/426788-just-add-women-and-stir-a-perfect-recipe -for-dashed-hopes.

74. Smith et al., "Obstacles and Opportunities."

75. C. J. Jung, *The Collected Works of C. J. Jung*, ed. Gerhard Adler, Michael Fordham, Herbert Read, and William McGuire (Princeton: Princeton University Press, 2014): 70–71.

76. Research and Markets, "Global Diversity and Inclusion (D&I) Market Report 2021: Market Is Estimated at $7.5 Billion in 2020, and Is Projected to Reach $15.4 Billion by 2026, Growing at a CAGR of 12.6%," Globe Newswire, January 27, 2022, https://www.globenewswire.com/en/news-release/2022/01/27/2374060/28124/en/Global-Diversity-and-Inclusion-D-I-Market-Report-2021-Market-is-Estimated-at-7-5-Billion-in-2020-and-is-Projected-to-Reach-15-4-Billion-by-2026-Growing-at-a-CAGR-of-12-6.html.

CHAPTER 8: THE LEADERSHIP CHARACTER STRESS TEST

1. Fred R. Shapiro, "Who Wrote the Serenity Prayer?," *Chronicle of Higher Education*, April 28, 2014, https://www.chronicle.com/article/who-wrote-the-serenity-prayer.

2. Carol Kinsey Goman, "5 Ways Body Language Impacts Leadership Results," *Forbes*, April 26, 2018, https://www.forbes.com/sites/carolkinseygoman/2018/08/26/5-ways-body-language-impacts-leadership-results/?sh=7a91a536536a.

3. "Body Language for Leaders," MindEdge, https://catalog.mindedge.com/courses/courses/1526/body-language-for-leaders.

4. Editors, "Emmanuel Macron Warns Europe: NATO Is Becoming Brain-Dead," *The Economist*, November 7, 2019, https://www.economist.com/europe/2019/11/07/emmanuel-macron-warns-europe-nato-is-becoming-brain-dead; Michael Idov, "The Improbable Rise and Endless Heroism of Volodymir Zelensky," *GQ*, February 27, 2022, https://www.gq.com/story/improbable-rise-endless-heroism-volodymyr-zelensky.

5. Idov, "Improbable Rise."

6. Franklin Foer, "A Prayer for Volodymyr Zelensky," *The Atlantic*, February 26, 2022, https://www.theatlantic.com/ideas/archive/2022/02/volodymyr-zelensky-ukraine-president/622938.

7. Leo Sands, "Sunken Russian Warship *Moskva*: What Do We Know?," BBC News, April 18, 2022, https://www.bbc.com/news/world-europe-61103927.

8. Foer, "Prayer for Volodymyr Zelensky."

9. James H. Andrews, "Churchill. A Volcano of Words in the Wilderness Years Before War," *Christian Science Monitor*, November 2, 1988, https://www.csmonitor.com/1988/1102/dblion.html.

10. John Gray, "Churchill, Chance and the 'Black Dog,'" BBC News, September 23, 2011, https://www.bbc.com/news/magazine-15033046.

11. Gray, "Churchill, Chance and the 'Black Dog.'"

12. John P. Kotter, "Leading Change: Why Transformation Efforts Fail," *Harvard Business Review*, May–June 1995, https://hbr.org/1995/05/leading-change-why-transformation-efforts-fail-2.

13. Tammi L. Coles, "The Luck Bluff," Global Network Perspectives, October 23, 2020, https://globalnetwork.io/perspectives/2020/10/luck-bluff.

14. Ruth Umoh, "Saying 'No,' Being Spontaneous and Other Lessons Learned from a $650,000 Lunch with Warren Buffett," CNBC, August 31, 2018, https://www.cnbc.com/2018/08/31/3-things-two-men-learned-from-their-650000-lunch-with-warren-buffett.html.

15. Richard Rumelt, *Good Strategy/Bad Strategy: The Difference and Why It Matters* (United Kingdom: Profile Books, 2011), 14.

16. Iain McCall, "Timeline of Apple Product Launches," September 30, 2019, https://4dproducts.co.uk/timeline-of-apple-product-launches.

17. "Don't Zoom in Too Close: 30% of Us Are Wearing PJs in Work Meetings, Some No Pants at All!," Business Wire, March 23, 2021, https://www.businesswire.com/news/home/20210323005490/en/Don%E2%80%99t-Zoom-in-Too-Close-30-of-Us-are-Wearing-PJs-in-Work-Meetings-Some-No-Pants-at-All.

18. Linda Crampton, "Serendipity: The Role of Chance in Scientific Discoveries," Owlcation, July 5, 2022, https://owlcation.com/stem/Serendipity-The-Role-of-Chance-in-Making-Scientific-Discoveries.

19. Howard Markel, "The Real Story Behind Penicillin," PBS, September 27, 2013, https://www.pbs.org/newshour/health/the-real-story-behind-the-worlds-first-antibiotic.

20. Crampton, "Serendipity."

21. "Discovering the Gold Standard of Cancer Drugs," MSU Today, August 1, 2018, https://msutoday.msu.edu/news/2018/discovering-the-gold-standard-of-cancer-drugs.

22. Levi King, "9 Proven Steps to Effective Leadership," *Inc.*, September 19, 2017, https://www.inc.com/levi-king/9-proven-steps-to-effective-leadership.html; Jerry Kurtz, "Want to Be an Effective Leader? Follow These 12 Steps," *Fast Company*, August 21, 2022, https://www.fastcompany.com/90776514/want-to-be-an-effective-leader-follow-these-12-steps.

23. Allison Quinn, "Ukrainian President Refuses to Evacuate, Tells U.S. He Needs Ammo, 'Not a Ride,'" *Daily Beast*, February 26, 2022, https://www.thedailybeast.com/ukrainian-president-volodymyr-zelensky-refuses-to-evacuate-tells-us-he-needs-ammo-not-a-ride.

24. Jessica Caporuscio, "What Are the Most Popular Strains of Cannabis?," Medical News Today, June 9, 2020, https://www.medicalnewstoday.com/articles/marijuana-strains.

25. Robin Wigglesworth and Harriet Agnew, "BlackRock Surges Past $10tn in Assets Under Management," *Financial Times*, January 14, 2022, https://www.ft.com/content/7603e676-779b-4c13-8f46-a964594e3c2f.

26. Matt Turner, "BlackRock's Larry Fink Told CEOs That 'Quarterly Earnings Hysteria' Is Bad for Business—Here's the Letter He Sent Them," *Business Insider*, June 14, 2016, https://www.businessinsider.com/blackrock-ceo-larry-fink-letter-to-sp-500-ceos-2016-6.

27. Mindy Lubber, "Ending Quarterly Capitalism," *Forbes*, February 21, 2012, https://www.forbes.com/sites/mindylubber/2012/02/21/ending-quarterly-capitalism/?sh=1b1ca25b77a6.

28. Kevin Coyne and Edward J. Coyne Sr., "Surviving Your New CEO," *Harvard Business Review*, May 2007, https://hbr.org/2007/05/surviving-your-new-ceo.

29. Paola Albornoz, "What Is Disruptive Leadership?," PDA, April 5, 2019, https://blog.pdainternational.net/en/what-is-disruptive-leadership.

30. Amir Kabir, "Why 52% of Fortune Companies Disappeared?," Grey Knight, April 9, 2023, https://greyknight.co.uk/why-52-of-fortune-500-companies-disappeared/.

31. KPMG, *Growing Pains: 2018 US CEO Outlook*, KPMG, 2018, https://assets.kpmg.com/content/dam/kpmg/us/pdf/2018/05/kpmg-ceo-outlook-2018.pdf.

32. Tim Zanni, *The Changing Landscape of Disruptive Technologies*, KPMG, 2018, https://assets.kpmg.com/content/dam/kpmg/pl/pdf/2018/06/pl-The-Changing-Landscape-of-Disruptive-Technologies-2018.pdf.

33. Drake Baer, "Mark Zuckerberg Explains Why Facebook Doesn't 'Move Fast and Break Things' Anymore," *Business Insider*, May 2, 2014, https://www.business insider.com/mark-zuckerberg-on-facebooks-new-motto-2014-5.

34. Tom Eisenmann, "Why Start-Ups Fail," *Harvard Business Review*, May–June 2021, https://hbr.org/2021/05/why-start-ups-fail.

35. KPMG, *Growing Pains*.

36. Jack Dorsey, "I Love Twitter," Twitter, April 25, 2022, https://twitter.com/jack/status/1518772753460998145.

37. Laurie Penny, "Every Time We Take an Uber We're Spreading Its Social Poison," *The Guardian*, March 3, 2017, https://www.theguardian.com/commentisfree/2017/mar/03/uber-spreading-social-poison-travis-kalanick; Eric Hegedus, "Elizabeth Holmes Halloween Costumes Spark Black Turtleneck Shortage," Fox News, October 31, 2019, https://www.foxnews.com/lifestyle/elizabeth-holmes-halloween-turtleneck-shortage.

38. Alexandra Frean, "Bitcoin Will Become the World's Single Currency, Twitter Chief Says," *The Times*, March 21, 2018, https://www.thetimes.co.uk/article/bitcoin-will-become-the-worlds-single-currency-tech-chief-says-66slm0p6b.

39. "Jack Dorsey's Square Changes Its Name to Block," BBC News, December 2, 2021, https://www.bbc.com/news/technology-59505516.

40. Jane C. Timm, "The 141 Stances Donald Trump Took During His White House Bid," NBC News, July 26, 2016, https://www.nbcnews.com/politics/2016-election/full-list-donald-trump-s-rapidly-changing-policy-positions-n547801.

41. Mini Tandon and Andrea Giedinghagen, "Disruptive Behavior Disorders in Children 0 to 6 Years Old," *Child and Adolescent Psychiatric Clinics of North America* 26, no. 3 (2017): 491–502, https://doi.org/10.1016/j.chc.2017.02.005.

42. Emily Bazelon, "Why Ruth Bader Ginsburg Refused to Step Down," *New York Times Magazine*, September 30, 2020, https://www.nytimes.com/2020/09/21/magazine/ginsburg-successor-obama.html.

43. Annie Karni, "G.O.P. Blocks Feinstein Swap, Leaving Democrats in a Conundrum," *New York Times*, April 18, 2023, https://www.nytimes.com/2023/04/18/us/politics/republicans-dianne-feinstein-judiciary.html.

44. Zach Schonfeld, "Grassley Has Already Filed for Reelection Bid in 2028," *The Hill*, November 17, 2022, https://thehill.com/homenews/campaign/3740578-grassley-has-already-filed-for-reelection-bid-in-2028.

45. Paul Kane, "Senate's Octogenarians Face the Age Question and Whether It's Time to Exit," *Washington Post*, December 12, 2020, https://www.washingtonpost.com/powerpost/senate-age-grassley-mecconnell-feinstein/2020/12/11/1f33b60a-3bd3-11eb-9276-ae0ca72729be_story.html.

46. Steve Lohr, "One Day You're Indispensable, the Next Day. . . ," *New York Times*, January 17, 2009, https://www.nytimes.com/2009/01/18/weekinreview/18lohr.html.

47. Thomas Barta and Patrick Barwise, "Why Effective Leaders Must Manage Up, Down, and Sideways," McKinsey & Company, April 27, 2017, https://www.mckinsey.com/featured-insights/leadership/why-effective-leaders-must-manage-up-down-and-sideways.

48. Jason Cowley, "From a Young Age Boris Johnson Longed to Be World King—but the Gods Are Mocking Him," *New Statesman*, November 4, 2020, https://www

.newstatesman.com/politics/uk-politics/2020/11/young-age-boris-johnson-longed-be
-world-king-gods-are-mocking-him.

49. "Leadership Potential Indicator," My Skills Profile, 2020, https://www
.myskillsprofile.com/testsV4/lpi.

50. *Korn Ferry Assessment of Leadership Potential*, Korn Ferry 2015, https://www
.kornferry.com/content/dam/kornferry/docs/article-migration/KFALP_Technical
_Manual_final.pdf.

51. Fi Phillips, "Korn Ferry Assessment of Leadership Potential (KFALP)," Psy-
chometric Success, January 22, 2023, https://psychometric-success.com/aptitude-tests
/test-types/kfalp.

52. "Princeton Review's 'SAT 1400+ Guaranteed*' Test Prep Program: Note the
Asterisk," Truth in Advertising, December 9, 2022, https://truthinadvertising.org
/articles/the-princeton-reviews-sat-1400-guaranteed-test-prep-program.

53. "Ace Your Korn Ferry Leadership Assessment Test with Accurate Practice
[KFALP, KF4D, UIT]," Job Test Prep, https://www.jobtestprep.com/korn-ferry
-leadership-test?idev_id=125&idev_username=psychosucc&utm_source=usaffiliate
&utm_medium=psychosucc&utm_campaign=125.

54. "Ace Your Korn Ferry Leadership Assessment Test."

55. "Leadership Assessment Test—the Complete Guide," Job Test Prep, https:
//www.jobtestprep.com/leadership-assessment-test.

56. Robert N. Raskin and Calvin S. Hall, "A Narcissistic Personality Inventory," *Psychological Reports* 45, no. 2 (1979), https://doi.org/10.2466/pr0.1979.45.2.590;
M. R. Levenson et al., "Assessing Psychopathic Attributes in a Noninstitutionalized
Population," *Journal of Personality and Social Psychology* 68, no. 1 (1995): 151–158, https:
//doi.org/10.1037//0022-3514.68.1.151.

57. Robert A. Emmons, "Factor Analysis and Construct Validity of the Narcissistic Personality Inventory," *Journal of Personality Assessment* 48, no. 3 (1984): 291–300,
https://doi:10.1207/s15327752jpa4803_11.

58. Wiley W. Souba and David W. McFadden, "The Double Whammy of
Change," *Journal of Surgical Research* 151, no. 1 (2009): 1–5, https://doi.org/10.1016/j.jss
.2008.11.808.

CHAPTER 9: THE CURE (IF YOU CAN AFFORD IT)

1. Daniel Goleman, "What Makes a Leader?," *Harvard Business Review*, January
2004, https://hbr.org/2004/01/what-makes-a-leader.

2. Katie Heaney, "What Kind of Person Fakes Their Voice?," The Cut, March 21,
2019, https://www.thecut.com/2019/03/why-did-elizabeth-holmes-use-a-fake-deep
-voice.html; Vanessa Friedman, "Hey Silicon Valley, Maybe It's Time to Dress Up, Not
Down," *New York Times*, December 13, 2022, https://www.nytimes.com/2022/12/13
/style/sam-bankman-fried-style.html.

3. George E. P. Box, "George's Column," *Quality Engineering* 5, no. 3 (1993): 517–
524, https://doi.org/10.1080/08982119308918991.

4. Shannon Selin, "Superstitious Napoleon," Military History Now, July 8, 2016,
https://militaryhistorynow.com/2016/07/08/superstitious-napoleon-did-bonaparte
-really-believe-in-evil-spirits-omens-and-lucky-charms.

5. Charles Vallance, "Business Leaders Who 'Leave Nothing to Chance' Attract
Bad Luck and Missed Opportunities," *The Telegraph*, April 20, 2014, https://www

.telegraph.co.uk/finance/comment/10777363/Business-leaders-who-leave-nothing
-to-chance-attract-bad-luck-and-missed-opportunities.html.

6. Lydia Ramsey Pflanzer, "How Elizabeth Holmes Convinced Powerful Men Like Henry Kissinger, James Mattis, and George Shultz to Sit on the Board of Now Disgraced Blood-Testing Startup Theranos," *Business Insider*, March 19, 2019, https://www.businessinsider.com/theranos-former-board-members-henry-kissinger-george-shultz-james-mattis-2019-3; Marco Quiroz-Gutierrez, "SBF Wanted the FTX Celebrity Spending Spree to Include a $100 Million Taylor Swift Sponsorship," *Fortune*, December 7, 2022, https://fortune.com/crypto/2022/12/07/sbf-ftx-taylor-swift-celebrity-sponsorships-lawsuits-bankruptcy; John Reed Stark, "Celebrity Crypto-Hawkers Should Get a Close Look," *New York Times*, December 17, 2022, https://www.nytimes.com/2022/12/17/opinion/crypto-ftx-crash-celebrity.html.

7. Kai Bird, "Jimmy Carter's Presidency Was Not What You Think," *New York Times*, February 20, 2023, https://www.nytimes.com/2023/02/20/opinion/kai-bird-jimmy-carter-life.html; "Carter Center Accomplishments," Carter Center, https://www.cartercenter.org/about/accomplishments.html; "Carter Work Project," Habitat for Humanity, https://www.habitat.org/volunteer/build-events/carter-work-project.

8. Rebecca Greenfield, "The $100,000 Anti-Burnout Program for CEOs," *Bloomberg*, March 27, 2017, https://www.bloomberg.com/news/articles/2017-03-27/the-100-000-anti-burnout-program-for-ceos.

9. Ken Favaro et al., "The $112 Billion CEO Succession Problem," PWC Strategy+ Business, May 4, 2015, https://www.strategy-business.com/article/00327#succession.

10. Greenfield, "$100,000 Anti-Burnout Program."

11. Greenfield, "$100,000 Anti-Burnout Program."

12. Nate Bennett and G. James Lemoine, "What VUCA Really Means for You," *Harvard Business Review*, January–February 2014, https://hbr.org/2014/01/what-vuca-really-means-for-you.

13. Mark Terry, "Johnson & Johnson's $100,000 Anti-Burnout Program for Top Execs," BioSpace, March 29, 2017, https://www.biospace.com/article/johnson-and-johnson-s-100-000-anti-burnout-program-for-top-execs-.

14. Lucy Kellaway, "Cheap Ways to Prevent Executive Burnout," *Financial Times*, April 16, 2017, https://www.ft.com/content/eb0c0a92-2035-11e7-a454-ab04428977f9.

15. Derek Saul, "CEOs Made 324 Times More Than Their Median Workers in 2021, Union Report Finds," *Forbes*, July 18, 2022, https://www.forbes.com/sites/dereksaul/2022/07/18/ceos-made-324-times-more-than-their-median-workers-in-2021-union-report-finds/?sh=3e3d5765ac52.

16. Investopedia, "Is a One Million Dollar Nonprofit CEO Salary as Bad as It Sounds?," *Forbes*, January 23, 2013, https://www.forbes.com/sites/investopedia/2013/01/23/is-a-one-million-dollar-nonprofit-ceo-salary-as-bad-as-it-sounds/?sh=1ee2187442c7.

17. "Let's Lead Boldly," AACSB, https://www.aacsb.edu.

18. West Catholic High School, "Preparing Future Leaders," 2020, YouTube video https://www.youtube.com/@grwestcatholic.

19. "Vision, Mission and Values," DeAnza College, https://www.deanza.edu/about-us/mission-and-values.html.

20. "Higher Education," FranklinCovey, https://www.franklincovey.com/solutions/education/higher-education.

21. "Our Guiding Vision," US Naval War College, https://usnwc.edu/About/Mission.

22. Tiny Leader's Children's Center, https://hs.ocfs.ny.gov/DCFS/Profile/Index /803001; "Home," Little Leaders Institute, https://littleleadersphl.com; "Lil' Leaders Childcare," Yelp, https://www.yelp.com/biz/lil-leaders-childcare-san-mateo; Tomorrow's Leaders Childcare, https://tomorrowsleaderschildcare.com (site discontinued); "Future Leaders Christian Learning Center Inc.," Great Philly Schools, https://www.greatphillyschools.org/schools/0011N00001TQzneQAD/future-leaders -christian-learning-center-inc.

23. "Future S.T.E.A.M Leaders Academic Child Care," Care.com, https://www .care.com/b/l/future-s-t-e-a-m-leaders-academic-child-care/moreno-valley-ca.

24. "About NAEP," National Assessment of Educational Progress, https://nces .ed.gov/nationsreportcard/about.

25. Lauren Camera, "Pandemic Prompts Historic Decline in Student Achievement on Nation's Report Card," *US News and World Report*, October 24, 2022, https://www .usnews.com/news/education-news/articles/2022-10-24/pandemic-prompts-historic -decline-in-student-achievement-on-nations-report-card.

26. Susan Cain, "Not Leadership Material? Good. The World Needs Followers," *New York Times*, March 24, 2017, https://www.nytimes.com/2017/03/24/opinion /sunday/not-leadership-material-good-the-world-needs-followers.html.

27. Curt Brungardt et al., "Majoring in Leadership: A Review of Undergraduate Leadership Degree Programs," *Journal of Leadership Education* 5, no. 1 (2006), https: //doi.org/10.12806/V5/I1/RF1; Sydney Lake, "10 Executive Leadership Programs That Should Be on Every Business Leader's Radar," *Fortune*, April 24, 2021, https://for tune.com/education/articles/10-executive-leadership-programs-that-should-be-on -every-business-leaders-radar.

28. Jill Barshay, "The Number of College Graduates in the Humanities Drops for the Eighth Consecutive Year," Hechinger Report, November 22, 2021, https: //hechingerreport.org/proof-points-the-number-of-college-graduates-in-the -humanities-drops-for-the-eighth-consecutive-year.

29. Winston Churchill, "1940: The Finest Hour: We Shall Fight on the Beaches," International Churchill Society, https://winstonchurchill.org/resources/speeches/1940 -the-finest-hour/we-shall-fight-on-the-beaches.

30. Bright Little Leaders Daycare, Inc., Facebook page, https://www.facebook .com/brightlittleleadersdaycare; "What Is Leader in Me?," Leader in Me, https://www .leaderinme.org.

31. Tim Bontemps, "Michael Jordan Stands Firm on 'Republicans Buy Sneakers, Too' Quote, Says It Was Made in Jest," ESPN, May 3, 2020, https://www .espn.com/nba/story/_/id/29130478/michael-jordan-stands-firm-republicans-buy -sneakers-too-quote-says-was-made-jest.

32. Paul Babiak et al., "Corporate Psychopathy: Talking the Walk," *Behavioral Sciences and the Law* 28, no. 2 (March 2010):174–193, https://doi.org/10.1002/bsl.925.

INDEX

DR. ELIAS ABOUJAOUDE is a Stanford psychiatry professor, author, researcher, and internet scholar. In 2006, at the height of our culture's love affair with the internet, he led the first large-scale study of internet addiction and sounded an early alarm in the heart of Silicon Valley: internet-related technologies are causing serious psychological harm. His subsequent book, *Virtually You: The Dangerous Powers of the E-Personality* (2011 *New York Times* Editors' Choice), made the case for the general audience, warning about internet-mediated aggression, narcissism, and privacy invasions, and predicting, with eerie prescience, how psychological forces unleashed online would polarize societies, compromise cognitive faculties, rock educational paradigms, and threaten democracy by encouraging demagogues.

Beyond decrying our psychological fate in the digital age, Dr. Aboujaoude also searched for a silver lining to internet-related technologies. Recognizing in his role as Stanford University physician and clinical faculty member the obstacles that patients face in accessing treatment, he cofounded in 2009 the first Silicon Valley company to deliver video-enabled counseling. Other projects explored the roles of virtual reality and artificial intelligence in treatment interventions. Well before COVID-19 forced an overnight shift to remote mental health treatment delivery, Dr. Aboujaoude was researching and publishing scholarly books and peer-reviewed articles on the technology-enabled treatments that would come to dominate psychological and psychiatric care.

More recently, Dr. Aboujaoude's work has focused on delineating the coaching movement from mental health treatment, understanding the psychology of leadership, and challenging the notion that what he calls the leadership industrial complex can reliably produce good leaders who can lift society and address the myriad problems we face. This has resulted in peer-reviewed research publications, articles for *Fortune* and *Psychology Today*, and an exposé for the British literary magazine *Aeon*.

Dr. Aboujaoude has lectured in over twenty countries to audiences that have included university-wide convocations, the Department of Defense, public libraries, and GAFA shareholder groups. His work has been broadly covered, including by the *New York Times*, *Wall Street Journal*, *Financial Times*, *Harvard Business Review*, *Congressional Quarterly*, *Washington Post*, *USA Today*, *The Atlantic*, *Fortune*, *Politico*, *Huffington Post*, *Wired*, *Newsweek*, and *Time*, as well as on NPR, CNN, BBC, ABC, and FOX.

PublicAffairs is a publishing house founded in 1997. It is a tribute to the standards, values, and flair of three persons who have served as mentors to countless reporters, writers, editors, and book people of all kinds, including me.

I. F. STONE, proprietor of *I. F. Stone's Weekly*, combined a commitment to the First Amendment with entrepreneurial zeal and reporting skill and became one of the great independent journalists in American history. At the age of eighty, Izzy published *The Trial of Socrates*, which was a national bestseller. He wrote the book after he taught himself ancient Greek.

BENJAMIN C. BRADLEE was for nearly thirty years the charismatic editorial leader of *The Washington Post*. It was Ben who gave the *Post* the range and courage to pursue such historic issues as Watergate. He supported his reporters with a tenacity that made them fearless and it is no accident that so many became authors of influential, best-selling books.

ROBERT L. BERNSTEIN, the chief executive of Random House for more than a quarter century, guided one of the nation's premier publishing houses. Bob was personally responsible for many books of political dissent and argument that challenged tyranny around the globe. He is also the founder and longtime chair of Human Rights Watch, one of the most respected human rights organizations in the world.

·   ·   ·

For fifty years, the banner of Public Affairs Press was carried by its owner Morris B. Schnapper, who published Gandhi, Nasser, Toynbee, Truman, and about 1,500 other authors. In 1983, Schnapper was described by *The Washington Post* as "a redoubtable gadfly." His legacy will endure in the books to come.

Peter Osnos, *Founder*